All Mine!

All Mine!

HAPPINESS, OWNERSHIP, AND NAMING IN ELEVENTH-CENTURY CHINA

STEPHEN OWEN

Columbia University Press

New York

Columbia University Press wishes to express its appreciation for assistance given by the Chiang Ching-kuo Foundation for International Scholarly Exchange in the publication of this book.

Columbia University Press
Publishers Since 1893
New York Chichester, West Sussex
cup.columbia.edu

Library of Congress Cataloging-in-Publication Data
Names: Owen, Stephen, 1946– author.
Title: All mine! : happiness, ownership, and naming in eleventh-century China / Stephen Owen.
Description: New York : Columbia University Press, [2021] | Includes bibliographical references and index.
Identifiers: LCCN 2021020189 (print) | LCCN 2021020190 (ebook) | ISBN 9780231203104 (hardback) | ISBN 9780231203111 (trade paperback) | ISBN 9780231554879 (ebook)
Subjects: LCSH: Chinese literature—Song dynasty, 960–1279—History and criticism. | Literature and society—China—History—To 1500.
Classification: LCC PL2293 .O94 2021 (print) | LCC PL2293 (ebook) | DDC 895.109/0042—dc23
LC record available at https://lccn.loc.gov/2021020189
LC ebook record available at https://lccn.loc.gov/2021020190

Columbia University Press books are printed on permanent and durable acid-free paper.
Printed in the United States of America

Cover image: The Garden for Solitary Enjoyment, 1515–1552, Qiu Ying.
The Cleveland Museum of Art, John L. Severance Fund 1978.67.
Courtesy of The Cleveland Museum of Art.
Cover design: Lisa Hamm

CONTENTS

All Mine!

INTRODUCTION

The famous Ouyang Xiu (1007–1072) once wrote down a joke that he had heard and was probably already old when he told it. Like all old jokes, it is probably better retold than translated. We have the wit and the straight man, both court ministers in an imperial Secretariat during the Five Dynasties. Minister He Ning noticed that Minister Feng Dao (whose pseudonym was "Ever-Happy Old Guy" 長樂老) was wearing new shoes and, pointing to his foot, asked: "How much did that cost?" Feng Dao lifted his leg to show his new shoe and said: "Nine hundred cash." He Ning at once summoned his aide and began to angrily berate him: "How come my new shoes cost eighteen hundred cash?!" After He Ning had given his aide a thorough tongue-lashing, Feng Dao smiled and lifted his other leg and pointing to that shoe said: "This one cost nine hundred too." At that the whole hall broke into thunderous laughter.[1]

At the end, Ouyang Xiu adds: "At the time it was said that if court ministers behaved like that, how could they maintain their authority over their subordinates?"

There is much to reflect on in this joke. If English and many languages didn't make that pesky distinction between singular and plural, the joke has universal appeal among shoe-wearing peoples whose shoes must be purchased. A Turkish speaker would immediately think this was a story about Nasreddin Hoca (Afanti in modern Chinese). In Chinese the fact that the comic pair are high ministers of state adds to the humor.

What might strike a modern reader as strangely incongruous is the concluding judgment. Ouyang Xiu is obviously writing this down for the joke, but something within him cannot let this pass without striking a note of critical disapproval. He finds in the joke a moral lesson about the proper behavior for high government officials, which some modern critics expand to a reflection of the decadence of government in the Five Dynasties period.

The joke does not need this particular setting in a government office, and there is little reason to take its historical specificity as anything more than gossip, an added point of humor to tie the joke to high officials and to Feng Dao in particular, living up to his pseudonym. But it also produces a discomfort that requires that it become a moral lesson.

Drawing moral lessons from stories had been part of the tradition since ancient times. There is nothing new about that. What is new is the disparity between the obvious force of the story and the lesson drawn. Immediately before Ouyang Xiu's remark disapproving such behavior, we have the scene of laughter in the hall of the Secretariat: "Thereupon the whole hall roared with laughter." Noting the laughter of the audience is a common form of closure when narrating a joke, encouraging the reader to join in the community of laughter. This scene, however, flips the narrative from joke to scandal, as Ouyang Xiu imagines a roomful of subordinates laughing at their superiors. The twist follows from an instinctive surveillance for lapses in behavior, and even the usually protected realm of a joke is not immune to immediate reproach.

The joke itself presents other problems. These "gentlemen," high officers of the court, are discussing money and doing so in public. The Five Dynasties setting in this case helps, by distancing the scene into the past. The world of money was, however, everywhere in Ouyang Xiu's own time, even though most formal writing was discreetly silent on the topic. We will never know if Ouyang Xiu was really sleeping with his "niece," but he evidently did put his tax-exempt name on property purchased with her money.[2]

When Wang Anshi's (1021–1086) economic reforms had been put in place, the emperor Shenzong (r. 1068–1085) showed a remarkable concern with the possibility of earning interest on state loans to hard-pressed peasants (though government loans had considerably lower interest than the 100 percent per annum charged by professional moneylenders).[3]

The ancient Confucian philosophical work *Mengzi* opens with a famous dialogue between Mengzi (Mencius) and the king of Liang (IA.1):

> 孟子見梁惠王。王曰: 叟不遠千里而來，亦將有以利吾國乎。孟子對曰:王何必曰利，亦有仁義而已矣。

> Mengzi met with King Hui of Liang. The king said: "Sir, you came without thinking that a thousand leagues was too far. Might you have some way to be of

> profit to my domain?" Mengzi answered: "Why must Your Majesty say 'profit'? The only thing to consider is fellow-feeling and what is right."

Although no joke is involved, this is an ancient version of the moralist's "intervention" in discourse. The Northern Song world was dividing under the weight of these two opposed and irreconcilable forces: on the one side was profit and a cheaper pair of good shoes; on the other side was a moral purity that considered interest in profit to be base and not to be considered. There were some who were fully committed to one or the other of these forces, but most people lived with both forces within them, and the easiest reconciliation of the conflict was hypocrisy—or, to be more generous, a split between distinct spheres, within each of which one force ruled. Public discussion of the price of shoes by the ministers in the Secretariat was an illicit contamination of one sphere by another.

The first force, profit, was in part unleashed by a humble seed—or, rather, twenty Chinese bushels (*dan*) of humble seeds—imported from Southeast Asia, known as "Champa rice," which ripened considerably more quickly than the strain of rice that had previously been grown in the rich agricultural region of the lower Yangzi River. This allowed two crops annually rather than one. Two crops annually were a bonanza for an empire founded on surplus carbohydrates. Along with improvements in other strains of rice and foodplants, which enabled farming on what had been marginal land, this led to an economic boom. Economic booms tend to make the rich richer and the poor poorer.

The problem for all farmers in temperate zones is surviving the period between autumn harvest and the first spring crop, while conserving enough surplus seed for spring planting. Merchant moneylenders were at hand with loans at exorbitant interest. Some farmers were flourishing, but a significant percentage were slipping into poverty and turning their lands over to the great estates, which often had tax-exempt status. When their land was transferred to large landowners, the peasants remained bound to that land, in what looks a great deal like "serfdom."

Those in charge of a large and ancient polity gradually came to feel the need to manage the economy. As ingenious as they were, they were amateurs at this, and especially with managing the economy of a very large country with an essentially medieval technology. Their only solution to problems was to issue edicts and try to enforce them, which, of course, brought out all the unforeseen problems inherent in any given edict. Such problems, in their turn, further persuaded the opponents of the policy that this was not the proper role of government, which should be the moral education of the populace. In short, we have problems of "profit" again encountering righteousness.

This brings us to the counterforce, which was government-sponsored printing and distribution of the Confucian Classics on an unprecedented scale. Two of the states in the Five Dynasties had already tried this—printing being less expensive than carving the Classics in stone, as had been done in the ninth century under the Tang. The reason given for carving the Classics in stone had been to stabilize their texts, whose accuracy tended to vary in their manuscript copies. The early Song government imprints had their own textual errors, but at least these errors were widely shared, rather than each of a thousand manuscript copies introducing its own copying errors.[4]

The Tang had recruited officials in large measure from families with a history of service to the dynasty, and the children of these families grew up understanding the workings of the government. The lower gentry, especially those from the provinces, made up only a small percentage of officeholders, and they were often employed only in lower echelon posts.

The Song actually put into practice the meritocratic ideals that have been projected back on the Tang, staffing their bureaucracy largely with those who passed the *jinshi* examination (without stacking the deck with scions of great families) and including a substantial representation from the provinces. These young men had had a largely moral education in the Classics, supplemented by the histories, which were understood no less in ethical terms.

The consequence of such an education began to show itself through the eleventh century in the constant impulse to draw moral lessons and an instinct to forestall criticism when it was anticipated, as we will see in several of the texts discussed in this volume. The stridency of such critical judgments of people and texts increased dramatically into the twelfth century.

The texts we will discuss directly concern neither the changing social world, permeated by money and acquisition, nor the world of Confucian ethical thought, fully realized in Daoxue, "the study of the Way," also called "Neo-Confucianism." Rather, these texts are situated in the contact zone between the two forces, where the impulse to think of "happiness" through acquisition and possession meets voices, both inner and outer, of moral criticism. When the austere moralist Cheng Yi (1033–1107) seeks to explain the *Analects*' distinction between "loving learning" and "being happy in learning," he explains that the former is like visiting someone else's garden and the latter is like being in one's own garden. When we see such an analogy, we realize how deeply these opposed forces have interpenetrated each other.

The essays in this volume are gathered around the question of happiness, whether actual or speculative, being contingent on having something in this world. The counterforce is happiness in the Way. Names are often strangely mixed in with the reflection on happiness—giving names, the stability of names, and value accrued by having a "name."

HAPPINESS 樂

China had a long and interesting discourse on happiness, beginning in the *Analects* of Confucius, *Lunyu* 論語, and carried through particularly in *Mengzi* 孟子, which was gaining status in the Song dynasty as one of the Confucian Classics in its own right. After antiquity, the discourse on happiness appeared sporadically, returning to prominence only in the eleventh century, during the Northern Song.

I'm sure happiness was always there as a fact: people were always sometimes happy and sometimes unhappy. The living fact is different from a discourse, which is not simply declaring that one is happy but thinking what the conditions of happiness are, what makes a person happy. In pre-Qin discourse one might be happy in the Way, happy in Heaven, happy in study, ritual, and right action, but the idea that "things" or possessions might be part of happiness was not usually a question in the ancient period. It *did* become an issue in the Song.

The interest in happiness was often situated in a larger sphere of instrumentality: doing something or having something that would lead to happiness. This was often expressed in the speculative future ("I'll go buy land there") or, if one is already happy, celebrating the conditions that have enabled happiness. Daoxue philosophers might celebrate their happiness in the Way, most notably Shao Yong 邵雍 (1011–1077) in his poetry.[5] Many others were concerned with more material contingencies of happiness. I do not mean that everyone believed that "having" certain things brought about happiness; some people clearly thought that clinging to things brought unhappiness instead. But these opposed beliefs were both based on a question about the relationship happiness and things.

In the *Analects* happiness shifts between a state attached to conditions and one that transcends conditions. Indeed, the very first entry in the *Analects* names a condition for happiness, albeit not a material one: "The Master said: 'Is it not a pleasure to study and from time to time to put it into practice? Does it not make one happy when friends come from afar?'" 子曰：學而時習之，不亦說乎？有朋自遠方來，不亦樂乎？ (I.1). The parallel between *yue* 說, "to be pleased with," and *le* 樂, "to be happy," seems like a simple variation in which "to be happy" is not a weighty term. Nevertheless, we should note that the sense of contingent happiness in Confucian thought often tends to be sociable; in the Northern Song texts we will discuss, contingent happiness is often "solitary happiness," *dule* 獨樂, a loaded term that flies in the face of the sociable happiness of the *Mengzi*.

Elsewhere in the *Analects* happiness is often more absolute, following from one's nature rather from a restricted circumstance. "Those who are wise are made happy by waters; those with fellow-feeling are made happy by mountains. Those who are wise take action; those with fellow feeling are tranquil. Those who are wise are happy; those with fellow-feeling live long" 知者樂水；仁者樂山。知者動；仁者靜。知者樂；仁者壽 (VI.21). The first pair of the term *le* (translated "made happy by"), as transitive verbs with an object, applies both to those who understand and to those who have fellow-feeling. The final *le* is a state of happiness, which is restricted to only those who understand.

The impulse to make happiness a general and higher condition can be seen in one of Confucius's favorite "good, better, best" series: "The Master said: 'Those who understand it are not so good as those love it, and those who love it are not so good as those who are happy in it'" 子曰：知之者不如好之者，好之者不如樂之者 (VII.8). To "love" or "like" something, *hao* 好, leaves open a gap of desire, as "being happy" does not. It is not difficult to see how easily such a distinction can underwrite the desire for acquisition and possession.

Happiness as the condition of a certain kind of person may be best represented in indifference to adversity. The best-known text invoking such happiness is Confucius's comment on his favorite disciple, Yan Hui: "The Master said: 'Virtuous indeed is Hui, with a single bamboo plate of food and a single ladle of water in a ramshackle lane; others could not endure their distress, but Hui does not change his happiness'" 子曰：賢哉回也！一簞食，一瓢飲，在陋巷。人不堪其憂，回也不改其樂 (VI.9). Confucius was interested in enduring adversity, but the phrasing here is worth note. The fact that Hui does not "change" his happiness implies that such happiness was an enduring condition that was not contingent on external circumstances. It was happiness as a state of being that attracted Daoxue thinkers; this was a happiness indifferent to the usual attractions of the world as well as to the discomforts of poverty.

The sociability of happiness, shared happiness, returns as an important topic in the *Mengzi*. The famous case is in the "Liang Huiwang" 梁惠王 chapter (IA.2).

> 孟子見梁惠王。王立於沼上，顧鴻鴈麋鹿。曰:賢者亦樂此乎。孟子對曰:賢者而後樂此。不賢者，雖有此不樂也。詩云: 經始靈臺，經之營之，庶民攻之，不日成之。經始勿亟，庶民子來。王在靈囿，麀鹿攸伏。麀鹿濯濯，白鳥鶴鶴。王在靈沼，於牣魚躍。文王以民力為臺為沼，而民歡樂之。謂其臺曰靈臺。謂其沼曰靈沼。樂其有麋鹿魚鱉。古之人與民偕樂，故能樂也。

Mengzi had an interview with King Hui of Liang. The king was standing by his pond and looking at the swans, wild geese, and deer. He asked: "Do the virtuous too find happiness in this?"

Mengzi answered: You can find happiness in this only if you are already virtuous. Someone who is not virtuous would not be happy even if he had all this. As the *Classic of Poetry* tells us:

They measured and began the Spirit Terrace.
Measured it and set to work;
The common folk labored at it;
In less than a day they finished it.
Measuring, beginning, they did not hurry,
The common folk came as children.[6]

The king was in the Spirit Park,
Where the does are crouching.
The does are plump and sleek;
The white birds are pristine.
The king was at the Spirit Pond,
with leaping fish abounding.

By the labor of the common people King Wen made his terrace and pond, and the common people rejoiced and were happy at this. They referred to his terrace as the "Spirit Terrace" and to his pond as the "Spirit Pond," and they were happy in his possession of deer, fish, and turtles. Men in ancient times shared their happiness with the common people, and thus they themselves were able to be happy.

Echoes of this passage and the issues raised in this passage appear in many of the works discussed in these essays. By its very nature ownership is not sharing, except as the owner permits. The famous Sima Guang 司馬光 (1019–1086) has to defend this principle when criticized for the name of his "Solitary Happiness Garden." The issue in the *Mengzi*, however, is not sharing the terrace and pool, but rather sharing the happiness with the common people. The king's question to Mencius is interesting because it suggests that a "virtuous man" might be above such common happiness. Mengzi characteristically redirects the question so that only a virtuous person can enjoy such happiness; however, the happiness is not essentially in the park itself and not contingent on having the park, but rather in sharing the common people's happiness at his having the park. While this may seem a too fine philosophical distinction, several of the essays turn on this question.

This same question returns in an equally famous passage in *Mengzi* IB.1.[7]

曰:獨樂樂，與人樂樂，孰樂。曰:不若與人。曰:與少樂樂與衆樂樂，孰樂。曰:不若與衆。

He said: "Which is greater happiness?—to find solitary happiness in music or to share happiness in music with others?" He answered: "It is better with others." He said: "Which is greater happiness?—to find happiness in music with few or to share happiness in music with many?" He answered: "It is better with many."

"Solitary happiness" 獨樂 is a problematic happiness, and it was to become very much so in the Northern Song.

Suppose, however, that I am walking alone in the mountains and come upon a beautiful scene. I sit down to look and feel happy. This also is "solitary happiness" 獨樂, but it does *not* fall under the implicit criticism of solitary happiness in *Mengzi*. The question of solitary happiness, as opposed to "happiness shared with many" 與眾樂, can arise only in regard to something you possess, something in which you have the power to exclude others—and that is very close to one definition of "ownership."

OWNERSHIP 擁有

It is hard to talk about ownership in classical Chinese. It is hard to talk about ownership in many premodern languages. In Western European languages, a fully developed discourse of ownership came only with capitalism and the philosophical "theory of right." Perhaps the closest term in classical Chinese is *jiyou* 已有, roughly "one's own." In modern Chinese, "ownership" becomes *yongyou* 擁有, the first citation for which in the monumental dictionary *Hanyu da cidian* is Mao Zedong (and is, no doubt, a translation term).

When we think about the discourse of "having" 有 and "ownership" 擁有, there are interesting distinctions to make. Suppose I say, "I have a glass of beer" or "I have a bunch of green vegetables." If you try to take away my beer or my vegetables, I may say: "That's mine," which is essentially a claim of "ownership," *yongyou*. But if I don't drink the beer in a few hours or cook the green vegetables within a few days, they are not worth "having." If I say I "have" a hundred dollars, it's similar: we all know that I will use it or consume it. If someone takes it, I will report them to the police.

But now suppose I say that I have hundred million dollars. It is not something I am going to consume in a month. It becomes part of my identity, changing the way others think of me and the way I think of myself. Suppose I say that I have a fine collection of Shang bronzes; they may be worth a large amount of money, but we know that—unless I am an art dealer or in hard straits—I am never going to sell what I have, no matter how valuable. Transferring ownership in this case becomes a significant act: if I give the collection to children, it is a family legacy, something that stays with the family; if I give it to a museum, there will almost certainly be a little sign saying: "Gift of Stephen Owen." Suppose I have a famous garden that everyone likes to visit; everyone knows to whom it belongs, and when they think of me, they may think of me as the owner of the garden, or conversely, when they visit the garden, they may think of me. "Self" and "garden" each becomes a central attribute of the other.

Thus there is a changing relation between people and their possessions. There are different kinds of value, and the more value that accrues to a thing, the more likely it is that I become identified with what I possess and identify myself with what I possess. When I say this, I am halfway to the obsessive collectors, like Wang Shen in Su Dongpo's "Account of the Hall of Precious Paintings" 寶繪堂記 or Zhao Defu in Li Qingzhao's (1081–c. 1141) "Afterword" to *Records on Metal and Stone*.

At this point you may be thinking: This is very interesting, but what does it have to do with Chinese literature? Suppose then I say: "I have ten thousand *juan* (scrolls, book sections) of books, a thousand old rubbings and copies of inscriptions, a zither, a chess set, and a jug of ale." Who am I?

> 吾家藏書一萬卷，集錄三代以來金石遺文一千卷，有琴一張，有碁一局，而常置酒一壺。

> My home library is of one myriad scrolls and I have gathered one thousand scrolls of records of texts surviving on metal and stone since the Three Dynasties; I have one zither and one chess set; and one jug of ale is always set out before me.

You may remember that I began with "having" a glass of beer. You should notice the difference between "having a glass of beer" and "one jug of ale always set out before me" 常置酒一壺: the jug comes from an apparently inexhaustible store that is always renewed. That is a different kind of "having"—it is more clearly *yongyou*.

NAMING 命名

I will come back to "The Biography of the Retired Layman Six Ones" 六一居士傳, just quoted, where happiness, naming, and ownership all are linked together. If possession is a difficult discourse in Chinese, both "happiness" and "names" have a long history that is too complicated to cover here in detail. I will simply raise a few questions.

One of the most famous passages on naming in the *Analects* was when Duke Jing of Qi asked Confucius about governing, to which Confucius tersely replied: "The ruler, a ruler; the subject, a subject; the father, a father; the son, a son" 齊景公問政於孔子，孔子對曰:君君臣臣父父子子 (XII.11). This initiated a long tradition focused on "getting the names right," *zhengming* 正名, matching name and fact: "a ruler should behave like a ruler should," and so on. For the moral development of an individual, this meant internalizing one's role in the proper sense; for those who gave an account of the world in writing history, it meant calling things by their right name. Thus Confucianism came to be called the "doctrine of names," *mingjiao* 名教.

If things are called by their right names, then the name should be stable so long as the thing or the relationship through which the thing is named is stable. In the literary tradition, giving a name is often a reflective act that requires explanation of why the name is the right name. From an outside perspective, the Chinese fascination with giving names to all sorts of sites and things is an interesting phenomenon, particularly considering that in China names have been so often unstable. The names of people are various, and the names of places often changed. Acts of naming and the etiology of names take on a reflective weight as writers negotiate a world that would be perspicuously intelligible if only one got all the names right—or if one understood why the existing names are the "right" ones. Thus the Retired Layman Six Ones 六一居士 tells us why his earlier self-naming (*hao* 號) was wrong and why his new name is the right name.

To name something is a form of taking possession, attaching one's own name to a site. The "Drunken Old Man," Zuiweng 醉翁, Ouyang Xiu's first pseudonym, names a pavilion "The Pavilion of the Drunken Old Man" 醉翁亭. He did not build the pavilion; it is presumably not "his"; but he claims it by naming it for himself. Even when giving a name that is not the name of the person who names, if there is a text to accompany the name and that is distributed to friends, "naming," *mingming* 命名, becomes "having a name/fame" 有名. The building can fall into disrepair and collapse, but names are often more enduring than buildings; such sites attached to a durable name were often rebuilt, indeed continuously rebuilt, so that the name creates the place as much as a place has a name. Naming and possession are closely related: to name something is to stake a claim.

As the art market grew in the Northern Song in junction with other markets in a money economy, a "name" acquired commercial value. However much a gentleman might not want to engage in crass commerce, his very name might trap him in the marketplace.

THE ESSAY

I have always been interested in the "genres" of scholarship. The very word "genre" evokes a groan in scholars, both literary and otherwise. It may prove less boring when it turns back on ourselves as a force that shapes not just our writing but the forms of thought we use. If we have learned anything in the past half century, we should know that we do not freely "use language" but rather are shaped by received habits of language and discourse that we have internalized.

When we think of "genre" in scholarly writing, it is a set of habitual procedures, requirements, and prohibitions that guide a "well-formed utterance" for a particular situation within a particular community. Scholars from one community or discipline often feel dissatisfied with discourse in another discipline. It is the mastery of just one scholarly genre that allows entry into the various guilds of the academy.

When such genres become fully internalized and routine, they are no longer fully available as objects for reflection in their own right. Like all genres, they are based on learned blindness, on phenomena not considered. For example, one thing that is sometimes hard, but not impossible, to see is how our current scholarly genres are contingent on earlier genres with their own limitations. In other words, our current disciplines are constructs of the interests and limits of the available record. There are silences that can be recognized as silences but are, more often than not, simply treated as if they are not there.

One scholar may organize extensive evidence in such a way as to prove a particular point. Guild members, usually with only passing knowledge of the same evidence, may read and approve the execution of a well-formed scholarly discourse. But a well-formed scholarly argument bears an uncertain relation to truth. Another scholar may know the same or proximate evidence and write a second discourse to counter the first scholar and give a different conclusion. One often tends to credit the second scholar's work because it is later, and there is vested interest in a larger teleology within which we improve and supersede the works of predecessors. Is the execution of a scholarly genre by the rules a guarantee of truth? Some believe so, and there may be some validity in such a guarantee of truth. But only if we accept the learned blindness of each protocol.

Or, perhaps, we should lend credence to an argument in inverse proportion to the number of intuitively important factors that are excluded from consideration by the protocols of a discipline.

There may be an advantage in increasing the kinds of scholarly genres with different rules. For example, I confess to an interest in questions greater than my interest in answers. Indeed, I am most interested in questions that keep arising for which no answer seems adequate.

The nature of discourse makes it impossible to do everything, but a multiplicity of different ways to think about historical phenomena would be a constant reminder of the limitation of our habitual procedures.

This suggests Montaigne's idea of the "essay," as "trying out" or an "attempt." We try out different ways to account for salient questions.

I like to think of cultural and historical phenomena as ecosystems or solar systems in constant change, each particular changed by and changing the whole. In such systems, causality becomes mathematically "complex," and when causality is mathematically "complex" it is indistinguishable from accident. It is a good way to understand how the meaning of things changes. For example, two instances of an argument may seem very close, indeed so close that one seems modeled on the other. But within the surrounding text, the second case may be deploying the argument for different, even incommensurate reasons. This sounds good but raises distinct problems for linear arguments and thought processes that are deeply embedded in linear arguments.

Like the early Tang historiographer Liu Zhiji, I prefer the mindlessly chronological order of *Zuo zhuan* to Sima Qian's centered narratives. It returns history to "one damn thing after another." It disables any single linear narrative by too many crisscrossing narratives, some without consequence, some simply stopping rather than concluding, some taking bizarre turns. Within this chaos appear the voices of moral historians seeking a level of coherence, with a retrospective knowledge of consequences, making accurate predictions based on contradictory premises.

A reader familiar with recent work on Song literature may be surprised that I do not address the question of literature's response to Daoxue (Neo-Confucianism), which was hostile to literature and responsible for considerable reflection on literature's place in the changing intellectual landscape of the Song. Fine work has been done in this, but it works through a limited set of questions that are strictly cordoned off from a larger view of the changes in both society and in literature. That point of view appears in the criticisms from the moralist interlocutors in some of these texts, whose intervention so often forces concession from the author as speaker. Such concessions are the shadow of the larger argument between moralizing Daoxue and literature, with literature unable to respond effectively to a critique posed in Daoxue's terms. And yet these authors keep writing things that invite such critiques, critiques even from within themselves. It is not the age of Daoxue to the exclusion of other interests—that inner force of resistance keeps resurfacing, and the only way to escape moralist surveillance must be either to hide or to lie.

The Song dynasty in the eleventh century is a good ground on which to reflect on these issues. We have different forces in play, and a policing of boundaries of discourse that tell us what contemporaries themselves recognized as uncomfortable topics. By this I mean that there is attention to what is controversial and to what should not be said, whether the censorship comes from within the author, from friends, or from enemies.

For *all* writing in this age, the most important event was Su Dongpo's trial in 1079 for slandering the emperor, primarily through his poetry but also in his prose. The dossier of the Censorate case survives.[8] The dossier contains readings of his poetry to demonstrate his opposition to the policies supported by the emperor; some interpretations are credible, but many are ridiculous. Here we see the kind of hostile surveillance that could be turned on any writing. The trial was important in its own right as the culmination of forces already widely at work in elite society. The dossier itself is not treated in these essays; rather, we see the background and the variety of forces of which this is only one instance. What is safe to write and what is not safe to write? When that question arises, silences are outlined and sometimes more significant than what is actually said.

These essays move back and forth across about sixty years of the Northern Song. Sometimes we will not observe chronology, but other times we will focus on it, suggesting changes that are occurring. Without pinpointing beginnings, it is hard to speak of causes; and beginnings are elusive because discursive moves that look the same can have a very different significance in a different context.

In the background of these texts, the policies advanced by Wang Anshi and his followers loom large, with a very vocal group of dissenters now called the "conservatives." The ensuing factional struggles had a profound impact on many of the writers included here. This was not the cause of the changes described in these essays but itself a large instance of such changes attempting to redefine the role of the government in the empire. Wang Anshi's reforms were themselves an "essay" in trying to configure a medieval polity to take centralized control of the economy.

If we see texts returning again and again to "happiness," this does not mean, as Yoshikawa Kojiro would have it, that the Song dynasty was happier than the Tang. Rather it means that happiness had become a question; and that, in turn, implies that whatever happiness is, it is neither realized nor easily within reach.

"What's in a Name" begins with the question of naming oneself by one's favorite possessions, claiming that they are the means by which the writer, Ouyang Xiu, can escape the public world and enjoy happiness. An imagined interlocutor criticizes his argument, and poor Ouyang Xiu has no adequate defense against his own inner critic. In the second essay, the "Magistrate of Peach Blossom Spring," we go back three decades to a younger Ouyang Xiu, exiled to the position of governor of the isolated but largely self-sufficient prefecture of Chuzhou, in the backwaters of what is now Anhui. Here Ouyang Xiu tries to reconcile happiness and empire (though never raising the question of taxation or corvée labor, the latter being the very means by which he undertook the "public works" that occasioned some of the essays). The prefecture is idyllic, echoing Tao Yuanming's account of "Peach Blossom Spring" from seven centuries earlier. "Peach Blossom Spring" was the beguiling vision of society without the state, and Ouyang Xiu's task was to write the state and its hierarchy of power back into the happy society.

"Missing Stones" begins with Ouyang Xiu still in Chuzhou, faced with a local name, the "Six Rocks of Ling Creek." This presents a problem for the governor who wants to "get the names right," because there is only one rock of the famous six left at Ling Creek. The rest have been taken by collectors. The question of taking possession enters idyllic Chuzhou; Ouyang Xiu has the last rock hauled away and taken to the prefectural seat. Thus, in the end all six rocks of Ling Creek are no longer at Ling Creek.

Su Dongpo was another rock collector, and in passing through Hukou he discovered a rock that he very much wanted to buy. He was on his way to exile and, since he couldn't take it with him, decided he would buy it when returning. But when he returned, he found that the rock had already been purchased by another collector. The saga of that now famous rock, "Nine Blossoms Mountain in a Jug," its name given by Su Dongpo, followed the fate of the dynasty, eventually entering the imperial collection, and perhaps ending up as a catapult stone, shot at the Jurchen army besieging the capital.

"All Mine" brings us to Sima Guang's "Solitary Happiness Garden," a name that flew in the face of Mengzi's "shared happiness." This is a wonderful story of names, advertising, and commercial value, as Sima Guang wrote a famous prose account and many poems about his "solitary happiness" garden, which in turn brought paying visitors every year. Here too the moralist interlocutor attacks the "name," until Sima Guang—after arguing that bringing others might use up the available happiness provided by the garden—is finally forced concede.

"The Stone That Tells Its Name" concerns another "rock" that Su Dongpo encountered in Hukou—this one, a little mountain in the lake with the name "Stone Bell." This was the rock that could not be carried away by a collector. Su Dongpo investigates the name to understand why it was the right name. The famous prose account he left marked the mountain forever with Su's own name, so that even now any mention of Stone Bell Mountain will immediately bring up the name of Su Dongpo.

Then we come to Su Dongpo's friend and disciple Huang Tingjian, writing an account for the garden of a merchant—and probably writing it for money. The "Account of Pine and Chrysanthemum Pavilion" returns to the "shared happiness" of ancient King Wen, discussed earlier. Huang Tingjian gives a vision of prominent and wealthy local merchant re-creating the idyllic polity on a local level and using his wealth to help his community, even as the dynasty was faltering. The final essay, "The Bamboo in the Breast and in the Belly," brings us to the artist's signature, to joking fantasies of wealth, and to laughter and death.

Earlier versions of the first five essays in this volume were given as the inaugural "Hu Shi Lectures" at Beijing University, May–June 2010. An earlier version of the first essay appeared as "Happiness, Ownership, Naming: Reflections on Northern Song Cultural History" in *Frontiers of Literary Studies in China* 5, no. 1 (March 2011): 3–24. An earlier version of "The Magistrate of Peach Blossom Spring" appeared in *Zhongguo wenxue xuebao*, no. 1 (December 2010): 61–82. The Chinese versions of the original Hu Shi lectures finally appeared as part of an essay collection, *Huayan* (A splendid banquet), published by Nanjing University Press in 2020. An earlier version of the sixth essay was presented on various occasions and was given as the Tang Prize Lecture in Taipei in September 2018, and one of the Reischauer Lectures at Harvard University in October 2018.

The texts discussed include some of the most famous prose works of the Northern Song, and two excellent books in English treating these texts and related issues deserve general mention. The first of these is Yang Xiaoshan's *The Metamorphosis of the Private Sphere: Gardens and Objects in Tang-Song Poetry* (Cambridge, Mass.: Harvard University Asia Center, 2003). The second is Ronald C. Egan's *The Problem of Beauty: Aesthetic Thought and Pursuits in Northern Song China* (Cambridge, Mass.: Harvard University Asia Center, 2006). I have tried to keep notes to a minimum, but in each case where the texts in our discussions overlap, I refer the reader to the discussion or discussions in those books. It always seems to me as though we are all three passing through the same sites on different itineraries, and what we see is in each case shaped by the particular itinerary. I have also included a "Further Readings" section at the end of the book.

1

WHAT'S IN A NAME?

The Biography of the Retired Layman Six Ones

Self-naming is an interesting act. In the Northern Song it became a common practice for gentlemen to assume pseudonyms, *hao* 號. There was no escaping the names given by one's parents—the demeaning but apotropaic child name, the *ming* 名, and the more formal *zi* 字 names. For the prominent few, a posthumous appellation was carefully considered but certainly beyond an individual's control. The *hao* or pseudonym was an opportunity to advertise one's more personal or private side, to say something about oneself.

While still in his thirties, Ouyang Xiu (1007–1072) had named himself Zuiweng 醉翁, "Drunken Old Man." This may not have been quite the proper image for a younger civil servant still in disgrace and exile, but it was perfectly all right for a *hao*. By his sixties—when he actually was an old man, still with a fondness for drink—he felt that to name himself "Drunken Old Man" in his thirties was not quite right. But rather than retaining the "old man," late in life he changed his *hao* to one far more peculiar: "The Retired Layman Six Ones" (or "One of Six") 六一居士.[1]

Such a name strikes a whimsical balance between simultaneously hiding oneself and advertising oneself. It is hard to say whether "The Biography of the Retired Layman Six Ones" 六一居士傳 (1070) was written to explain the name or the name was chosen to invite the "Biography." It is not a standard "biography," *zhuan* 傳, with one's native place, lineage, and life. Rather it is a biography of the person as he defined himself by that name. The choice of pseudonym invites the question: "What do you mean by that?" Lest someone fail to ask, Ouyang Xiu brings in a "visitor," *ke* 客, to pose the required question within the biography itself.

Although it is an untypical "biography," the work is not without precedent. About seven centuries earlier there was a tongue-in-cheek "biography" of someone whose "name" was given for five things, which would have made "six" with the addition of the person himself. This was Tao Yuanming's 陶淵明 (365?–427) "Biography of Master Five Willows" 五柳先生傳. According to Ouyang Xiu's logic, Tao Yuanming could have also been "Master Six Ones" 六一先生 if Tao had written as Ouyang Xiu did: "By adding this one old man, me, aging among these five things, how can this not make six ones?" 以吾一翁，老於此五物之間，是豈不爲六一乎?

Ouyang Xiu's readers would not be surprised by "The Biography of the Retired Layman Six Ones" because this literary transformation of the biography genre was well established; but Tao Yuanming's version was more appropriate for "Master Five Willows" because he had no history, no deeds, no hint of the choice or change from the political man that justified calling oneself "retired layman," *jushi* 居士. Master Five Willows was nothing more than a series of observed traits, with the only stable mark of identity being the five willows by his home. The name was mere contingent chance that meant nothing more than the contingency of all names. Anyone could have five willows by their home. We need to consider Master Five Willows first in order to understand the Retired Layman Six Ones.

Tao Yuanming, Biography of Master Five Willows

先生不知何許人也，亦不詳其姓字。宅邊有五柳樹，因以爲號焉。閑靜少言，不慕榮利。好讀書，不求甚解，每有會意，便欣然忘食。性嗜酒，家貧不能常得。親舊知其如此，或置酒而招之。造飲輒盡，期在必醉，既醉而退，曾不吝情去留。環堵蕭然，不蔽風日。短褐穿結，簞瓢屢空，晏如也。常著文章自娛，頗示已志。忘懷得失，以此自終。

We don't know what age the master lived in, and we aren't certain of his real name. Beside his cottage were five willow trees, so his name (*hao*) was taken from them. He lived in perfect peace, a man of few words, with no desire for glory or gain. He liked to read but didn't try too hard to understand. Yet whenever there was something that caught his fancy, he would be so cheerful he would forget to eat. He had an ale-loving nature, but his household was so poor he couldn't always get hold of ale. His friends, knowing how he was, would invite him to drink. And whenever he drank, he finished what he had right away, hoping to get very drunk. When drunk, he would withdraw, not really caring whether he went or stayed. His dwelling was a shamble, providing no

> protection against wind or sun. His coarse clothes were full of holes and patches; his plate and pitcher were always empty; he was at peace. He often composed literary works for his own amusement, and these gave a good indication of his aims. He forgot all about gain or loss and in this way lived out his life.

Whenever a writer evokes a famous earlier text as an analogy for himself, he calls attention to the differences as well as to the similarities. Both Master Five Willows and the Retired Layman Six Ones like books: for one, "He liked to read but didn't try too hard to understand. Yet whenever there was something that caught his fancy, he would be so happy he would forget to eat"; for the other, "My home library is of one myriad scrolls" 吾家藏書一萬卷. Both Master Five Willows and the Retired Layman Six Ones like to drink: for one, "He had an ale-loving nature, but his household was so poor he couldn't always get hold of ale. His friends, knowing how he was, would invite him to drink. And whenever he drank, he finished what he had right away, hoping to get very drunk. When drunk, he would withdraw, not really caring whether he went or stayed"; for the other, "one jug of ale is always set out before me" 常置酒一壺.

It is obvious that Master Five Willows and the Retired Layman Six Ones have a profoundly different relationship to the things they like. The happiness of Master Five Willows is unmediated; that is, he is represented enjoying what he has when he has it. The Retired Layman Six Ones possesses things in anticipation of using them and enjoying them. He may enjoy reading his books, but he takes delight in how many books he has. He may enjoy drinking, but he takes delight in the knowledge that he always has ale to drink close at hand. His delight is prospective, guaranteed by possession, and is transferred from the experience of consumption to possession of the means to consume and enjoy. Moreover, in contrast to Master Five Willows's poverty, the Retired Layman Six Ones enjoys abundance. His jug of ale is always present and always refilled.

Another profound difference between the two biographies is that Tao Yuanming, the author, creates an anonymous narrator from the community to tell the story of Master Five Willows, whose proper name and life are unknown. The first thing that the narrator tells us is that not only is his name unknown, even the time of Master Five Willows is unknown. He does not seem to be a contemporary of the narrator, who informs us at the end that he "lived out his life," *zi zhong* 自終, in the manner described. To those who knew him he had no other name. Not so for the Retired Layman. He does not try to hide the fact that he does have another name, a surname and a given name: he is Ouyang Xiu, one of the most prominent political figures and intellectuals of the day. As the interlocutor will remind him, there is no escaping that name and the personal history that goes with it.

Ouyang Xiu opens the biography by informing us that he is changing his pseudonym.

> 六一居士初謫滁山，自號醉翁。既老而衰且病，將退休於潁水之上，則又更號六一居士。

> When the Retired Layman "Six Ones" was banished to the mountains of Chuzhou, he called himself "The Drunken Old Man." When he became old, frail, and sick, he was going to retire to the waters of the River Ying. Then he once again changed how he called himself: the "Retired Layman Six Ones."

"Name" here is, of course, only a *hao*, a name chosen by a person to reflect his sense of identity. He begins, however, recalling an earlier time when he took on a different name, "The Drunken Old Man," Zuiweng 醉翁, a name that we know from other writings involved the joy that he shared with others in the context of the general happiness brought on by the imperial peace. That "happiness shared with many" 與眾偕樂 of the *Mengzi* has disappeared entirely in "The Biography of the Retired Layman Six Ones," whose identity seems closely tied to "solitary happiness" 獨樂. The things in "The Biography of the Retired Layman Six Ones" are his possessions, rather than sites where the governor and the people can gather.

"Getting the names right" is a question. In an earlier poem "On the Pavilion of the Drunken Old Man at Chuzhou" 題滁州醉翁亭, he told us a truth about that name, how the name didn't quite match the real situation: "Forty is not yet considered old" 四十未為老. Likewise, in the prose "Account of the Pavilion of the Drunken Old Man," "Zuiweng ting ji" 醉翁亭記, from the same period, he claimed the name simply because he was the oldest of the group, and he disclaimed the implications of the other component of his chosen name, "drunken" 醉, saying that drinking was only something in which he could "lodge" other, more serious concerns. Here in "The Biography of the Retired Layman Six Ones," he touches on the inaccuracy of his earlier name with a wry humor: now that he is actually frail and old, he discards the name "Old Man." From this opening statement, the promise of the biography is that the name and the person will somehow be reconciled. We know, however, that names can be problematic.

客有問曰:六一，何謂也。居士曰:吾家藏書一萬卷，集録三代以來金石遺文一千卷，有琴一張，有碁一局，而常置酒一壺。客曰:是爲五一爾，奈何?居士曰:以吾一翁，老於此五物之間，是豈不爲六一乎?

> It happened that someone asked him: "What do you mean by 'Six Ones'?" The Retired Layman said: "My home library is one of myriad scrolls and I have gathered one thousand scrolls of records of texts surviving on metal and stone since the Three Dynasties; I have one zither and one chess set; and one jug of ale is always set out before me." The person then said: "This is just five 'ones'; what about that?" The Retired Layman then said: "By adding this one old man, me, aging among these five things, how can this not make *six* ones?"

The presence of an interlocutor, or literally "visitor" 客, is a significant device in Chinese prose that touches on the presumptions of knowledge in the Chinese tradition. In a "discourse," *lun* 論, the author may offer a direct exposition of impersonal knowledge; but there is another kind of knowledge, particularly about oneself, that is authorized only by being elicited by someone else's challenge. He knows the name is strange; he needs someone to give him the opportunity to explain it. Someone must ask him the meaning of this peculiar name Liuyi 六一, "Six Ones"—a public name whose meaning is based on private knowledge that requires exegesis. To give oneself such an enigmatic name is to invite interrogation and the occasion to explain, and we can see how the initial questions are staged by the act of self-naming and the first incomplete explanation that reveals only five of the six terms—the library, the epigraphic collection, the zither, the chess set, and the jug of ale.

The explanation of the name that Ouyang Xiu gives himself should tell us who the person "is"; but Ouyang Xiu tells us only what he "has," which turns out to be only "five ones." This inevitably provokes the interlocutor to ask about the missing "one," which turns out to be Ouyang Xiu himself, growing old among the other five. Here in the five-plus-one-person we recognize the presence of "Master Five Willows" behind the Song writer's identity. We may point out yet another profound difference between Master Five Willows and the Retired Layman Six Ones. Tao Yuanming's five willows were just there, and they were all of the same kind. The willows were a coincidental presence, a convenience by which others could "place" the otherwise nameless free-spirit and eccentric. Ouyang Xiu, by contrast, has genteel possessions, accumulated over time, by which he names himself.

Master Five Willows' willows are literally rooted; they define the person by a stable place. The Retired Layman Six Ones' things are an entourage that follows him if he moves from place to place, a portable identity. They define a space into which the owner only pretends to disappear as one among many, even as he reminds us of the basic distinction between a "me," *wú* 吾, and outer "things," *wù* 物.

When a fire burned up Tao Yuanming's homestead, he was able to discover that he was unchanged despite the loss of all the material possessions he had; even more, if Master Five Willows had lost his five willows, he would have been indifferent. Even though Ouyang Xiu defines himself by the particular prestige things he chooses—the books, copies of inscriptions, zither, chess set, and ale of leisure pursuits—he still defines himself by his possessions, which in this new Song world are often the conditions of happiness. If he loses these things—the books, rubbings, zither, chess set, and ale-he loses his name and identity as the Retired Layman Six Ones.

The apparent austerity of "five" things is, of course, only an illusion of words. Two of the "ones" are merely counters for large numbers: "one myriad / ten thousand" *juan* 卷 of books (about a thousand modern books) and "one thousand" old rubbings or copies of inscriptions. The appearance of a recluse's contentment with limitation and limited possessions in fact represents a considerable estate. Ouyang Xiu's contemporary Sima Guang, author of the huge *Comprehensive Mirror for Government*, *Zizhi tongjian*, claimed a library only half the size of Ouyang Xiu's for the study hall in his Luoyang garden. Granted that Ouyang Xiu may have only one zither and one chess set (what would one do with more than one of either?), the "one" jug of ale is no less only an illusion of limitation—he may have one jug "always" set before him, but there seems little doubt that it can be refilled as often as he wants. This "retired layman" is far from Tao Yuanming, who gets his "one jug" only occasionally and must often do without. The rhetoric of limitation exposes its own untruth, and this new name assumed by the writer is no less problematic than his earlier appellation "Drunken Old Man."

This man "owns" things and identifies himself by what he owns. The theoretical problem is embedded in the name. To own things may result in being defined by what one owns, thus the self is both an owner and, at the same time, himself contingent on his possessions. The *liu* 六, the sixth member of the assemblage, seeks to solve that by simply adding himself to the other "five"; but as a very particular "one," *yi* 一, among the *liuyi*, "Six Ones," we know that he has a different status than the other five.

The interlocutor, hearing Ouyang Xiu's explanation of his name, comes up with the anticipated objection, playing on the range of meaning of *ming* 名 as "name" and "fame" or "reputation" (in English expressed as a private possession, "to make a name for oneself):

> 客笑曰:子欲逃名者乎，而屢易其號，此莊生所誚畏影而走乎日中者也；余將見子疾走大喘渴死，而名不得逃也。居士曰:吾固知名之不可逃，然亦知夫不必逃也。吾爲此名，聊以志吾之樂爾。

> The person then laughed, saying: "Do you really want to escape from having a name/fame? To so often change how you call yourself is what Zhuangzi made fun of as 'someone who fears his shadow yet runs in the sunlight.' As I see it, you are running swiftly, panting, dying of thirst, yet you will never manage to escape your name."
>
> The Retired Layman replied: "I know quite well that having a name cannot be escaped; nevertheless, I also understand that one doesn't have to escape it. I made this name ("Six Ones") just to commemorate my happiness."

For the interlocutor to "change how you call yourself" seems to be a version of "escaping your name." To be a *jushi* 居士, a "retired layman," is to withdraw from the public eye, to seek to have one's "name" not known; but in changing his name and choosing this peculiar new pseudonym, Ouyang Xiu is, in fact, advertising himself. Ouyang Xiu responds that he knows "name" cannot be escaped—and here, I think, he means name as reputation in a general sense—so it does not matter if he changes the particular name. Of the motive for choosing the name he says: "I made this name just to commemorate my happiness" 吾為此名，聊以志我之樂爾. The claim of casualness or offhandedness (*liaoyi* 聊以) in the phrasing is to counteract the suspicion that a name exists to be made known. Yet the verb *zhi* 志, translated here as "commemorate," implies a motive of publicity or to keep something from being forgotten. This name, like the earlier name "Drunken Old Man" 醉翁, is centrally concerned with happiness. The Drunken Old Man's happiness was reflexive, a happiness in the happiness of others. Here, in response to the interlocutor's request that Ouyang Xiu describe his happiness, we see it is something quite different:

> 客曰:其樂如何？居士曰:吾之樂可勝道哉？方其得意於五物也，太山在前而不見，疾雷破柱而不驚；雖響九奏於洞庭之野，閱大戰於涿鹿之原，未足喻其樂且適也。然常

患不得極吾樂於其間者，世事之爲吾累者衆也。其大者有二焉，軒裳珪組勞吾形於外，憂患思慮勞吾心於内，使吾形不病而已悴，心未老而先衰，尚何暇於五物哉。雖然，吾自乞其身於朝者三年矣，一日天子惻然哀之，賜其骸骨，使得與此五物偕返於田廬，庶幾償其夙願焉。此吾之所以志也。

The other person asked: "What is that happiness like?" The Retired Layman replied: "Can my happiness ever be fully told? When I find satisfaction among these five things, Mount Tai can be right in front of me, but I don't see it; peals of thunder can smash a column, but I won't be alarmed. Even the echoes of the Nine Shao in the wilderness of Dongting or viewing the great battle on the plain of Zhuolu are inadequate to figure such happiness and contentment. Still I have always counted it a misfortune not to be able to enjoy the fullest measure of happiness among them, for many were the worldly concerns that have encumbered me. On the outside, carriage, gown, badge, and ribbons tasked my physical form; on the inside, worries, troubles, concerns, and cares tasked my mind. These made my physical form decrepit though not sick and my heart waste away though not old—what free time was there for my five things? Even so, for three long years I begged for my person from the court; then one day the Son of Heaven sympathetically felt my distress and granted me back my bones, making it possible for me to go back to my cottage in the fields together with these five things. And I hope that I can enjoy the fulfillment of this abiding desire here. This is why I commemorated it."

A discourse on happiness may try to explain the causes of happiness or its nature. Keeping in mind that the interlocutor here is probably a figment of Ouyang Xiu's own imagination, this is precisely the question that the interlocutor poses. Ouyang Xiu's answer is a peculiar one. Perhaps the condition of happiness cannot be put into words, but it can be inferred by the external viewer's observation, by the complete absorption in his happiness—in Ouyang Xiu's case, conditioned by the presence of his things. As we will see in the following essay, in his younger years his happiness was also conditioned by his surroundings. Then it was other people being happy; now it is a complete absorption that excludes other people and the outside world altogether. Absorption can be described only negatively: in order to say that you do not notice what is going on outside the assemblage of self and possessions, you must name what you do not notice.

This is, of course, the same paradox of Tao Yuanming's fifth "Drinking Ale" 飲酒: "I made a cottage in the human realm, / yet there was no noise from horse and wagon" 結廬在人境，而無車馬喧. You must name the presence of the sound that you do not hear in order to claim that you do not hear it. But for Ouyang Xiu the supposedly unnoticed claims on his attention are exaggerated and hyperbolic. Mount Tai is right there before him, but he doesn't see it; thunder and lightning crash, but he doesn't heed it. However, the two scenes that are given as inadequate to "figure," *yu* 喻, his happiness are of particular interest. The first is the great musical performance held by the Yellow Emperor on the wilds of Dongting, recounted in the "Cycles of Heaven" 天運 chapter of *Zhuangzi*:

> 北門成問於黄帝曰:帝張咸池之樂於洞庭之野，吾始聞之懼，復聞之怠，卒聞之而惑，蕩蕩默默乃不自得。
>
> Beimen Cheng once asked the Yellow Emperor, "My Lord, when you performed Heaven's Pool music in the wilderness of Dongting, I was at first terrified by what I heard; then as I heard more, I felt a sense of apathy; finally, in the last part, I was all in confusion, swept along in a state of blankness, stupefied."

The Yellow Emperor tells Beimen Cheng that this was the progression of responses intended in the music; but "terror," "apathy," and a final "state of blankness"—while arguably a rare case of the sublime in the Chinese tradition—hardly seem to be overwhelmed by the intimate happiness of absorption in examining rubbings or playing chess. The second case, the cosmic battle between the Yellow Emperor and the rebel Chiyou on the plain of Zhuolu, is an even stranger comparison with scholarly pastimes. The term that can link these figures to Ouyang Xiu's happiness is the assumed power of external events to command attention and absorption that can be counteracted only by the depth of Ouyang Xiu's own absorption.

We are, in fact, uncomfortably close to thinking of Ouyang Xiu's possessions as *youwu* 尤物, "infatuating creatures/things," originally used to refer to femmes fatales, but in the Song dynasty, commonly used to describe possessions, real or speculative, whose attraction results in a destructive disregard for the rest of the world. The common critique of such is that in the long run they do not bring happiness, but rather discontent. It is also important to keep in mind that these "five things" are not chance presences like Tao Yuanming's five willows but are indeed possessions acquired with money, gifts, or, in the case of Ouyang Xiu's copies of inscriptions, collected personally.

According to the description of his absorption, the "five things" have power over him as he has power over them. This seems to be the balance of power that makes Ouyang Xiu not simply an owner of things but brought to their level as "one of six": the "five things" command him as he commands them; the master is mastered, and that balance of mutual mastery and the enclosure it creates is the aging Ouyang Xiu's understanding of happiness.

Ouyang Xiu scarcely needs to go on to tell us that such happiness in enclosure is negative; that enclosure is also exclusion. It is an escape not just from name, but also from the external burdens of office and the internal anxieties that accompanied them. It is the desire for a space of autonomy within social whole—not the recluse as the isolated self, but a new, peculiarly constituted community. It is a space of long-standing desire (夙願), which at last, with the emperor's blessing, can be fulfilled.

Such desire leads the interlocutor to the next and obvious objection, that Ouyang Xiu's ties to the "five things" are no less an entanglement than his ties to public life.

> 客復笑曰:子知軒裳珪組之累其形，而不知五物之累其心乎？居士曰:不然。累於彼者已勞矣，又多憂；累於此者既佚矣，幸無患。吾其何擇哉？於是與客俱起，握手大笑曰:置之區區不足較也。
>
> 已而歎曰:夫士少而仕，老而休，蓋有不待七十者矣。吾素慕之，宜去一也。吾嘗用於時矣，而訖無稱焉，宜去二也。壯猶如此，今既老且病矣，乃以難彊之筋骸，貪過分之榮祿，是將違其素志而自食其言，宜去三也。吾負三宜去，雖無五物，其去宜矣，復何道哉。熙寧三年九月七日，六一居士自傳。

> The other person once again laughed, saying: "You understand that carriage, gown, badge, and ribbons encumber your physical form, but don't you also understand that the five things encumber your heart?" The Retired Layman said: "It's not that way. To be encumbered by the former is indeed being put to task, and in addition brings many cares; to be encumbered by the latter is an indulgence and fortunately brings no misfortune. What is there to choose between the two?" Thereupon I stood up together with my visitor, clasped his

> hand, and said with a loud laugh: "Let's drop the matter. These petty things are not worth comparing."
>
> After that I gave a sigh and said: "A gentleman takes service in his youth and retires when he is old. There are indeed those who do not wait until they are seventy. I've always yearned to do so—that's the first reason that it is appropriate to quit. I have indeed been employed in my day yet have done nothing of note—that's the second reason it is appropriate to quit. I was still this way when I was in my prime, and now I am old and sick; in fact, to be greedy for fame and salary with these old bones and sinews that are so hard to force would be to go against my lifelong aims and to eat my own words—that is the third reason it is appropriate to quit. Given these three reasons that it is appropriate to quit, it would be indeed appropriate to quit even without these five things. What more is there to say!"
>
> The third year of the Xining reign, seventh day of the ninth month, the self-account of the Retired Layman Six Ones.

The interlocutor's objection would be that of any thinker of the day; it was an objection that would be made by Su Dongpo in "An Account of the Hall of Precious Paintings" 寶繪堂記 of 1077: happiness should not be contingent on any object, and particularly not on external things. The encumbrance of Ouyang Xiu's attachment to his favorite possessions is no less an encumbrance than holding public office. Ouyang Xiu characteristically counters the more abstract truth with the obvious experiential truth: service makes him miserable, while his "five things" make him happy. The term he uses, however, is an interesting one: he calls his absorption in his possessions an "indulgence" or "escape," *yi* 佚, a term that can be used in a pejorative sense and associated with "letting go." It can be a term of excess and is easily associated with more bodily excesses than books, inscriptions, a zither, a chess set, and a single jug of ale. Perhaps he is uneasy about letting oneself go in engagement with things; he says it "fortunately brings no misfortune," 幸無患, and abruptly breaks off the line of thought, trying to drop the conversation. If the interlocutor is indeed his own creation, this is a strange thing to do, making himself uncomfortable by his own imagined objections.

He then essentially surrenders, offering three reasons why it was appropriate for him to retire. We note that he has redirected the critique away from his happiness with his things to his decision to retire. The first of these reasons is his inclination. For the other two reasons he offers public pieties—and then, as if realizing that he has gone too far in stating his pleasure in the "five ones," says that he should have retired even without them. We have an interesting transformation from following an "abiding desire," *suyuan* 夙願, to doing what is "appropriate," *yi* 宜. With which he terminates the discourse.

Even conjuring a voice from the outside to ask about his happiness, poor Ouyang Xiu is forced to surrender his claim of happiness in absorption and take recourse in the "appropriateness" of his retirement. The interlocutor first is led to ask Ouyang Xiu's staged questions; but the interlocutor's objections, a form of self-examination, gradually cut to a point where the author is embarrassed and breaks off the dialogue, then defends himself. What he has confessed is self-indulgence, tacitly reaffirming the claims of public duty that call into question all private pleasures and invoke the very encumbrances that he was trying to escape.

Behind the façade of the "biography," *zhuan* 傳, as the etiology of a name, with the precedent of Tao Yuanming in the background, there is another genre of even greater antiquity. This genre was sometimes called the *shelun* 設論, in which a fictive interlocutor, literally a "visitor," appears to criticize the behavior of the author, thus allowing the author to defend his life choices—an "apology" in its older sense. The rhetorical term is *procatalepsis*. Most of "The Biography of the Retired Layman Six Ones" is taken up by this, with the interlocutor conjured up from an imagined community within him that is always watching and judging.

There is, however, a dark twist in Ouyang Xiu's version. While the earliest *shelun* conclude with the author-protagonist vindicating himself, we cannot escape the feeling that Ouyang Xiu has somehow lost the argument. He began with happiness. When he was pressed on the point, happiness turned into radical enclosure and absorption in his things. Then pressed by the interlocutor's claim that his attachment to his things is no less an entanglement than the demands of public life, he can only respond that he likes his things and they do him no harm. Finally, he changes the topic, changing his justification from happiness to "appropriateness" and that he does not need the five things by whose company he defined himself.

He is defeated and grudgingly concedes defeat. Four of his five possessions could be for private enjoyment or "solitary happiness," providing the kind of perfect enclosure of which he seems to have been speaking. One of those possessions, however, opens a space to the outside world: the chess set, the only one of his five "things" that cannot be enjoyed alone but needs a *ke* as "visitor" and opponent.

From within himself he imagines the surveillance of society, of his peers. The vision of complete enclosure that promises oblivion to all that happens outside fails him.

There is no harm if an old man, who had served the empire all his life and was to die only a few years later, had leisure to enjoy his "cultural objects" and his ale. But by 1070 China was coming into a new age in which every utterance was to be judged by new and stricter moral standards. Ouyang Xiu's claims in "The Biography of the Retired Layman Six Ones" could provoke some contemporary intellectuals to criticize his affection for external things and judge that Ouyang Xiu was "not someone who possessed the Way" 非有道者. The magnitude of such a charge, criticizing Ouyang Xiu's moral nature and attainments, is bizarrely out of proportion to his whimsical celebration of his retirement and favorite pastimes. Ouyang Xiu had been a pioneer in the renewed study of the Confucian Classics, a major historian, the creator of a supple, straightforward style of "old-style prose," and an important political figure. All this, however, could be dwarfed by his playful choice of a pseudonym.

Su Dongpo, who himself criticized attachment to things, came to his old patron's defense in "Written After 'The Biography of the Retired Layman Six Ones'" 書六一居士傳後:[2]

> 蘇子曰:居士可謂有道者也。或曰:居士非有道者也。有道者無所挾而安。居士之於五物，捐世俗之所爭，而拾其所棄者也，烏得為有道乎。蘇子曰:不然。挾五物而後安者，惑也；釋五物而後安者，又惑也。且物未始能累人也，軒裳圭組，且不能為累，而況此五物乎。物之所以能累人者，以吾有之也。吾與物俱不得已而受形於天地之間，其孰能有之。而或者以為己有，得之則喜，喪之則悲。今居士自謂六一，是其身均與五物為一也。不知其有物耶，物有之也。居士與物均為不能有，其孰能置得喪於其間。故曰:居士可謂有道者也。雖然，自一觀五，居士猶可見也。與五為六，居士不可見也。居士殆將隱矣。

> Master Su says: The Retired Layman may be thought of as one who possesses the Way. Some have said: "The Retired Layman is not someone who possesses the Way." One who possesses the Way is at peace without holding onto anything. In his relation to his five things, the Retired Layman gave up what ordinary people in the age struggle for yet picked up what they rejected—how can this be considered possessing the Way?
>
> Master Su says: This is wrong. One who is at peace only after holding onto these five things would be deluded, and one who is at peace only after letting go

of these five things would be also deluded. For material things have never had the capacity to encumber a person; even coach and uniform and seal and ribbons of office don't have the capacity to be encumbrances, much less these five things. The reason why things have the capacity to encumber a person is because "I" possess them. Both I and external things could not help receiving form in this world, so who has the capacity to possess them? Yet there are some who consider them their own; they are happy when they gain such things and sad when they lose them.

Now the Retired Layman refers to himself as "Six Ones," which is to say that his person is just one together with the five things. I don't know whether he possesses the things, or the things possess him. And if the Retired Layman and his things equally do not have the capacity to possess, then who can put questions of gain and loss to them? This is the reason I say: The Retired Layman may be thought of as one who possesses the Way. Nevertheless, in observing the five from the perspective of one, the Retired Layman still can be seen; joining the five to become six, the Retired Layman cannot be seen. The Retired Layman has virtually become hidden.

Su Dongpo was always a genius with the clever argument. To feel the necessity to let go of things in order to find peace is no less a dependency on things than the need to hold onto them; in either case, things, whether in their presence or in their absence, become determining factors in human happiness. Su Dongpo was always smarter than those who offered the naïve moralizing Confucian point of view, who saw mere possession as an inherent danger. Su understood that renunciation essentially reinforces the belief in the power of external things to take control of a person. "The reason why things have the capacity to encumber a person is because 'I' possess them" 物之所以能累人者，以吾有之也. From this premise, Su Dongpo ingeniously grants to Ouyang Xiu the only perfect solution: possession that is dissolved in the uncertainty of who is the owner and who is owned 不知其有物耶，物有之也. Yet despite his ability to contest naïve moralizing, Su Dongpo already belongs to a world in which the criterion of judgment is whether one does or does not "possess the Way" 有道.

There is, however, a wrinkle here. Sent from post to post, arrested and thrown into prison on a capital offense, then sent to a backwater prefecture in exile, Su Dongpo was to write in a song: "I always resent how this body of mine is not my own." "Not my own" is a variation on the "I possess," *wu you* 吾有, in the passage quoted. This is a stunningly direct way to rephrase the cliché used by Ouyang Xiu: "for three long years I begged for my person [*shen* 身, my body] from the court" and "one day the Son of Heaven . . . granted me back my bones."

The young scholars sent to the capital to take the *jinshi* examination were part of the local tribute levee. They were "local products" for the emperor to use or discard at his pleasure. The fact that they were imperial possessions was built into their clichés, and to Su Dongpo this proved experientially true—or, at least, subjectively so.

Ouyang Xiu stood on the margin of a new world. The ideological world of nascent Daoxue and the larger world of Northern Song social values had not yet come apart as radically as they would. On one side, many "gentry," *shidafu* 士大夫, were collecting and acquiring valuable things (keeping in mind that prestige cultural objects had come to have considerable commercial value); on the other side, there was a discourse that disdained "possessing things" 有物, with the only legitimate possession, *you* 有, being *you Dao* 有道, "possessing the Way." Many people were truly hypocritical, passionately acquiring possessions while disdaining the idea of possession. Some people cheerfully acquired; some people truly disdained possessions. There is a problem when social practice and ideology split. Ouyang Xiu stands on the edge of this split, honestly admitting that he enjoys what he has and that it makes him happy. It is not vast wealth, but he has much. He doesn't want more; he doesn't want to lose what he has. He was to die a few years later. He was close enough to the new world of values to feel uneasy that he enjoyed his possessions so much. Yet his happiness in his "things" was almost innocent, however much he was aware that it might look like vulgar ownership.

ENGAGING THE PAST

"The Master did not discuss weird things, force, disorder, or divine beings" 子不語怪力亂神 (*Analects* VII.20). In fact, the Master did not discuss a great many things, too numerous to mention—including personal possessions. However, what the Master *did* discuss helped to outline the field of Daoxue discourse.

The eleventh century was a cusp of change; but in a constantly changing world, cusps of change are almost everywhere. Literary men of the period attempted to maintain their links with the past, but tectonic changes were occurring, and cracks in the ground were showing. New, less formal genres of writing were appearing everywhere with a simplicity of discourse that finally justifies the term "classical" for the older, more established genres. In one of those newly established genres, the colophon, Su Dongpo famously wrote: "I am, indeed, Tao Yuanming, and Tao Yuanming is indeed me" 我即淵明，淵明即我 ("Written After Reading Yuanming's 'There Is a Gentleman in the East'" 書淵明東方有一士後).[3] The statement of perfect identity only reminds us of how different Tao Yuanming and Su Dongpo were. Perhaps the most profound difference is that Tao Yuanming, who so often held up earlier figures as personal models, would never have written: "I am, indeed, so-and-so; so-and-so is me" 我即某，某即我. If it is hard to measure change in the short duration, the magnitude of difference is immediately obvious over longer spans.

Likewise, Ouyang Xiu, *desiring* utter absorption in immediate engagement with what he was doing, evoked Tao Yuanming's Master Five Willows with his absorption and oblivion to his surroundings: "His friends, knowing how he was, would invite him to drink. And whenever he drank, he finished what he had right away, hoping to get very drunk. When drunk, he would withdraw, not really caring whether he went or stayed." The person we most want to resemble is inevitably the person we can never quite be.

The large shifts over a longer span of history inevitably create conflicts of values between the "now" where the writer stands and the "then" of his imagined counterpart in the past. One obvious example is in Ouyang Xiu's rhetoric of limitation. The new name he gives himself tells us that he has five single things, which is to say that he has only five things. But when we examine those five "ones," they represent abundance rather than limitation. He is proud of possessing much but wants to appear as a Tao Yuanming, who has little. Both are real values for Ouyang Xiu, and they cannot be reconciled, except through the ingenious pseudonym, which is the means to affirm both values simultaneously. In the same way he is both fleeing "name," *ming* 名, and making his name even more known, as the interlocutor tells him. Again, there are two contradictory values that can coexist only through the text.

Even though at the end of the "Biography" Ouyang Xiu surrenders his claim for absorption in his five things along with the claim of happiness, by creating a scene of possession, he entered a realm that the "Master did not discuss"—nor would the Master have discussed. For all the popularity of the "Biography," the pleasure in one's possessions left an odor that bothered the moralists. Here is another "Master," this one from the twelfth century:

> "The prose of Six Ones has discontinuities and passages that do not follow that seem as though there are characters missing. . . . The ideas in 'The Biography of the Layman Six Ones' are commonplace and the prose is flaccid." . . .
>
> When someone asked what [work of Ouyang Xiu] the Master [Zhu Xi] did like, he said, "The Account of the Pavilion of Abundance and Happiness."
>
> 六一文有斷續不接處，如少了字模樣。 . . . 六一居士傳意凡文弱。 . . . 問先生所喜者。云：豐樂亭記。
>
> Zhu Xi, *The Sayings of Master Zhu* 朱子語類

2

THE MAGISTRATE OF PEACH BLOSSOM SPRING

"The Biography of the Retired Layman Six Ones" was written two years before Ouyang Xiu's death in 1072. Ouyang Xiu had, in fact, been writing about happiness for most of his writing career. In 1036 he had been exiled to Yiling County 夷陵 in Xiazhou 峽州, where he gave a humorous account of what a primitive place it was: the market was so cramped that the local magistrate had to get out of his carriage, and the smell of the fish shops so awful that he had to rush through holding his nose ("When passing the market, even the magistrate always had to get down from his coach and hurry through holding his nose" 雖邦君之過市，必常下乘，掩鼻以疾趨). But the local magistrate had prepared comfortable quarters for him, so that instead of the appropriate misery of repentance for the misdeeds that brought about his exile, he felt quite comfortable.[1]

> 夫罪戾之人，宜棄惡地，處窮險，使其憔悴憂思，而知自悔咎。今乃賴朱公而得善地，以偷宴安，頑然使忘其有罪之憂，是皆異其所以來之意。
>
> It is appropriate that someone who is guilty of an offense be cast away into some awful place and dwell in some backwater, so that he can think sadly on his miserable state and learn to regret his transgression. But now, in fact, thanks to Lord Zhu, I have a fine spot, by which I steal some peace and quiet, stupidly brought to forget any sadness at my offense. This is, in every way, quite otherwise than the purpose for which I was brought here.

These words are part of a commemoration known as "An Account of the Hall of Perfect Delight in Yiling County" 夷陵縣至喜堂記. A hall called "Perfect Delight" 至喜 discursively resists imperial power to make an official miserable and repentant. Note the term Ouyang Xiu uses to mark the difference between what he is supposed to feel and what he actually feels: it is "appropriate," *yi* 宜, to feel penitent and reflect on his errors. This is the same term he was to use late in life when forced to surrender his claim of happiness in retirement in favor of an argument based on the "appropriateness" of retirement. We can enjoy something of the irony in his sense of the word.

Su Dongpo surely had this account in mind when he wrote his "Account of the Terrace of Going Beyond" 超然臺記 in 1074:[2]

> 余自錢塘移守膠西，釋舟楫之安，而服車馬之勞；去雕墻之美，而蔽采椽之居；背湖山之觀，而適桑麻之野。始至之日，歲比不登，盜賊滿野，獄訟充斥，而齋厨索然，日食杞菊。人固疑余之不樂也。處之期年，而貌加豐。髮之白者，日以反黑。

> When I left Qiantang [Hangzhou] to take up the administration of Jiaoxi [Mizhou], I forsook the steadiness of a boat and submitted to the difficulties of going by horse and coach. I left behind the attractions of carved walls and took shelter in a dwelling with plain beams. I turned my back on vistas of lakes and mountains to walk through a wilderness of mulberry and hemp. On the day I arrived, I found that the harvest had been bad for several years running. There were bandits everywhere in the outlands, and complaints clogged the courts. I kept to a plain diet, each day eating only wolfberry and chrysanthemums. People obviously suspected I was unhappy. But when I had been there for a full year, my features looked increasingly healthy, and the white in my hair every day progressively reverted to its former black.

There is, however, a basic difference between Ouyang Xiu's and Su Dongpo's happiness in adversity. For Ouyang Xiu, happiness needs some object, edifice, or place in the world to which it can attach itself. In Yiling it is the relatively comfortable lodgings provided by the magistrate. Su Dongpo, however, makes the claim that the happiness comes purely from within himself, as in the "Account of the Terrace of Going Beyond."

"Going Beyond" is, in this context, being beyond the weight of potential administrative worries, which are carefully enumerated for his reader. The terrace itself was not the cause of his happiness, which came from within, but naming the edifice offered an occasion to reflect on his happiness in writing, just like Ouyang Xiu claimed to commemorate his happiness in the "Biography." Su Dongpo casts himself as the latter-day Yan Hui, happy in adversity, but unlike the case with Yan Hui, only adversity can bring out Su's happiness.

In Ouyang Xiu's "Account of Painted Boat Studio" 畫舫齋記, the perils of travel by water become converted to happiness by the studio built to imitate a boat:[3]

> 乃忘其險阻，猶以舟名其齋，豈真樂於舟居者邪。
>
> In fact, I forgot the perils and difficulties and still named the studio after a boat—but how could one truly be happy staying on a boat?

But then he thinks that being in a boat might be a condition for happiness after all:

> 然予聞古之人，有避世遠去江湖之上終身而不肯反者，其必有所樂也。苟非冒利於險，有罪而不得已，使順風恬波，傲然枕席之上，一日而千里，則舟之行豈不樂哉。
>
> Nevertheless, I've read that among the ancients there were those who fled society and went far away to spend their whole lives on the rivers and lakes and were never willing to go back—so there must have been something about it that made them happy. So, unless one is braving perils for profit or compelled to do so for some offense, then supposing one goes a thousand leagues in a single day, with fair winds and calm waves, proudly resting on pillow and mat, how then can traveling by boat not be happy?

The building and giving it a name are central to the process of thinking, by which distress or unhappiness turn, not to happiness itself, but to understanding why one could be happy.

The most famous and engaging texts on happiness and naming come from Ouyang Xiu's term as governor of Chuzhou 滁州 in the mid-1040s. "The Account of the Pavilion of Abundance and Happiness" 豐樂亭記 from 1045 begins: "It was in summer of the year after I took up the governorship of Chuzhou that I first drank Chu's water and found it sweet." 修旣治滁之明年，夏，始飲滁水而甘.[4] We know that Ouyang Xiu was a careful stylist, and it is always worth paying close attention to how he phrases things. His genius was reinventing "old-style prose," *guwen* 古文, and making it straightforward and simple. He might have simply told us that the water of Chuzhou was sweet—earlier in the Tang, tea-drinking had encouraged a discourse on the connoisseurship of water. But he represents the sweetness of the water as an experience and discovery. He does so by the phrase *yin er gan* 飲而甘: *gan*, "sweet," was normally an intransitive verb, but used in parallel with *yin*, "drink," it is forced into a transitive, considerative sense, "found it sweet." This had been characteristic prose in antiquity (and was used in the revival of "old-style prose" in the Tang). Here it gives an unobtrusive flavor of antiquity to the sweetness of the water.

This opening anticipates the theme of the account, concerning things that are so "close at hand" 近 and habitual that they are overlooked. Once Ouyang Xiu notices that the water is "sweet," he seeks out the source (*yuan* 源/原), which in this case is literally a "source," a spring. The source of sweet water becomes linked to the overlooked "source" 原 of happiness of the people of Chuzhou.

> 修既治滁之明年，夏，始飲滁水而甘。問諸滁人，得於州南百步之近。其上豐山，聳然而特立；下則幽谷窈然而深藏；中有清泉滃然而仰出。俯仰左右，顧而樂之。於是疏泉鑿石，闢地以爲亭，而與滁人往遊其間。

> It was in summer of the year after I took up the governorship of Chuzhou, that I first drank Chu's water and found it sweet. I asked the locals about it and found it nearby, a hundred paces south of the prefectural seat. Above was Abundance Mountain, rising up and standing apart. Below was Secluded Valley, keeping it deeply hidden. Between these two was a clear spring, coming out upward from the ground and welling over. Looking about, above and below and all around, I was delighted. Thereupon I had a channel dredged and had the rock cut, opening the spot in order to make a pavilion. And I would go there on excursions with the natives of Chuzhou.

The stream's source is close at hand (得於州南百步之近). Usually things of value either come from afar or go far (*yuan* 遠). The most expensive objects come from "far places," the best plans consider "what is far ahead"; profound implications are "far-reaching." All are encompassed by the same word, *yuan*.

The *Analects* opens by Confucius's remark about friends coming from "afar." But also in the *Analects*, the disciple Zixia 子夏 recommended "thinking about what is close at hand," *jin si* 近思, as an important part of fellow-feeling (*ren* 仁): "Zixia said: 'To study widely and be focused in one's aims, to ask earnestly and think about what is close at hand—fellow feeling can be found in this'" 子夏曰：博學而篤志，切問而近思，仁在其中矣 (XIX.6). Thinking about what lies close at hand was indeed the virtue of Song intellectuals, from the natural science of Shen Gua to the philosophical observations of the Confucian thinkers. Knowledge does not necessarily lie in what is far away but can be found by investigating and reflecting on what lies close around one and how that is linked to oneself and to the larger world.

Although close at hand, the presence of the spring is not at all obvious; in fact, it is represented as if it were in some remote place. Abundance Mountain looms above it; Secluded Valley lies below; and the spring is hidden by the vegetation in between. Here the governor builds a pavilion for his own pleasure and that of the residents of Chuzhou. He literally uncovers what is hidden.

I want to pause a moment over Secluded Valley, presumably a descriptive place name. It may be "keeping it deeply hidden" 窈然而深藏, but Ouyang Xiu publicizes it. As we will see in the next essay, the area around the spring is where Ouyang Xiu set up the larger rock from Ling Creek for everyone to appreciate. If he had left the rock in any ordinary "secluded valley," then the act would have been strange indeed (he writes: "Had I left it to sink away in someplace remote and secluded, it would have been too bad" 棄沒於幽遠則可惜). The geography—even of "secluded" spaces like Secluded Valley—becomes perspicuous in an imperial geography of named places, and a place named "Secluded" can be put on a map and is distinct from any unnamed "secluded place."

It is not enough simply to find the source of sweet water; a space must be cleared, the flow of the water must be controlled and directed (as Great Yu 大禹 did on a larger scale when he cut channels for the rivers of China), a building must be constructed, and it must be named. Part of the "secluded" or "hidden" landscape becomes "civilized" as it enters an imperial map of named sites.

The name Ouyang Xiu gives the pavilion has two components: "abundance" 豐 for the name of the mountain on which the spring was located, as well as the abundant harvests that the folk of Chuzhou enjoy, and "happiness" 樂, presumably for the joy Ouyang Xiu and the residents of Chuzhou had on excursions to the pavilion. Wild nature is cleared away, and the spring is made accessible. And through writing, the governor opens up the "sources" of both their sweet water and their happiness for the residents.

The source of the sweet water has to be discovered; the source of the happiness of the people of Chuzhou also needs to be uncovered, but it is more complicated than simply finding a spring. It awaits the governor Ouyang Xiu to make it clear. As he moves out of the city to the spring hidden in the landscape, the discourse suddenly turns to the past, which is also hidden in the landscape.

> 滁於五代干戈之際，用武之地也。昔太祖皇帝，嘗以周師破李景兵十五萬於清流山下，生擒其將皇甫暉、姚鳳於滁東門之外，遂以平滁。修嘗考其山川，按其圖記，升高以望清流之關，欲求暉鳳就擒之所，而故老皆無在者。蓋天下之平久矣。自唐失其政，海内分裂，豪傑並起而爭，所在爲敵國者，何可勝數。及宋受天命，聖人出而四海一。嚮之憑恃險阻，剗削消磨，百年之間，漠然徒見山高而水清。欲問其事，而遺老盡矣。

> During the warfare of the Five Dynasties, Chuzhou had been a place of battle. Long ago our emperor Taizu had once led the Zhou army and smashed one hundred and fifty thousand troops of Li Jing at the foot of Clearcurrent Mountain and captured the generals Huangfu Hui and Yao Feng outside the eastern gate.[5] Thereafter Chuzhou was pacified. I have studied the mountains and rivers, checking them against maps and accounts, and I climbed a high place to view Clearcurrent Pass, hoping to find the spot where Huangfu Hui and Yao Feng were captured—but no old people survive from that time. Truly the world has been at peace for a long time. From the time that the Tang government collapsed, and the world split apart with bold, outstanding men rising everywhere in contention, how can one count all the places that became enemy realms? When the Song dynasty received the Mandate of Heaven, a Sage Ruler emerged, and the sea-girt world became one. The defensible fastness on which they once relied has been obliterated and wiped away; and in the span of a hundred years one sees only a blur of high mountains and clear rivers. And if one wants to ask about what happened here, the old survivors of that age are all gone.

Shifts of topic and attention are interesting, and traditional critics of Chinese prose paid attention to them. They represent the way in which the mind makes associations.[6] All of a sudden our attention is directed out into the landscape around Chuzhou, to Clearcurrent Mountain 清流山 and the battle that took place there at the end of the Five Dynasties, then to the east gate of Chuzhou where the Southern Tang generals Huangfu Hui and Yao Feng were captured by the founder of the Song dynasty, when he was still a general of the Later Zhou kingdom. We later realize that Ouyang Xiu is searching for *yuan* 原/源, looking for the "source" of the happiness of the prefecture, just as he searches for the source of sweet water. What is close at hand leads to what is far-reaching. But when he sets out to investigate the traces of this "source," unlike the source of the stream, those traces are nowhere to be found. And Ouyang Xiu marvels how, during the intervening century, the sites of those heroic deeds have so utterly vanished, even from local memory. History has left no traces in the natural beauty of the landscape.

今滁介於江淮之間，舟車商賈，四方賓客之所不至。民生不見外事，而安於畎畝衣食，以樂生送死，而孰知上之功德，休養生息，涵煦百年之深也。

Now Chuzhou is bounded by the Yangzi and the Huai, a place where boats and wagons and merchants and visitors from all over do not come. The people see nothing of what happens outside, but they are content with the food and clothing provided by their fields, whereby they are happy during their lives and see off their dead. Who among them understands the depth of the Emperor's achievement and virtue, nurturing them and giving them ease, achievements and virtue that have shed grace on them for a hundred years?

We come then to a peculiar situation in which the people, by their very isolation, lead lives of contentment; yet in another context, the geography that gives them such isolation (a "defensible fastness") made them a site of battles. They live in peace without realizing or remembering enough to know that their happiness depends on the peace of the empire. As he uncovered the spring or "source" (*yuan* 源 /原) hidden beneath the vegetation, here he publicizes for them the buried historical past and the source of the current happiness of the people of Chuzhou.

修之來此，樂其地僻而事簡，又愛其俗之安閑。既得斯泉于山谷之間，乃日與滁人仰而望山，俯而聽泉。掇幽芳而蔭喬木，風霜冰雪，刻露清秀，四時之景無不可愛。又幸其民樂其歲物之豐成，而喜與予遊也。因爲本其山川，道其風俗之美，使民知所以安此豐年之樂者，幸生無事之時也。

夫宣上恩德，以與民共樂，刺史之事也。遂書以名其亭焉。慶曆丙戌六月日，右正言知制誥知滁州軍州事歐陽修記。

When I came here, I was happy with the remoteness of the place and the simplicity of its affairs; I also loved the contentment and ease of local customs. Having found this spring between the mountain and the valley, I daily join the people of Chuzhou in gazing up at the mountain and listening to the spring run down below. Whether picking secluded blossoms and being shaded by tall trees, or in frosty wind or ice and snow, it reveals its pure excellence—the scenery of all the four seasons is lovable. I also feel fortunate in how the people are

> happy in the abundance of their harvests and enjoy going on excursions with me. Thus I have told the basics of their mountains and rivers and stated the beauty of their customs, so that the people will know why it is that they can be content in the happiness of this abundant year and feel fortunate that they are living in these times without problems.
>
> To proclaim the Grace and Virtue of the Sovereign in order to share happiness with the people is the business of the governor. Consequently, I wrote this to name the pavilion. An account made on a certain day of the sixth month of the sixth year of the Qingli reign by Ouyang Xiu.

Then we come back to Ouyang Xiu's happiness, which is now happiness in the simplicity of the people and the rareness of problems. The account becomes the means to make the people understand the larger context and cause of their contentment. And though the district is "without business/problems," *wushi* 無事, whereby the governor does not have the usual problems, it becomes then the business of the governor to make imperial grace manifest and—in a peculiar formulation that echoes *Mengzi*, "thereby to share happiness with the people" 以與民共樂.

This happiness is something very different from the pleasures of visiting the pavilion with the governor and different again from being left in isolation and knowing nothing but contentment in what is close at hand. In this final version, happiness involves knowing *why* you are happy, the contingency of happiness, hard-won from war and suffering and, by implication, a happiness easily lost. The governor comes from the outside—from outside the locale and with knowledge of a past that has been locally forgotten. His "business" is to bring in that outside knowledge and cast a shadow on the happiness of the local people so that they will treasure it all the more and feel gratitude to the empire that otherwise leaves them alone.

When King Wen 文王 of the ancient Zhou dynasty "shared the people's happiness," it was the same kind of happiness as the innocent happiness of the people of Chuzhou, even though King Wen needed to share it in order to be able to be happy himself. Ouyang Xiu is aware that happiness comes in different kinds; in fact, there is a hierarchy of happiness corresponding to the hierarchies of society. The higher one is in the hierarchy, the more self-conscious one is about happiness.

For Ouyang Xiu, the scene of happiness has a distinct shape, in which the hierarchy of happiness appears in concentric circles. He declares a site, gives it a name, and occupies the center; others gather around, and he appreciates his central position. His naming a site contributes to his own name. The minimal shape is like the

Retired Layman Six Ones, surrounded by his five "things," with his new name (*hao*) adding himself to the assemblage as the sixth. In Chuzhou, surrounded by mountains, he names a site like the Pavilion of Abundance and Happiness 豐樂亭 or the Pavilion of the Drunken Old Man 醉翁亭, where he is surrounded by the happy populace and the rocks that he has brought in from Ling Creek. Outside those mountains is the empire, within which he circulates his writing to his friends. We have the poems responding to "The Account of the Pavilion of Abundance and Happiness" by Cai Xiang 蔡襄 (1012–1067), Su Shunqin 蘇舜欽 (1008–1048), and Mei Yaochen 梅堯臣 (1002–1060). Near at hand in Chuzhou he had Zeng Gong 曾鞏 (1019–1083), the adoring disciple, to write an account of a second pavilion, an account in which Ouyang Xiu is still central.

Zeng Gong's account in every way represents the voice of the disciple. The pavilion on which he writes in 1047, the Pavilion That Sobers the Mind 醒心亭, was built after the Pavilion of Abundance and Happiness.[7] Its purpose was to serve as a place to sober up after having become drunk at the earlier pavilion. His own account "enables me by writing to commit my own name in sequence after His Excellency's [Ouyang Xiu] writing" 得以文詞託名於公文之次.

Zeng Gong, An Account of the Pavilion That Sobers the Mind

滁州之西南，泉水之涯，歐陽公作州之二年，搆亭曰豐樂，自為記，以見其名之意。既又直豐樂之東幾百步，得山之高，搆亭曰醒心，使鞏記之。

凡公與州賓客者遊焉，則必即豐樂以飲，或醉且勞矣，則必即醒心而望。以見夫羣山之相環，雲烟之相滋，曠野之無窮，草樹衆而泉石嘉，使目新乎其所覩，耳新乎其所聞，則其心洒然而醒，更欲久而忘歸也。故即其所以然而為名，取韓子退之北湖之詩云。噫。其可謂善取樂於山泉之間，而名之以見其實又善者矣。

雖然，公之樂，吾能言之:吾君優游而無為於上，吾民給足而無憾於下，天下學者皆為才且良，夷狄鳥獸草木之生者皆得其宜，公樂也。一山之隅，一泉之旁，豈公樂哉?乃公所以寄意於此也。若公之賢，韓子歿數百年而始有之。今同遊之賓客，尚未知公之難遇也。後百千年，有慕公之為人，而覽公之跡，思欲見之，有不可及之歎，然後知公之難遇也。則凡同遊於此者，其可不喜且幸歟?而鞏也，又得以文詞託名於公文之次，其又不喜且幸歟?慶曆七年八月十五日記。

Southwest of Chuzhou on the bank of a stream, Master Ouyang, in the second year of his governorship of the prefecture, constructed a pavilion called

"Abundance and Happiness" and himself wrote the account to show the significance of the name. Thereafter, several hundred paces directly east of "Abundance and Happiness" reaching the heights of the mountain, he constructed another pavilion called "Sobers the Mind"; and he had me, Gong, write the account for it.

Whenever His Excellency and his guests from the prefecture come on an excursion, they always go to "Abundance and Happiness" to drink; and when they happen to get drunk and uncomfortable, they always go to "Sobers the Mind" for the view. By seeing all the mountains circling around, made lush by the clouds and mist, the endlessness of the broad wilderness, the multitude of plants and trees and the excellence of rocks and streams, it makes their eyes renewed by what they observe and their ears renewed by what they hear. Then their minds grow expansive and sober up, and they stay on longer, heedless of going back. Thus, he gave it a name for how it is there, borrowing what Han Yu had said in his poem on North Lake.[8] Indeed, he may be considered good at finding happiness among the mountains and streams, but he is someone even better at giving names that show the reality.

Still I am able to tell of His Excellency's happiness: Our Ruler is at perfect ease and governs by nonaction above; our common folk are well-provided and have no resentments below; all over the world men of learning are universally talented and virtuous; all living things, frontier peoples, birds and beasts, plants and trees, attain what is appropriate for them—all this is His Excellency's happiness. How could His Excellency be made happy merely by a nook in a mountain or a streamside? In fact, this is why His Excellency only invests his thoughts in such. One of worthiness such as that of His Excellency has been found only after several centuries following the death of Han Yu. The guests who go on excursions with him scarcely realize how rare it is to encounter His Excellency. In the centuries and millennia to follow, some will adore the kind of person His Excellency was; and in looking on his traces, they will yearn to see him and sigh that they are too late. Only after this will they understand how rare it is to encounter His Excellency. Can all those who come on excursions here with him not feel delighted and fortunate? And can I, Zeng Gong, being able to add my own name by writing in sequence after His Excellency's writing, not feel even more delighted and fortunate? An account on the fifteenth day of the eighth month in the seventh year of the Qingli reign.

As the disciple, Zeng Gong also assumes the role of the master's exegete: "I am able to tell of His Excellency's happiness" 公之樂，吾能言之. Of course, Zeng Gong's explanation is that Ouyang Xiu's happiness is not in the immediate circumstance but in the imperial peace itself, a happiness that finds expression in the natural scene. Perhaps there was a wry humor in the inebriate governor's choice of such a very sober author for a pavilion named "Sobers the Mind."

This is an interesting twist of what Ouyang Xiu himself says, which is that the imperial peace is the precondition rather than the object of happiness. It is a subtle but profound difference. Zeng Gong explicitly denies that Ouyang Xiu finds happiness in the natural scene and the pleasures of the excursions (一山之隅，一泉之旁，豈公樂哉). Ouyang Xiu himself never says such a thing; the pleasures of the landscape and excursions are indeed the occasions of happiness; he recognizes, however, that this happiness is possible only because of and through the imperial peace. For Zeng Gong, happiness in the here and now should be nothing more than a figurative instantiation of happiness in the Way. Perhaps the most revealing indication of Zeng Gong's essentially abstract object of happiness is the final clause of the description of Ouyang Xiu's happiness: the imperial peace, the contentment of the common folk, the abundance of virtuous men, and "all living things, fish and fowl, birds and beasts, plants and trees, attain what is appropriate for them—all this is His Excellency's happiness." As Chinese poets have often correctly observed, the natural world is indifferent to human suffering and the success or failure of the polity. Zeng Gong's addition of this clause is significant, making the natural world only another circumstantial instantiation of the Way. We cannot but notice that Zeng Gong's interpretation of Ouyang Xiu, that his happiness is the consequence of what is "appropriate," is actually quite different from Ouyang Xiu's clear distinction between the appropriate and happiness. In his "Account of the Pavilion of the Drunken Old Man," Ouyang Xiu, the humorous empiricist, suggested a very different relationship between human beings and Nature: "When the visitors leave, the birds are happy" 遊人去而禽鳥樂也. While he represents the necessity of the empire for human happiness, he also realizes that the birds care nothing for people or their empire, except that they would rather be left alone.

Tao Yuanming's "Account of Peach Blossom Spring" 桃花源記 describes a fisherman discovering a village people who were descendants of people who had fled the wars in the breakup of the Qin dynasty five centuries earlier. They knew nothing of the outside world and its history. The image of such a village was powerfully seductive in Chinese culture because it imagined a society without the state, an internally sufficient social space that was not part of the empire. It was a hole in a totalizing empire. The very name that was given to the village came from the traces of peach blossoms in the flowing water that led to its discovery from the outside.

Ouyang Xiu is our "magistrate of Peach Blossom Spring." "Surrounding Chuzhou everywhere are mountains" 環滁皆山, just as Peach Blossom Spring is surrounded by mountains and cut off from the outside world. Chuzhou is the place to which few outsiders come; it is vaguely utopian, and its inhabitants seem unaware of history and the doings of the outside world just like the villagers of Peach Blossom Spring. The fisherman in the "Account of Peach Blossom Spring" tells the villagers what had happened in history since Qin; in "The Account of the Pavilion of Abundance and Happiness," Ouyang Xiu reminds the people of Chuzhou of their own forgotten history—of the battles and violence that occurred nearby only a century before—but in doing so, he reminds them of how their blissful happiness depends on the imperial peace. Once the fisherman left Peach Blossom Spring, he could never find it again, and the village remained outside the empire. Ouyang Xiu is the agent of empire coming from the outside, ordering construction of public buildings around the prefectural seat inscribed with names and dates, sites of shared pleasure that teach the locals the history and hierarchy that make them only a small part of a greater whole. If the contentment of the people of Chuzhou were completely autonomous, the empire would not be necessary. By reminding them of the violence that they have forgotten, their contentment is to the credit of the empire; and the governor's sharing their happiness becomes the celebration of the imperial system and a reinscription of a hierarchy of power in a world that was oblivious to it.

Ouyang Xiu's most famous piece of this period is the "Account of the Pavilion of the Drunken Old Man" 醉翁亭記, from 1046, a year after "The Account of the Pavilion of Abundance and Happiness."[9] Here we see the same issues returning in a new configuration. The "Account of the Pavilion of the Drunken Old Man" continues the theme of a hierarchy of power that is related to a hierarchy of knowledge and thus a hierarchy of happiness.[10] This is closely related to the authority to identify and name.

環滁皆山也。其西南諸峯，林壑尤美。望之蔚然而深秀者，琅邪也。山行六七里，漸聞水聲潺潺，而瀉出于兩峯之間者，釀泉也。峯回路轉，有亭翼然，臨于泉上者，醉翁亭也。作亭者誰？山之僧智僊也。名之者誰，太守自謂也。

> Surrounding Chuzhou everywhere are mountains. The forests and ravines of the many peaks to the southwest are especially beautiful. The place rising with thick verdure in one's gaze is Langya. When you go six or seven leagues into the mountain, the burbling sound of water gradually comes to ear, and what spills forth between the two peaks is Brewer's Stream. The peak turns, the road bends around, and there is a pavilion with wings outspread; looking out over the stream is the Pavilion of the Drunken Old Man. Who was it made the pavilion?—a monk of the mountain known as Zhixian. Who was it named the pavilion?—the governor claims this for himself.

The style of the account is both peculiar and justly famous, but it is worth asking just what the repeated use of the copula ("as for X, it is Y," X 者, Y 也) does. It is an authoritative voice that locates a place and names it. The opening passage focuses in on a single spot in the landscape, identifying and naming, until finally it names the governor as the person with the power to give names. The account also closes by naming the author and identifying the governor as Ouyang Xiu. He is identified not simply as such, as is the norm in accounts—but as the one person among all Chuzhou's things and people who has the ability to write this, an ability that comes to him as the representative of the outside world. He both is at the center of things, with all attention focused on him, and has a view from the outside that sees himself at the center of things. As the empire is a circle with the emperor in the center, so its outlying prefectures are little circles centered on the representative of the greater whole that "puts them in their place."

We should look closely at how this works. Chuzhou was the scene of collective happiness in "The Account of the Pavilion of Abundance and Happiness," achieved by discovering the hidden "source." The "Account of the Pavilion of the Drunken Old Man" even more theatrically focuses on a single spot hidden in the vegetation. Ouyang Xiu begins with the large perspective of Chuzhou itself, surrounded by a panorama of mountains. The scene focuses on one quadrant in the panorama, then on one spot, hidden in greenery. At once we are entering that enclosed spot, directed first by the sound of a stream and then by the stream itself, which leads to the pavilion, which will be the stage of the happy excursions of the people of Chuzhou. If there is a lesson in this theatrically controlled movement of vision, it is that the specific place—the scene of happiness—is contained in the larger world. Just as he traced the source of sweet water in the earlier account, here he follows the sound to the stream itself and follows the stream to the pavilion, a site already built, awaiting only his act of naming.

The stream already has a name, Brewer's Stream. The stream in turns leads to the pavilion, first identified by its maker, a local monk. The governor then takes for himself the right not only to name the pavilion, but to name the pavilion after himself (his pseudonym)—or perhaps to name himself for the name he gives to the pavilion. The speaker in the text asks questions that ultimately lead back to himself as the answer, developed in a scene in which he holds center stage. The new name for the pavilion, in conjunction with the name Brewer's Stream, affirms the imperial order of origins and consequences: the water of Brewer's Stream makes ale, and the ale makes the governor drunk. And the governor is the giver of names.

The monk who "made" the pavilion almost certainly did not make it with his own hands; he had it made. Unless he was a carpenter-monk, the resources that enabled him to build the pavilion probably came from donations. It is hard to call such donations entirely "free," motivated by the desire for blessing or the fear of retribution; but they were at least more free than imperial taxation and corvée labor. The possessions of the Buddhist church (*sangha*) have here been symbolically appropriated by the state as a theatrical set on which to stage a resonantly archaic scene of good government. As we will see, on the same authority to act for the common good, Ouyang Xiu appropriated the last rocks of Ling Creek.

We might pause on the passage: 名之者誰? 太守自謂也, translated as "Who was it named the pavilion?—the governor claims this for himself." The second clause means both: "The governor refers to himself as such" (a statement that does not answer the question unless we take 名之者誰 to mean something like "who lent his name to it?"), and "The governor himself referred to it as such." Both seem to be apparently true. As with the Retired Layman Six Ones, self-naming spreads out and attaches itself to adjacent things. Moreover, the instability of "referring," *wei* 謂, turns into the stability of "name," *ming* 名. A name requires an etiology: the first part of the name comes from the occasion of getting drunk, and the second part, "old man," *weng* 翁, is justified by the fact that he is the oldest person present. To be the senior in a group does not justify the term "old man," and we soon find out that the term "drunken" also has its problems.

> 太守與客來飲於此，飲少輒醉，而年又最高，故自號曰醉翁也。醉翁之意不在酒，在乎山水之間也。山水之樂，得之心而寓之酒也。

> The governor comes and drinks here with his guests; and no sooner does he drink a little than he gets drunk. And being also the most advanced in years, he calls himself the "Drunken Old Man." The Drunken Old Man's thoughts are not in the ale but in this space of mountains and waters. The happiness of the mountains and waters is attained in the heart and invested in the ale.

Master Five Willows is, of course, again in the background: "And whenever he drank, he finished what he had right away, hoping to get very drunk. When drunk, he would withdraw" 造飲輒盡，期在必醉，既醉而退. The "Drunken Old Man" gets drunk on far less: "no sooner does he drink a little than he gets drunk" 飲少輒醉. But these new Song dynasty names are all only relative and figural: this is not "getting the names right" 正名 but giving names that point to something else. The "old man" 翁 is merely the eldest, which belies this particular appellation. Drunkenness is not even itself, but only a displaced signifier: "The Drunken Old Man's thoughts are not in the ale but in this space of mountains and waters. The happiness of the mountains and waters is attained in the heart, and invested in the ale" 醉翁之意不在酒，在乎山水之間也。山水之樂，得之心而寓之酒也. This is a characteristically Song move: liking to get drunk is morally suspect, and he feels compelled to explain that his interests are not really in drinking but actually in the landscape. Even interest in the landscape might be suspect, for we have seen how Zeng Gong denied such interests in Ouyang Xiu and explained that his real interests were in the ambiance of good government and not in the landscape.

Let me add that for Master Five Willows his "purposes" are actually in the ale itself; for Tao Yuanming it is not a world of displaced signifiers, but a desire to drink: if there is a larger meaning, it is in the person. Like the name that is transferred from the governor himself to the pavilion, what is in the governor's mind is transferred from the landscape to the ale. There is a process by which the space of the landscape (in which Ouyang Xiu places himself linguistically "in this space of mountains and waters" 在乎山水之間也, as he later did with his five objects of pleasure as the Retired Layman Six Ones) is converted to joy, which is first achieved in the heart and then "invested" or "lodged temporarily" (also "figured") in the ale. The ale is not the "means" of pleasure merely but its figurative, external expression.

If we compare Tao Yuanming's world with Ouyang Xiu's world, the differences are striking. In Tao Yuanming, the physical world that he inhabits is primarily what it seems to be. Tao Yuanming looks at the vapor on the mountain in the setting sun and finds a "truth" there:

> 山氣日夕佳，飛鳥相與還。 此中有真意，欲辨已忘言。

> The vapor on the mountain in numinous at twilight,
> birds in flight join together in return.
> In this there is some truth—
> I want to analyze it but have lost the words.

Tao Yuanming's "truth" is experienced as *in* the physical world, not "lodged" in it by the mind of the viewer. In Ouyang Xiu, the physical scene is named and described not entirely as a world of things, but as a world of signifiers that require explanation. Meaning is not stable: new explanations are always produced. Here he speaks of his "happiness in the landscape" 山水之樂; but by the end it is his "happiness in the happiness of others" 太守之樂其樂也.

> 若夫日出而林霏開，雲歸而巖穴暝，晦明變化者，山間之朝暮也。野芳發而幽香，佳木秀而繁陰，風霜高潔，水落而石出者，山間之四時也。朝而往，暮而歸，四時之景不同，而樂亦無窮也。

> When the sun comes out, the haze in the forest lifts, and when the clouds come back, the crevices in the cliff darken. These transformations of darkness and light are the dawns and dusks in the mountains. Wildflowers come out and secluded spots grow fragrant; fine trees burgeon and their thick leafage casts shade. The wind and frost are high and pure, then the water level sinks and rocks emerge. These are the four seasons in the mountains. At dawn we set off and at twilight we return; and though the scenery of the four seasons is not the same, the happiness in it is endless.

Tao Yuanming's Peach Blossom Spring was an idyll, a place that knew only the regular changes of the day and the seasons; it was out of history and did not belong to the empire's time, measured in the reigns of rulers. Ouyang Xiu wants to make Chuzhou an idyll within the empire and at the end of the account omits the reign date that binds cyclical time to the linear time of the state. If, in "The Account of the Pavilion of Abundance and Happiness," Ouyang Xiu reminds the people of troubled historical past that they have forgotten, here in the "Account of the Pavilion of the Drunken Old Man" he allows history to be forgotten, evoking a constancy of happiness through regular diurnal and seasonal change. In this account there is only happiness constantly renewed, as if the whole prefecture were on an eternal holiday.

> 至於負者歌于途，行者休於樹，前者呼，後者應，傴僂提攜，往來而不絕者，滁人遊也。臨溪而漁，溪深而魚肥；釀泉爲酒，泉香而酒冽，山肴野蔌，雜然而前陳者，太守宴也。宴酣之樂，非絲非竹，射者中，弈者勝，觥籌交錯，起坐而喧嘩者，衆賓歡也。蒼顔白髮，頽然乎其中者，太守醉也。

> Those carrying things sing on the path; those just walking rest among the trees. The ones in front shout; the ones behind answer; hunched down and leading by the hand, they go back and forth continuously—these are the excursioners of Chuzhou. Standing by the stream and fishing: the stream is deep and the fish are fat; brewing spring water to make ale; the spring waters are sweet and the ale is cold and sharp; herbal relishes from the mountains and greens from the wilds, all mixed together and set before us: this is the governor's feast. The music when the feast gets tipsy is neither of strings nor woodwinds. The tosspot player gets one in the pot; the chess player wins a game; goblets and forfeit tallies lie mixed up together; the buzz of chatter as they get up and sit down—these are the guests having a good time.[11] Darkening complexion and white hair, collapsed in their midst—this is the governor, drunk.

We see the people streaming out to the pavilion singing and happily carrying loads that make them bend their backs from the weight. At this point he introduces hierarchy into his mixed crowd: birds, "the people," and the governor. He repeats "governor" so often that we are compelled to think how this will be taken in the larger empire and would be taken by the emperor at the center. This is the sign of good government, with the people happy because of the governor and happy along with the governor. This is a happiness that will be to the governor's credit, just as the larger imperial peace is to the credit of the emperor.

> 已而夕陽在山，人影散亂，太守歸而賓客從也。樹林陰翳，鳴聲上下，遊人去而禽鳥樂也。然而禽鳥知山林之樂，而不知人之樂；人知從太守遊而樂，而不知太守之樂其樂也。醉能同其樂，醒能述以文者，太守也。太守謂誰？廬陵歐陽修也。

> At last the evening sunlight is in the mountains, and the shadows of the people scatter in confusion; the governor sets out for home, and the guests follow. The trees in the forest shade them over, with the sounds of birdsong above and below. The excursioners leave, and the birds are happy. However, the birds only know the happiness of the mountain forest, but they don't know the happiness of people; people know to follow the governor on his excursion and be happy, but they don't know the governor's happiness in their happiness. The one who can be drunk and share their happiness and who, sobering up, can give an account of it in writing is the governor. And who is the governor? Ouyang Xiu of Luling.

Finally we come to the famous passage on the hierarchy of being, which is also a hierarchy of happiness. On the lowest level are the birds, who find their joy when the people leave and are incapable of understanding or sharing the joy of the human beings—indeed, the completeness of their joy requires the removal of the human intruders. On the second level are the people, who come here in a crowd and have a good time but are incapable of understanding the governor's joy, which is a happiness in their happiness. This is an intensely political Confucianism, echoing the *Mengzi*'s reading of the Spirit Terrace in the *Classic of Poetry* 詩經: "Men in ancient times shared their happiness with the common people, and thus they themselves were able to be happy" 古之人與民偕樂，故能樂也. That may be the background of Ouyang Xiu's claim, but "sharing happiness" 偕樂 is not the same as "being happy in their happiness" 樂其樂, which is far more complicated.

At last we come to the final naming: from the "Drunken Old Man," we move to the "governor," who finally names himself as Ouyang Xiu. To describe oneself in the third person is not at all unusual, but this piece maintains third-person reference to himself throughout, as if in some final mediation in which the "I" finds his joy in the image of himself finding his joy in the joy of others. Ouyang Xiu is here not "Ouyang Xiu"; rather he is the "governor," a position in the imperial hierarchy. Once retired and removed from that location of self in the official hierarchy in which he had spent his entire life, it is no wonder that, in "The Biography of the Retired Layman Six Ones," he creates a new system of "things" in which to define himself.

We might return to Ouyang Xiu's "being happy in their happiness" and take note of an undated poem by one of his contemporaries, someone no less obsessed with happiness. This is Shao Yong 邵雍 (1011–1077), and the poem in question is "No Taking Pains in Composing Poems" 無苦吟:[12]

平生無苦吟，書翰不求深。行筆因調性，成詩為寫心。詩揚心造化，筆發性園林。所樂樂吾樂，樂而安有淫。

No taking pains in poems all my life,
in my writing I don't seek depth.
By my moving brush I temper my nature,
I complete a poem to describe my mind.
The poem brings out the mind's creation,
the brush shows forth my nature's garden.
What makes me happy is happiness in my happiness,
and in happiness how can there be any excess?

This a remarkably self-consciousness happiness, not just the need to know that you are happy in order to be happy, but the location of happiness itself not in primary experience, but in the secondary, reflective experience. It seems that Shao Yong suggests that more direct happiness is in danger of "excess," *yin* 淫, and only the distance of self-consciousness protects one against loss of control. It is a striking parallel and contrast with Ouyang Xiu's "being happy in their happiness."

The texts of this period echo one another and respond to recent earlier texts. As the people of Chuzhou affectionately gathered around Ouyang Xiu, his accounts circulated in the larger world; and his friends, both younger and older, sent in poems and sometimes prose, surrounding him with celebration of his happiness. Su Dongpo was another devoted younger friend; and, as we have seen, he defended the aging Ouyang Xiu against criticism. But Su Dongpo was also very competitive. In the mid-1040s Ouyang Xiu was governing mountainous Chuzhou; in 1061 the twenty-six-year-old Su Dongpo, recently having passed the examination, went to take up his first post as staff advisor (*qianshi panguan* 簽書判官) of the governor of Fufeng in dry Shaanxi. And in his "Account of the Pavilion of Delighting in the Rain" 喜雨亭記 (1062), he recalls and perhaps gently teases the author of "The Account of the Pavilion of Abundance and Happiness." This issue again begins with water.[13]

Su Dongpo, Account of the Pavilion of Delighting in the Rain

亭以雨名，志喜也。古者有喜，則以名物，示不忘也。周公得禾，以名其書；漢武得鼎，以名其年；叔孫勝狄，以名其子。喜之大小不齊，其示不忘一也。

余至扶風之明年，始治官舍，為亭於堂之北，而鑿池其南，引流種樹，以為休息之所。是歲之春，雨麥於岐山之陽，其占為有年。既而彌月不雨，民方以為憂。越三月乙卯，乃雨，甲子又雨，民以為未足，丁卯大雨，三日乃止。官吏相與慶於庭，商賈相與歌於市，農夫相與抃於野，憂者以樂，病者以愈，而吾亭適成。

於是舉酒於亭上，以屬客而告之曰:五日不雨，可乎？曰:五日不雨，則無麥。十日不雨，可乎？曰:十日不雨，則無禾。無麥無禾，歲且薦饑，獄訟繁興，而盜賊滋熾。則吾與二三子，雖欲優游以樂於此亭，其可得耶。今天不遺斯民，始旱而賜之以雨，使吾與二三子，得相與優游而樂於此亭者，皆雨之賜也。其又可忘耶？

既以名亭，又從而歌之。曰:使天而雨珠，寒者不得以為襦。使天而雨玉，飢者不得以為粟。一雨三日，繄誰之力？民曰太守，太守不有。歸之天子，天子曰不。然歸之造物，造物不自以為功。歸之太空，太空冥冥，不可得而名，吾以名吾亭。

The pavilion is named for the rain, commemorating my delight. When the ancients had cause for delight, they named things for it to show that it was not to be forgotten. When the Duke of Zhou got [auspicious] grain, he named one of his writings for it; when Emperor Wu of Han got a cauldron, he named the year for it; when Shusun vanquished the Di people, his son was named for it. Though these occasions for delight differed in magnitude, they were the same in showing that these were not to be forgotten.

In the year after I reached Fufeng, I first had my official lodgings taken care of and made a pavilion north of the hall. South of it I dredged out a pond, brought in a stream of water and planted trees to make it a place where I could rest. In the spring of that year, it had rained grain on the southern slopes of Mount Qi, and the prognostication was for a good harvest. But then it didn't rain for a full month, and the common people thought that was worrisome. By the eighth day of the third month it rained; on the seventeenth it rained again, but the common people thought that it wasn't enough. On the twentieth there was a big rain that lasted three days. Officials and clerks got together to offer congratulations in the courtyard; merchants got together to sing in the marketplace; peasants got together to clap their hands out in the wilds. Those who were worried became happy; those who were ill were cured; and it was then that my pavilion happened to be completed.

Thereupon I raised my ale-mug in the pavilion to urge my guests to drink and said to them: "Is it all right if it doesn't rain for five days?" They said, "If it doesn't rain for five days, there will be no wheat." "Is it all right if it doesn't rain for ten days?" They said, "If it doesn't rain for ten days, there will be no rice."

With no wheat and no rice, the harvest will fail, lawsuits will abound, and bandits will run amok. And if that happens, how will you and I get to take our ease, being happy in this pavilion, even if we want to? But now Heaven has not abandoned these common folk, first with a drought but then granting them the gift of rain; and the fact that you and I have been able to get together to take our ease and find happiness in this pavilion is entirely a gift granted by the rain. Can it be all right to forget that?

This said, I named the pavilion for it, and followed with a song about it:

Supposing Heaven rained pearls,
those who were cold could not make a jacket of them.
Supposing Heaven rained jade,
those who were starving could not use it as grain.
A rain that lasted three days long–
to whose power was that due?
The common folk say "the governor";
the governor says, "Not me!"
Then attribute it to the emperor;
the emperor says, "O no!"
So attribute it to the Maker of Things;
the Maker of Things won't take credit.
Then attribute it to the Great Void,
the Great Void is a dark mystery,
you cannot grasp it to give it a name,
and so I named my pavilion.

Unlike the bliss of Chuzhou, where everyone always seemed happy, at Fufeng there is a long interval of worry about the drought that turns to happiness with the rain—and it is at that moment that the pavilion is completed.

If it were Ouyang Xiu, he would be happy in the happiness of the people. What is represented as acting for the common good in Ouyang Xiu is for Su Dongpo treated as private advantage, *si* 私. Su Dongpo is not seriously declaring private advantage; rather, he is being playful. He treats the rain entirely in terms of his own personal benefit. He and a few friends want to enjoy themselves in the pavilion. If the drought continues and there is a famine, there will be social unrest, banditry, and all manner of problems for officials. In that case he and his friends won't be able to enjoy themselves. Su's anticipated relaxation is the gift of the rain, and he commemorates this by the name "Pavilion of Delighting in the Rain" 喜雨亭.

The major playful twist away from Ouyang Xiu is in the question of responsibility. For Ouyang Xiu, happiness follows from the founding of the dynasty and continued peace and good government, of which he is the representative. Su Dongpo uses the term of an imperial gift *cì* 賜. First it is a gift of Heaven: "Heaven has not abandoned these common folk, first with a drought but then granting (*cì*) them the gift of rain" 今天不遺斯民，始旱而賜之以雨. Then it is a gift from the rain itself to Su Dongpo and his friends: "the fact that you and I have been able to get together to take our ease and find happiness in this pavilion is entirely a gift granted by the rain" 使吾與二三子，得相與優游而樂於此亭者，皆雨之賜也.

When one uses the term "grant a gift," *cì* 賜, there must be a donor, someone to *thank* for the gift. This uncertainty about who or what is responsible leads to humorous meditation, characteristic of Su Dongpo, in a comic song on the search for agency. Thanks are due—primarily because Su Dongpo used the term "a gift granted" 賜—but no one knows whom to thank. The governor would be the first and obvious choice. Ouyang Xiu's Chuzhou pieces imply that the governor is the proximate agent of the happiness of the people of Chuzhou, but Ouyang Xiu refers the credit back to the dynasty and the emperor. Here the governor declines to take the credit, then the emperor, then the Maker of Things (the First Mover), until at last we come to the Great Void, which is silent on the matter, incomprehensible, and unknown. We chuckle because no one takes responsibility for a good deed. It is a world of chance. Sometimes there is happiness.

There is one more small thing to notice: So Dongpo says what Ouyang Xiu did not: "and so I named my pavilion" 吾以名吾亭. Su Dongpo calls it "*my* pavilion" 吾亭.

In the Tang, literary men did not write much about happiness—and certainly not often in prose. Bai Juyi 白居易 (772–846) might be an exception, but he was more broadly the "pre-Song Man," their underappreciated predecessor. Moreover, for Bai Juyi, "being comfortable" is more often an issue than "happiness" in a large sense. Before the Tang the writings of Tao Yuanming, who was indeed centrally concerned with the question of happiness, often loom in the background. But for a few generations in the eleventh century, literary men wrote a great deal about happiness, and its conditions.

We often read these as single texts, examples of "Song prose," but they were very much part of a "family" of texts, circulating in a community, with responses, criticism and refutation, mutual teasing, and reprises that, in apparent reformulation of a parent text, subtly but significantly change the terms. "Happiness" was no less a topic in nascent Daoxue, most notably in the poems of the philosopher Shao Yong. The Confucian Classics they studied so intently had much to say on the topic, but the version of happiness for philosophically inclined Confucian thinkers differed from the happiness of the more literary scholars, who were more deeply bound up in the social and public world.

We know that Su Dongpo is being playful in the "Account of the Pavilion of Delighting in the Rain," but we need to think of Ouyang Xiu's two famous essays from his term as governor of Chuzhou to fully appreciate the play. In an older version of Confucianism—one that still received lip service—the rain that saved the crops would have been attributed to Heaven's response to beneficent government, so that any of the possible actors in such a political drama of explaining the weather might have deserved thanks. Su Dongpo smiles and, in effect, says: "Who knows? It simply rained."

We cannot entirely rebuild the web of crisscrossing relationships and circulating texts, but we can find enough to see that it is a force guiding the production of texts (and, no doubt, encouraging the construction of pavilions to name and provide the occasion for new texts). Perhaps a better way to read Song literature might be not in individual texts or the "life and times" of a single author, but through these networks of circulation, within which the discursive personalities and the changes through their lives come out so clearly.

3

MISSING STONES

There are "living questions" at a particular moment in a culture, and there are "dead questions." For dead questions there is an answer—sometimes several answers—but the question disappears behind the answers. For living questions, however, the question itself keeps returning. Literature and thought form around the living questions, where even the wisest and most brilliant answers cannot stop the question from returning.

If you pay close attention to a text, you can tell when there is a living question. Even if a writer intends to be direct and simple, some force intervenes and he will say something unexpected or odd, the argument will take an unexpected turn, or the writer will simply break off and change the topic. Sometimes the writer will try to demonstrate why the oddness is, in fact, obvious. At other times the oddness will make us suspect that the writer is being humorous; we often can't be sure whether he means to be humorous, but humor often forms around living questions because there are contradictions that cannot be resolved. These are marks of living questions, where the question remains greater than any possible answer.

Let me offer an example.

Suppose an author begins an essay: "There are six rocks at Ling Creek" 菱谿之石有六. We soon learn that this is a very problematic statement: five of the six have been taken away and are no longer at Ling Creek; one of those missing rocks is nearby, but the other four have been taken to places unknown by one or more rock-lovers. The last rock, too large and difficult to move, is described as "fallen flat" 僵臥, as if even this rock is not in the "proper" position that merited it being counted as one of the "six rocks of Ling Creek." By the end of the essay the author tells us that he has taken away the last, supine rock himself—along with one of the missing rocks, the one who's nearby location he knows. In the middle of the essay we further learn that Ling Creek may be the wrong name, a relatively recent name for a stream once called Xìng Creek, or so they say; neither we nor Ouyang Xiu know if his informants are right. We are not even at all sure that the rocks were originally from the creek or were brought there in making a garden. Much of the account concerns the fact that these mostly missing rocks belonged to the estate of the rough tenth-century Wu general Liu Jin; but finally another, later text collides with this one and we learn that the "six rocks" may not have belonged Liu Jin at all, but to the subsequent Southern Tang owner of the estate, Feng Yanlu.

The interest in the rocks is linked to the question of ownership—by the putative original owner Liu Jin and by the collectors who later took the rocks for themselves, along with Ouyang Xiu's own implicit assertion of the governor's authority to take away the last rock and the smaller rock that was in the possession of a local commoner. His unease with the resemblance of his own appropriation of the last rocks to that of ordinary collectors leads him at last to one of the earliest discussions of the "public trust" in China—the state appropriation of something to make it available to all (or, at least, officialdom), but owned by none.

The text in question is Ouyang Xiu's "Account of the Rocks of Ling Creek" 菱谿石記 of 1046, again during his term as governor of Chuzhou.[1] He begins: "There are six rocks at Ling Creek" 菱谿之石有六. But this cannot be true: in mountainous Chuzhou there were surely rocks everywhere in Ling Creek, including large ones. There may have been six famous ones, but only one of those six was still there when Ouyang Xiu visited the site; and since that one had fallen over and was often submerged, how would he have known that it was one of *the* six? This was clearly local lore, and he needed someone to tell him that the often-submerged rock in the creek was one of the famous six. But how does the local person know? We come to the kind of local knowledge that so troubled the representatives of the empire when they wanted to write the definitive local history for the next governor and for the sake of the empire, in which the "local" was to be mapped down to the last famous rock.

> 菱谿之石有六。其四為人取去；其一差小而尤奇，亦藏民家；其最大者，偃然僵臥於谿側，以其難徙，故得獨存。每歲寒霜落，水涸而石出，谿旁人見其可怪，往往祀以為神。

> There are six rocks at Ling Creek. Four have been taken away by people; and there is one, quite small and remarkable, that is kept at a commoner's home. The largest lies fallen over by the edge of the creek; and being hard to move, it managed to be the only one to remain. Every year when the cold frosts fall, the water level sinks, and the rock emerges. Seeing how amazing it is, people by the creek often worship it as a god.

Ouyang Xiu will not take the rocks as his private possessions, but in some essential way he is no different previous collectors who took five of the six rocks away. As he tells us at the very beginning of his "Preface for the List of My *Records of Collected Antiquities*" 集古錄目序: "Things always are gathered by those who love them, and they are always obtained by the one with the greater strength" 物常聚於所好，而常得於有力之強。As the local governor, he is "the one with the greater strength." His power not only provides him the resources to move the largest rock that has proven so difficult for others to move, it also gives him the social power to take the remarkable smaller rock from the home of a commoner. If local commoners generally regarded the larger rock as a deity, the governor has the authority to have their deity transported to his Pavilion of Abundance and Happiness, so that the local Chuzhou gentry can appreciate it as an aesthetic object. The empire centralizes its treasures, whether this is done by a local governor or by the emperor Huizong 徽宗, who would collect the finest rocks from all over the empire for his imperial park, only to lose them all in the end–rocks, park, empire, and eventually his own life.

Everyone understood the principle of "gathering and keeping together," *ju* 聚, followed by "scattering" or "dispersal," *san* 散. Once upon a time General Liu Jin of the Wu regime during the Five Dynasties had the power to acquire the rocks and keep them together. After Liu Jin passed away–and the unmentioned appropriation of the estate in the Southern Tang–there was dispersal of what had been gathered. Others took the rocks away according to their means. Property depends on power–political, social, or moral–but not on an established sense of rights.

> 菱谿，按圖與經皆不載。唐會昌中，刺史李濆為荇谿記，云水出永陽嶺，西經皇道山下。以地求之，今無所謂荇谿者。詢於滁州人，曰:此谿是也。楊行密有淮南，淮人為諱其嫌名，以荇為菱。理或然也。

> On consultation, none of the maps or canonical texts record a "Ling Creek." In the Huichang reign of the Tang (841–846), the governor Li Fen wrote an

> "Account of Xing Creek," saying that the waters came from Yongyang Ridge and then went west at the foot of Huangdao Mountain. When one looks for it, there is now nothing called Xing Creek. I inquired of someone from Chuzhou, who said that it is this creek [that is, Ling Creek]. When Yang Xingmi occupied Huainan, the people of Huainan avoided the taboo on his name and changed Xing to Ling. That may be how it was.

Ouyang Xiu does what any good Chinese local official would do: he gets out his maps and records and checks for the site. There may have been six rocks at Ling Creek, but unfortunately, he discovers that, according to his records, there is no Ling Creek. What he does find is an account by a predecessor, an obscure mid-ninth-century governor of Chuzhou named Li Fen. This, however, is an "Account of *Xing* Creek," now Li Fen's only extant work. Li Fen's Xing Creek seems to follow roughly the same course as Ouyang Xiu's Ling Creek. Not only are rocks moving around, names are shifting as well. Li Fen commented on the splendid scenery and repaired a ruined pavilion in which to entertain his guests, but he didn't mention any remarkable rocks. This suggests that either Ouyang Xiu has the wrong creek, or the rocks were moved there after Li Fen's time, or no one noticed them earlier and associated them with the creek.

He asks the locals, who tell him that Xing Creek is, indeed, Ling Creek, and that the name was changed to avoid a taboo on the name of a local Wu ruler of the Five Dynasties, Yang Xingmi, who ruled for only three years. The problem is that locals often don't really know the history and often give an explanation that seems plausible but not reliable. In the "Account of Stone Bell Mountain," Su Dongpo wisely laughed at the locals' explanation of the name of the mountain, when they struck stones to explain the name's origin. In "The Account of the Pavilion of Abundance and Happiness," Ouyang Xiu noted that the locals seemed to know nothing of the major battles in the region that happened almost a century earlier in the Five Dynasties. If everyone in the Five Dynasties Wu Kingdom (including remote Chuzhou) had tried to avoid the sounds of the characters in Wu ruler Yang Xingmi's 楊行密 name, they would have lost not just *xìng* 行 (locally in the falling tone), but apricots *xìng* 杏, and indeed all good fortune *xìng* 幸.

The local explanation of the name of the creek is, at best, dubious; but Ouyang Xiu wants a history for this creek, just as he wanted the local people to know about the nearby battles. Ouyang Xiu accepts the explanation provisionally because he has no other explanation. It solves a problem of knowledge, with one textually documented creek missing in the landscape and an undocumented creek making an appearance. The explanation solves a problem but raises the possibility, in remote Chuzhou, there were creeks outside the textual record. In real local culture, moreover, a creek that has a name in one place may have a different name five miles upstream. The empire is an inventory of place names; these should be known and textually mapped. But famous rocks are moved; names change; creeks disappear. Ouyang Xiu wants to normalize the record, identify and name and create historical continuity. He centralizes, literally bringing the last rocks into imperial space, the prefectural capital.

Should we find it odd that the locals know so much about the very brief Wu regime, its taboo characters, and the estate of one of its generals but are ignorant of a major battle nearby late in the Five Dynasties, a battle between the much larger Southern Tang and the Later Zhou, whose general became the founder of the Song dynasty? For Ouyang Xiu, there is problematic local knowledge and the secure historical knowledge of the center and the empire. Perhaps there is only local knowledge, and in war the winners get to tell history as it seems to them. To put it in other terms, the "reliable," authorized history serves the interests of the dynasty.

Yet another instability in history is social mobility, nowhere as obvious as in the local generals of the Five Dynasties. As he stands by the creek, Ouyang Xiu has an indignant fantasy of absent and vaguely illicit splendor.

> 谿傍若有遺址，云故將劉金之宅，石即劉氏之物也。金，偽吳時貴將，與行密俱起合淝，號三十六英雄，金其一也。金本武夫悍卒，而乃能知愛賞奇異，為兒女子之好，豈非遭逢亂世，功成志得，驕於富貴之佚欲而然邪？想其陂池臺榭，奇木異草與此石稱，亦一時之盛哉。今劉氏之後散為編民，尚有居谿旁者。

> By the creek there seem to be some traces of ruins. They say that this was the home of the former general Liu Jin and that the rocks were in fact the possessions of the Liu family. Liu Jin was an exalted general of the illegitimate Wu regime, who rose in arms together at Hefei with Yang Xingmi. They were called the "Thirty-six Heroes," and Liu Jin was one of them. Jin was basically a military man and a tough soldier, and his capacity to appreciate marvelous things was a child's passion. How could this have occurred had he not encountered an age of turmoil, and, achieving deeds and fulfilling his aims, let his arrogance carry him into the unbounded desires of the rich and noble? I imagine his pools and

> terraces with kiosks, rare trees and wondrous plants, renowned along with the rocks—it was the splendor of a single moment. Now the posterity of the Liu family has scattered into the registry of commoners, and some still live beside the creek.

We come at last to ruins and the traces of the past. "They say," *yun* 云, that this was the estate of Liu Jin, one of Yang Xingmi's top generals, just as "they say" that there were six remarkable rocks at the stream. The mansion is in ruins, the rocks are mostly gone, the name of the creek has changed, and the powerful Liu family has sunk into the population registry as commoners 編民. In fact, in this strange account nothing, neither names nor things, is stable.

Ouyang Xiu cannot bear that the exquisite smaller rock has been left in the possession of a commoner, and he takes it away. Even less can he bear that such a splendid estate should have been the possession of a rough general like Liu Jin. He cannot see the estate, but he imagines its vanished splendor. In the middle of the ninth century, in the Late Tang, Liu Fen did not mention any remarkable rocks; after a moment of splendor early in the Five Dynasties, the estate has gone to ruin, its imagined gardens have been overgrown, and all but one of its remarkable rocks have been carried away. At the center of Ouyang Xiu's fantasy of one moment of glory is one thing that troubles him: that a rough military man could gather and possess such imagined beauty and splendor. When thinking of the military man, the connoisseur's "capacity to appreciate marvelous things" 愛賞奇異 is followed immediately by "a child's passion" 為兒女子之好, and then by extravagant excess: he "let his arrogance carry him into the unbounded desires of the rich and noble" 驕於富貴之佚欲, as would be appropriate for a military man. Ouyang Xiu had in his life seen many splendid gardens and approved of them because they belonged to cultivated gentlemen; this is a garden he never saw, but he disapproves of it because the owner had been a military man.

Ouyang Xiu's ideal social vision, which we find in the "Account of the Pavilion of Abundance and Happiness" and "The Account of the Pavilion of the Drunken Old Man," is the social order of benign civil power, with the governor at the center, surrounded by the local gentry, and below them, the bearers cheerfully doing their labors. If, as Ouyang Xiu himself says, "things always gather to those who love them, and they are always obtained by the one with the greater strength," what if "the one with greater strength" refers to a military man—as was often the case in the Tang and very much the case in the Five Dynasties? In the Tang, military men often moved into the civil realm; the class division was not rigid. But this is now the Song. Ouyang Xiu takes care to tell us that Liu Jin's descendants have been reduced to commoners. Unlike the gentry families who perpetuate their status by education, military men rise from commoners, and their descendants return to the status of commoners. Note that when Ouyang Xiu appropriates the exquisite smaller rock from the home of a commoner, he takes the unusual step to specify the commoner's surname, the Zhu family 朱氏. Why does he do this? It is the trace of a moment of anxiety about ownership; if the commoner owner had been surnamed Liu 劉, Ouyang Xiu might be taking a family heirloom, which would present an ethical problem even for someone with the power to do so. But the commoner's surname, usually overlooked, is given here to reassure the reader that this is not a descendant of Liu Jin, sunk to the level of commoner.

In a letter to Mei Yaochen from the year after he wrote the "Account of the Rocks of Ling Creek," Ouyang Xiu speaks of only the two rocks he moved to the Pavilion of Abundance and Happiness and says they were the "former possessions" (*jiuwu* 舊物) not of Liu Jin but of a Southern Tang official Feng Yanlu 馮延魯, brother of the courtier and lyricist Feng Yansi 馮延巳.[2] Feng Yanlu's political reputation may have been tarnished as a bad advisor, but Southern Tang taste retained a nostalgic appeal in the mid-eleventh century. If the Wu military regime had a bad odor, the Southern Tang carried immense cultural prestige and provided Ouyang Xiu a worthy former owner of the vanished estate that was so vivid in his imagination.

The historical truth is uncertain. Perhaps Ouyang Xiu did more research and found that the rocks came to the estate when it belonged to Feng Yanlu. Perhaps the locals liked to associate the site with the military hero Liu Jin rather than the courtier Feng Yanlu. But then perhaps the rocks and famous garden really did belong to Liu Jin, who might well have had an inborn instinct for the beauties of landscape gardening. We cannot know, and Ouyang Xiu himself probably could not have known with historical certainty. What is clear is that Ouyang Xiu eventually chose the account that best suited his notion of how the world should have been and lent a certain cultural aura to the rocks that adorned the environs of the Pavilion of Abundance and Happiness.

予感夫人物之興廢，惜其可愛而棄也。乃以三牛曳置幽谷；又索其小者，得於白塔民朱氏，遂立于亭之南北。亭負城而近，以為滁人歲時嬉遊之好。

> I then was moved at how people and things have their moments of glory and then decline, and I thought it a pity that something so attractive be left abandoned. I had three oxen haul it [the largest rock] away and put it in Secluded Valley. I also sought out the smaller one and found it at the home of the commoner Zhu family at White Pagoda. Then I set them [the rocks] up to the north and south of the pavilion. The pavilion has the city wall to its back nearby, and they can be good things for the seasonal excursions of the people of Chuzhou.

But now there are no more rocks at Ling Creek. Because of the account, these two rocks on either side of the Pavilion of Abundance and Happiness will probably be long known as the "rocks of Ling Creek"; they have not only been carried away, they have been given a name and a story, the memory of a single moment of splendor. A great many people read Ouyang Xiu's account; very few people probably read the letter to Mei Yaochen in which the identity of the former owner of the rocks seems to have been corrected. Just as he reminded them of the battles in the vicinity and the capture of the Southern Tang generals right by the gate of Chuzhou, the governor is giving names and history to the local populace. In making the rocks part of public space, Ouyang Xiu tries to stabilize them and take them out of a continuing process of gathering and scattering.

> 夫物之奇者，棄没於幽遠則可惜，置之耳目則愛者不免取之而去。嗟夫。劉金者雖不足道，然亦可謂雄勇之士，其平生志意，豈不偉哉。及其後世，荒堙零落，至於子孫泯沒而無聞，况欲長有此石乎？用此可為富貴者之戒。而好奇之士聞此石者，可以一賞而足，何必取而去也哉。

> If you leave the most remarkable things abandoned in some secluded and remote place, then it is a pity; but if you put one where it can be heard of and seen, then someone who covets it will inevitably take it away. Although Liu Jin is not worth consideration, still he may be considered a brave and heroic man; and his life's goals were certainly grand! But when it came to his posterity, they fell in the world to the point that his descendants disappeared from note and are not heard of. How much less could he want to hold onto these rocks forever. Let this be a warning for the rich and noble. Yet now gentlemen who love remarkable things and hear of these rocks may be satisfied just to come and appreciate them—why must they take them away?

At last Ouyang Xiu faces a paradox. If the rocks are left in their natural state in some secluded and remote place, then it would be a waste, because no one (except for worshipping commoners) will appreciate them; if attention is called to them, then they will be taken away. Ouyang Xiu's solution is a public trust: such things should be placed in view but as a possession of the state, so that many can enjoy them, but no one can take them away. The large rock is placed in Secluded Valley 幽谷, vaguely echoing "things abandoned in some secluded and remote place" 棄没於幽遠; but here Secluded Valley is just the name for a spot very close to the government seat in Chuzhou and, ironically unsecluded, accessible to all.

He tries to make it a lesson against ownership; and yet he is like the others in the act of taking something because he has the power to do so. The Song pleasure in possession is matched by the disapproval of possession, especially the prize possessions of others, or at least by an immense anxiety about possession. Everyone knew the principle of "gathering and scattering": what was accumulated would be dispersed. Things are held by power, not by right; and the power to hold onto things rarely lasts past death. Ouyang Xiu may have hoped that by establishing the Ling Creek rocks near the Pavilion of Abundance and Happiness, he was placing them under the protection of the state and the local public and his own name as the author of their account. "[Gentlemen] may be satisfied just to come and appreciate them" 可以一賞而足 anticipates Su Dongpo's argument for enjoying and letting go in "The Account of the Hall of Precious Painting." These were "living questions." Ouyang Xiu and others return to these same questions again and again.

The irony is that Ouyang Xiu's famous account adds widespread prestige to the rocks that they never before possessed. Eventually there will probably be someone with the will and the strength to come and carry the last rocks away.

Ouyang Xiu may have disapproved of privately collecting famous rocks, but he himself still desired to collect and possess, even though feeling a great anxiety about the pleasure of collecting and ownership. In the "Preface for the List of My *Records of Collected Antiquities*" 集古錄目序 of 1062, almost two decades after his term in Chuzhou, he tried to find a legitimate place for the pleasure of collecting.[3] To continue the passage quoted earlier, he begins with remarkable frankness about desire and power:

> 物常聚於所好，而常得於有力之強。有力而不好，好之而無力，雖近且易，有不能致之。

> Things are always gathered by those who love them, and they are always obtained by the one with the greater strength. If there is someone with the strength who doesn't love them or someone who loves them but lacks the strength, then he cannot acquire them, even if they are close at hand and easy.

In an age when acquisition and the happiness of collecting and possession were both spreading among the elite and coming under attack at the same time, Ouyang Xiu tried to make a space for his own passion for collecting copies of inscriptions and rubbings. He did so first by describing the vulgar acquisition of rare material treasures brought from distant places:

> 象犀虎豹蠻夷山海殺人之獸，然其齒角皮革，可聚而有也。玉出崑崙，流沙萬里之外，經十餘譯乃至乎中國。珠出南海，常生深淵，採者腰絙而入水，形色非人，往往不出，則下飽蛟魚。金礦於山，鑿深而穴遠，篝火餱粮而後進，其崖崩窟塞，則遂葬於其中者，率常數十百人。其遠且難而又多死禍，常如此。然而金玉珠璣，世常兼聚而有也。

> The elephant, rhinoceros, tiger, and leopard are man-killing creatures of the mountains and seas of foreign lands, yet their tusks and horns, and skins and pelts can be gathered and possessed. Jade comes from the Kunlun Mountains, ten thousand leagues beyond the Drifting Sands, and it reaches the heartland only after passing through over a dozen languages as it changes hands. Pearls come from the Southern Ocean, always growing in the deep abyss. Those who gather them tie a rope to their waists and dive into the water; they don't look like other people; and when often they don't come to the surface, then they have fed the sharks down below. Metals are mined in the mountains; they dig deep and tunnel far, going in only when they have torches and dried provisions; but when the mountain collapses and the tunnels are blocked, those who are consequently buried inside are usually dozens or hundreds. It is always this way with distances and hardships and, moreover, this causes frequent deaths. Nevertheless, people of the time always can gather together metal, jade, and pearls and possess them.

In contrast, he argues for the innocence and scholarly merit of the inscriptions and rubbings from antiquity on that he himself has collected.

> 皆三代以來至寶，怪奇偉麗，工妙可喜之物。其去人不遠，其取之無禍。然而風霜兵火，湮淪磨滅，散棄於山崖墟莽之間未嘗收拾者，由世之好者少也。幸而有好之者，

又其力或不足，故僅得其一二，而不能使其聚也。夫力莫如好，好莫如一。予性顓而嗜古，凡世人之所貪者皆無欲於其間，故得一其所好於斯。好之已篤，則力雖未足，猶能致之。

All are the most perfect treasures from the Three Dynasties [of high antiquity] on, marvels of exceptional beauty, things of rare workmanship that give delight. They are not far away from us, and no disaster is involved in obtaining them. Nevertheless, the fact that they have become buried and eroded by the frost and wind and fires of war, abandoned and scattered on mountainsides and in desolate wilderness, is because few in the age love them. And if by lucky chance there is someone who loves them but who at the same time lacks enough strength, then he can only get a few and cannot gather them.

Given the strength, nothing is better than loving something; and in loving something, nothing is better than single-mindedness. I am by nature naively simple and have a passion for antiquity; there is nothing I want among all those things that are avidly desired by the people of this age, so I am able to achieve a single-minded focus in loving these things. Being steadfast in my love for them, I am still able to acquire them, even though my strength is inadequate.

These antiquities are close at hand and abandoned because almost no one wants them. Moreover, they are not merely unappreciated; they are wearing away, so that the act of collecting becomes an act of virtuous preservation, just like relocating the rocks of Ling Creek. Those few who want such things don't have the power. Presumably Ouyang Xiu does have the power that he disclaims at the end. With this he makes the transition to the passionate single-mindedness of the collector: "in loving something, nothing is better than single-mindedness" 好莫如一. And he uses the loaded term *shì* 嗜, translated as "have a passion for," functionally equivalent to the "avid desire," *tan* 貪, that he uses for the things of superficial value that ordinary people want. As much as he wants to hold onto things, he knows his collection will be scattered, so the *Record of Collected Antiquities* will include as much as he can.

When Ouyang Xiu uses the phrase "having the strength" 有力, he calls to mind—wittingly or unwittingly—a famous passage in the "Great Teacher" 大宗師 chapter of *Zhuangzi*:

夫大塊載我以形，勞我以生，佚我以老，息我以死。故善吾生者，乃所以善吾死也。夫藏舟於壑，藏山於澤，謂之固矣。然而夜半有力者負之而走，昧者不知也。

> This Great Hunk of Dirt weighs me down with form and tasks me with life. It gives me some escape by old age and lets me rest by death. Thus, thinking that life is a good thing is, in fact, a reason to think death a good thing. You hide a boat in a ravine and hide the mountain in a swamp—and you think it is secure. Still at midnight someone with strength comes and carries it away, while you are ignorant of it and don't know.

The Song has great stories of collection. We have the emperor Huizong 徽宗, the passionate collector-emperor, who was himself "collected" along with all his precious objects by the Jurchen, who "had the greater strength" 有力之強. But the most cutting is Li Qingzhao's 李清照 (1081–c. 1141) critique in "Postface to *Records On Metal and Stone*" 金石錄後序, in which the collection she shared with her husband, Zhao Defu, became a weight on her marriage and seemed to acquire a greater value than its human collectors.[4]

> 右金石錄三十卷者何? 趙侯德父所著書也。取上自三代, 下迄五季, 鐘、鼎、甗、鬲、盤 、匜、 尊、 敦之款識, 豐碑大碣、顯人晦士之事蹟, 凡見於金石刻者二千卷, 皆是正偽謬, 去取褒貶, 上足以合聖人之道, 下足以訂史氏之失者, 皆載之, 可謂多矣。嗚呼! 自王播、元載之禍, 書畫與胡椒無異; 長輿、元凱之病, 錢癖與傳癖何殊? 名雖不同, 其惑一也。

> What are the preceding chapters of *Records on Metal and Stone*?—the work of the governor Zhao Defu. In it he took inscriptions on bells, tripods, steamers, kettles, washbasins, ladles, goblets, and bowls from the Three Dynasties of high antiquity all the way to the Five Dynasties; here also he took the surviving traces of acts by eminent men and obscure scholars inscribed on large steles and stone disks. In all there were two thousand sections of what appeared on metal and stone. Through all these inscriptions one might be able to correct historical errors, make historical judgments, and mete out praise and blame. It contains things which, on the highest level, correspond to the Way of the Sages, and on a lower level, supplement the omissions of historians. It is, indeed, a great amount of material. Yet catastrophe fell on Wang Ya and Yuan Zai alike; what did it matter that the one hoarded books and paintings while the other merely hoarded pepper? Changyou and Yuankai both had a disease; it made no difference that the disease of one was a passion for money, and of the other, a passion for the transmission of knowledge and commentary. Although their reputations differed, they were the same in being deluded.

Ouyang Xiu insists on the distinction between his single-minded passion for collecting inscriptions and a more "vulgar" passion for acquiring rare and costly goods. His urgency in making such a distinction is a sign that he already understands the critique that Li Qingzhao was to offer many decades later. The objects of single-minded acquisition and their cultural status do not matter. The passion easily slips into obsession and can corrupt a clear-headed assessment of different kinds of value, as happened with Zhao Defu, Li Qingzhao's husband.

Everyone knew the stories of those who, faced with ruin and death, could not let go. Emperor Yuan of the Liang burned his huge library so that it would not fall into the hands of his Northern Zhou conquerors. Taizong, emperor and one of the founders of the Tang, ordered that the most famous piece of calligraphy in history, Wang Xizhi's copy of the "Preface to the *Lanting Collection*," be buried with him. Even if stories like this are not historically true, they suggest the compelling interest in those who could not let go of what they had.

In defense of the aging Ouyang Xiu, Su Dongpo argued that renouncing attachment to things was basically the same as passionate attachment to things, in that both assumed the "infatuating" power of external things, with one side succumbing to that power and the other side fearful of it, along with the fear of loss. What they sought was a middle ground. Ouyang Xiu proposed limitation, "knowing what is enough," *zhi zu* 知足. Later in the "Preface for the List of My *Records of Collected Antiquities*" the anticipated critic enters to chide Ouyang Xiu on the vanity of collection. In response, Ouyang Xiu says: "This satisfies what I love; it's all right to enjoy such things and grow old in them" 足吾所好，玩而老焉可也. He declares it's "enough" and grants himself permission to enjoy what's enough. He has found a place to stand in human contradiction. Perhaps it is being unfair to the old man, but we cannot help noticing that this was written in in 1062; in the "Biography of the Retired Layman Six Ones" from eight years later, he had added a library of ten thousand scrolls, a chess set, a zither, and a refillable jug of ale to his requirements for "what is enough."

Critics, real or imagined, seem to show their heads everywhere through these texts. All he had to say was: "I don't really care about these things; I only care about the Way" or "I don't really care about these things; they are merely something in which I lodge my thoughts on the Way." Then he could collect as he pleased, free from carping criticism. There is an open invitation to hypocrisy.

Su Dongpo was another writer who could not keep his silence. Neither could he rest with Ouyang Xiu's "It's all right." As was so often the case, he tried to find a new way to resolve the question of possession and things.

In 1074, twelve years after the "Preface for the List of My *Records of Collected Antiquities*," Su Dongpo received a request from a friend, the imperial son-in-law, Wang Shen 王詵, to write an account for his new gallery of artworks, the Hall of Precious Paintings 寶繪堂. As was so often the case, Su Dongpo made a very smart argument, though with none of the very human contradictions that we see so often in Ouyang Xiu.[5] According to Su Dongpo:

> 君子可以寓意於物，而不可以留意於物。寓意於物，雖微物足以為樂，雖尤物不足以為病。留意於物，雖微物足以為病，雖尤物不足以為樂。

> It is all right if superior man lets his interests be temporarily invested in things, but it is not all right if he lets his interest remain in those things. If you temporarily invest your interest in things, then even humble things are enough to bring happiness, and even the most infatuating things are not able to be a sickness. If your interest stays in things, then even humble things can be a sickness, and even the most infatuating things are not enough to bring happiness.

Su Dongpo is attacking the passion for ownership itself: we can almost hear Ouyang Xiu in the background: "Now loving something is better than strength, and in loving something, nothing is better than single-mindedness. I am by nature naively simple and have a passion for antiquity; there is nothing I want among all those things that are avidly desired by the people of this age, so I am able to achieve a single-minded focus in loving these things." Such single-mindedness is precisely "letting one's interest remain in things." Su Dongpo is essentially offering the lesson of Buddhism in a nonreligious garb: with attachment the owner is owned. But the solution is not Buddhist renunciation, of which he has earlier offered a secular critique, but enjoying things without holding onto things. Ouyang Xiu had tried to make the argument that loving antiquities was better than loving ordinary treasures, but Su Dongpo counters that the passion is the same.

> 始吾少時，嘗好此二者，家之所有，惟恐其失之，人之所有，惟恐其不吾予也。既而自笑曰:吾薄富貴而厚於書，輕死生而重畫，豈不顛倒錯繆失其本心也哉。自是不復好。見可喜者雖時復蓄之，然為人取去，亦不復惜也。譬之煙雲之過眼，百鳥之感耳，豈不欣然接之，然去而不復念也。於是乎二物者常為吾樂而不能為吾病。

> At first when I was young, I loved these two [books and paintings]. As for what I already possessed, my only fear was that I would lose them; and my only fear

> about what others possessed was that they would not give them to me. But eventually I laughed at myself, saying: "I think so little of wealth and honor, yet care about books; I disregard life and death, but prize paintings. It's clear that I have things turned around and upside down and have lost my original mind." From that point on I didn't love them anymore. When I saw something that brought delight, I might collect it for a while, but when someone took it away, I didn't feel bad about it. Compare it to the clouds and mist passing before one's eyes or the birds in all their kinds stirring the ears—how can we help being cheered on encountering them?—nevertheless, when they go away, we don't brood on them anymore. Thus, these two things always made me happy, but were not able to be a sickness.

Now we have come to an interesting argument about the relation between possession and happiness. In the account of the rocks of Ling Creek, Ouyang Xiu was content to say that it was enough to enjoy the rocks without possessing them. Su Dongpo goes a step further, saying that possessing them necessarily makes one unhappy. He is closer to the Daoxue moralists than he would like to be. Su Dongpo says nothing about Wang Shen's real relation to his possessions. He speaks only of his own earlier passion for possession, which, according to Su's own account, could be far more extreme than that of Ouyang Xiu.

Su Dongpo's argument may have been ingenious one, but it was also perilous. He was essentially arguing for flirting with things and flirting with possession. He used the term "infatuating creature/thing" without wisely reckoning the power of infatuation. He foolishly believed that he was immune to infatuation and the erotics of possession. He who tried to teach Wang Shen a lesson was ripe for a lesson himself.

We come now to the most famous of all "missing stones," occasioning three poems that represent nexuses in a web of changes and whose meaning is inseparable from that web. The web has one clear story line, dotted with poems, and spreads out to a history of Su Dongpo's writings and the writings of others. The first part of the story has been well told elsewhere.[6] It is a story of happiness and unhappiness, possession, along with a name that gave value to a rock and stayed with it through its travels. I will summarize the first part of the story.

Su Dongpo, who had warned Wang Shen about the perils of infatuation with possessions, the "infatuating things" that could be a woman or a painting or even a rock, became himself the victim of what he warned about. In 1092 he came into possession of two rocks that became part of an assemblage he named "Qiu Pond."

One of the two main rocks had a hole in it, a "cave," and the name that he gave refers to the fourteenth poem of Du Fu's "Miscellaneous Poems in Qinzhou" 秦州雜詩:[7]

萬古仇池穴，潛通小有天。

For all time the cave at Qiu Pond
secretly connects to There-is-a-little-Heaven.

By 1092 Su Dongpo had experienced youthful celebrity, political prominence, imprisonment, humiliation, and exile; he had had enough, and, as he discovered, there was no way out. Like so many others, the young man had yearned to enter public life, had succeeded, had been worn out, and discovered that there was no way out until the government decided to set him free. The current government was, however, vindictive and had no intention of setting him free. He wanted to get away, and his little assemblage of rocks offered an imaginary hole in the world, beyond which lay another, happier world—in miniature.

Like everything he touched, Su Dongpo's assemblage of rocks became famous, at which Wang Shen reentered the scene, asking to "borrow" them. Wang Shen was a notorious "borrower," who did not always return what he borrowed. After having been instructed by Su Dongpo not to cling to the "things" in his copious collections, but rather to enjoy them and let them go, it must have given Wang Shen a certain wicked pleasure to ask Su Dongpo to borrow his beloved rocks. Su consulted with friends as to what to do, and the friends responded in a remarkably public discussion of how to handle Su's problem. His friends even suggested that he might destroy the rocks rather than yielding them to Wang Shen—this might recall Emperor Yuan burning his library rather than losing it to the conqueror. Then in 1094, without surrendering his rocks to Wang Shen, Su was again exiled, this time to Huizhou in the far south.

On the way to Huizhou he passed through Hukou and found another remarkable rock that seemed to him to complement his Qiu Pond rock assemblage. This was another "infatuating thing," and he immediately fell in love, giving it the name "Nine Blossoms [Mountain] in a Jug." The first part of the name was for the rock's nine peaks, like the original Nine Blossoms Mountain in modern Anhui. The "jug" echoed the story of an old immortal who every night shrank and jumped into a jug in his possession. Inside was another world in miniature, which echoed the tiny "cave" that led to another world in one of the rocks that Su already had. He wrote his first poem on the rock after he left Hukou as he was continuing on to Huizhou.[8]

Su Dongpo, Nine Blossoms Mountain in a Jug 壺中九華詩[9]

湖口人李正臣蓄異石九峰，玲瓏宛轉，若牕櫺然。予欲以百金買之，與仇池石為偶，方南遷未暇也。名之曰:壺中九華，且以詩記之。

Li Zhengchen of Hukou had a rare rock with nine peaks, winding about with holes and openings like a window grillwork. I wanted to buy it for a hundred pieces of silver to be the companion of my rocks in Qiu Pond. Presently I am being transferred southward and don't have time. I called it "Nine Blossoms Mountain in a Jug" and wrote a poem to give an account of it.

清溪電轉失雲峯，夢裏猶驚翠掃空。五嶺莫愁千嶂外，九華今在一壺中。天池水落層層見，玉女牕明處處通。念我仇池太孤絶，百金歸買碧玲瓏。

The clear stream turns in a flash, I lost sight of its cloudy peaks,
but in dream I am still amazed how its azure sweeps the void.
In the Five Alps be not sad that it lies past a thousand cliffs,
Nine Blossoms now stays there in its single jug.[10]
In Heaven's Pool the water sinks, it reveals its every tier,
the Jade Maiden's windows are bright, opening through everywhere.
I brood on how my Qiu Pond is all too lonely,
For a hundred in silver I'll go back and buy its emerald twinkling.

In a boat, carried swiftly by the current on his way to Huizhou, he has lost sight of Nine Blossoms Mountain in the waking world, but can still admire it in dream. The "Five Alps" are the real mountains, a range that must be crossed to get to his place of exile in Guangdong. But though his desired rock is out of sight, in the fourth line he speaks with confidence, affirming it is still there. His confidence was misplaced.

"Heaven's Pool" was a name often given to pools high in the mountains, and like all Su Dongpo's names for his rocks, it is used for a part of the new rock or the assemblage. The striations become watermarks; the holes in the rock become the "Jade Maiden's windows," looking through from another world to this world.

At last he comforts himself by vowing to buy it when he returns. The literati often liked to avoid explicit reference to buying things, preferring barter, under the cloak of mutual gifting. But like the Retired Layman Six Ones and his five possessions, this was Su Dongpo's dream of contentment.

In this we begin to see why possession matters so much. Many possessions can be moved: they are the objects of the will of others. Su Dongpo himself was treated as the "possession" of empire; he could be moved here or there in imperial geography, sent off to Huizhou and on until he came at last to Hainan Island. As he says in a famous song lyric, "this body is not my own." He has been moved about in imperial geography, and he dreams of a topography that is a portal to elsewhere, a world of the immortals that will be his own. He will be the emperor of a small space, whose miniature mountains are named for famous mountains of the empire. The term that governs the whole poem is "going back and buying" 歸買, the acquisition that promises to make the speculative future of happiness into the real future.

Su Dongpo's dream of his "infatuating thing" and of his future acquisition is a slight poem, interesting only because it prepares us for the poem that follows, in which the fantasy is broken. Eight years later, after long exile in the far South, he returned to Hukou only to discover that someone else had purchased the rock, someone "with greater strength" (有力而強).[11]

予昔作壺中九華詩其後八年復過湖口則石已為好事者取去乃和前韻以自解云

Some time ago I wrote a poem on "Nine Blossoms Mountain in a Jug." Eight years later I again passed by Hukou, and the rock had already been taken away by a collector. Then I wrote a companion piece to the same rhymes to unburden myself. (1101)

江邊陣馬走千峰，問訊方知冀北空。尤物已隨清夢斷，真形猶在畫圖中。歸來晚歲同元亮，却掃何人伴敬通。賴有銅盆修石供，仇池玉色自玲瓏。

A line of horses by the riverside, a thousand peaks galloping,
asking what happened, I learned that Jibei is empty now.[12]
That infatuating thing is already cut off, along with my lucid dream,[a]

but the true shape is still there in a diagram.[b]
Returning home in my later years, the same as Tao Yuanming,
who, in declining visitors, is the match of Feng Yan?
All I have is my bronze basin to present my devotional gift of rock,
their jade colors in Qiu Pond are twinkling all by themselves.[c]

Su Dongpo's own notes:

a. Liu Mengde [Liu Yuxi, 772–842] considered [the real mountain] Nine Blossoms Mountain to be one of the most infatuating things of Creation 劉夢得以九華為造物一尤物.

b. The Daoist Canon has a "Diagram of the True Forms of the Five Marchmounts" 道藏有五嶽真形圖.

c. At home I have bronze basin in which I keep the Qiu Pond rocks; it is perfectly green, with a hole in the back. Also, I once gave strange rocks as a devotional offering. Reverend Foyin composed a work called the "Strange Rock Offering" 家有銅盆貯仇池石正綠色有洞穴達背予又嘗以怪石供佛印師作怪石供一篇.

When he was sailing in a boat swiftly past mountains, Su Dongpo liked the metaphor of mountains as galloping horses; and in this case he imagines Jibei, the native home of famous horses, as emptied because the horses have galloped away. But then the missing horses are also the missing mountain, his Nine Blossoms Mountain in a Jug. Writing to Wang Shen earlier, he had called those precious objects that were too much loved "infatuating things" *youwu*, a term often applied to beguiling women; here he recalls how Liu Yuxi called the real Nine Blossoms Mountain "one of the infatuating things of Creation." The beautiful object is now gone in a dream, and all that remains is the image in a map.

Su Dongpo next becomes Tao Yuanming, after serving, finally returning home to lead a quiet life, or the early Eastern Han Feng Yan 馮衍, who, after serving and getting into trouble, quit his position and retired, refusing to see visitors (Su writes literally 却掃, "refusing to sweep" [the path to his door]). Finally, we have the absent rock, "Nine Blossoms in a Jug," always present in his mind as awareness of the rock as the missing part of his rockery, leaving only his basin (the diminutive "pond" in Qiu Pond) with its fine pebbles, from which he offers a devotional gift to a Buddhist temple.

Even though Su Dongpo was, overall, the greater writer, Huang Tingjian's poem, written on visiting Hukou after Su Dongpo's death, is the most significant work of the three. Huang Tingjian is often understood as a poet of allusion, "allusion" in this case meaning references to Tang and earlier texts. In fact, Huang Tingjian was far more deeply engaged in recent and contemporary discourse; and, as we will see, his allusions often work through allusions made by his contemporaries. To appreciate Huang Tingjian, we must put him back in that world.[13]

> 湖口人李正臣蓄異石九峯。東坡先生名曰:壺中九華，并為作詩。後八年自海外歸，過湖口，石已為好事者所取。乃和前篇以為笑，實建中靖國元年四月十六日。明年當崇寧之元五月二十日，庭堅繫舟湖口，李正臣持此詩來，石既不可復見，東坡亦下世矣。感歎不足，因次前韻
>
> Li Zhengchen of Hukou kept a remarkable rock with nine peaks. Su Dongpo named it "Nine Blossoms Mountain in a Jug" and wrote a poem for it. Eight years later, returning from over the sea, he passed through Hukou, but the rock had already been taken away by a collector. He then wrote a companion piece for the earlier poem as a *jeu d'esprit*. This was the sixteenth day of the fourth month in the first year of the Jianzhong Jingguo reign. On the twentieth day of the fifth month of the following year, the first year of the Chongning reign, I moored my boat at Hukou, and Li Zhengchen brought this poem to me. The rock was no more to be seen, and Su Dongpo too had passed away. Unsatisfied by my sighs, I followed the earlier rhymes.
>
> 有人夜半持山去，頓覺浮嵐暖翠空。試問安排華屋處，何如零落亂雲中。能迴趙璧人安在，已入南柯夢不通。賴有霜鍾難席卷，袖椎來聽響玲瓏。
>
> Someone came at midnight and carried the mountain away,
> suddenly aware that sifting haze and azure warmth are empty.
> Let me ask, is being all set up in a splendid chamber
> better than being lost in a tumult of clouds?
> Someone able to bring back Zhao's jade disc—where is that person now?—
> he has already entered Southern Bough Land where no dreams reach.
> But we do have is that frosty Bell that can't be rolled up in a mat,
> bludgeon in sleeve, I'll go listen to its echoes clanging.

In the long title Huang Tingjian tells us: "The rock was no more to be seen, and Su Dongpo too had passed away," creating a parallel between the absent rock and the lost friend. The rock was taken by a passionate collector Guo Xiangzheng 郭祥正; and Huang Tingjian, who certainly knew Ouyang Xiu's "Preface for the List of My *Records of Collected Antiquities*," immediately made the connection between Ouyang Xiu's "having the strength," *you li* 有力, and the famous "someone with strength," *you li zhe* 有力者, of *Zhuangzi*, quoted earlier:

> This Great Hunk of Dirt weighs me down with form and tasks me with life. It gives me some escape by old age and lets me rest by death. Thus thinking life a good thing is, in fact, a reason to think death a good thing. You hide a boat in a ravine and hide the mountain in a swamp—and you think it is secure. Still at midnight someone with strength comes and carries it away on his back, while you are ignorant of it and don't know.

However much we try to protect life, death comes and carries it away, as the man with strength carries the boat away. We need to know this to hear the pained humor of the first line in the competitive, passionate collector—in Ouyang Xiu's terms the one with greater strength—who comes unseen by night and carries away not the boat but the mountain that hides it—or in this case, Su Dongpo's "Nine Blossoms Mountain in a Jug."[14] We read this, then, with an emphasis: "Someone came at midnight and carried the *mountain* away!" In the same way Su Dongpo himself was carried away by Death, the collector with the most strength of all.

"Nine Blossoms Mountain in a Jug" was the mountain that Su Dongpo wanted to buy, a miniature version of the recluse "buying a mountain," *mai shan* 買山, as a place to which to withdraw. Su Dongpo himself had written of "buying a mountain" in a poem entitled "Written on a Painting of Misty Rivers and Layered Cliffs in the Collection of Wang Dingguo [Gong]" 書王定國所藏煙江疊嶂圖.[15] In the poem, Su Dongpo examined the painting in detail and then commented:

不知人間何處有此境，徑欲往買二頃田。

> I don't know where in this mortal world there is such a scene as this—
> I want to off there at once and buy two acres of fields.

But the beginning of that ekphrastic poem was very strange for its description of the painting, and it is a strangeness that Huang Tingjian remembered in his own second line. Su Dongpo had written:

江上愁心千疊山，浮空積翠如雲煙。山耶雲耶遠莫知，煙空雲散山依然。

> Sad heart upon the river, mountains in a thousand folds,
> heaps of azure floating in emptiness like clouds and mist.
> Is it a mountain? Is it cloud? In the distance you cannot tell,
> then the mist is gone, the clouds scatter, and the mountain is there as ever.

To remark on the obvious, clouds do not usually disperse in paintings but may in poems on painting by Su Dongpo—but when the clouds scatter on Su Dongpo's return to Hukou, there is nothing there: "suddenly aware that sifting haze and azure warmth are empty." Someone has carried the mountain away, and only cloud and mist remain. The sad humor is given depth by the technical Buddhist term *dunjue* 頓覺, translated here in context as "suddenly aware," but in its more conventional rendering in a Buddhist context, it is "sudden enlightenment." Enlightenment is, of course, always the knowledge that the seemingly substantial world—as substantial as a mountain—is, in fact, "empty" *kong* 空.

This miniature missing mountain had by then no doubt been finely placed for the appreciation of its successful collector and his friends. Though it does not enter Huang Tingjian's poem, we might note here that although he lost the physical rock, Su Dongpo's act of naming staked a claim on the rock that could not be erased. The rock already belonged to Su Dongpo by virtue of his having named it, and the collector's acquisition was taking something that should have belonged to the one who named it—not simply making a higher bid on an unnamed rock.

Next Huang Tingjian offers a comment that has many parallels in the *Zhuangzi*. As far as the rock is concerned it is just as well off—or better off—left alone in the wilds rather than being set up on display in a splendid chamber. So too would Bian He's jade have been better off left in its natural matrix, rather than causing such suffering for the finder and such contention among humans to possess it after it was cut into a jade disk.

Like "Nine Blossoms Mountain in a Jug," Bian He's jade began as just another rock. Bian He found it and recognized that it was the matrix of an exceptional piece of jade. Twice he presented it to a king of Chu, but the king's experts examined it and said it was just a plain rock. Each time the king, angered by what he thought was deception, cut off one of Bian He's feet. Finally, with a new king, Bian He presented it one more time, and the jade expert recognized the most precious jade within. The cutting—of the matrix as well as the feet—showed the kind of stuff of which Bian He and the jade were made. The jade then was itself cut and made into a large jade disk with a hole in the middle, a *bi* 璧, an object with aura, for the possession of which the lords of the domains competed with one another.

The famous *bi* made from Bian He's jade came into the hands of the lord of Zhao. The king of Qin wanted to "collect" it—for Qin wanted to possess all things, including the domains themselves, and, in the famous words of the Han statesman Jia Yi, Qin wanted "to roll the world up in a mat" (see line 7 of the poem). Qin promised the lord of Zhao a string of cities in exchange for the *bi*, just as the Song collectors would trade with one another for their finest possessions. But just as Su Dongpo could not trust Wang Shen's claim that he wanted to "borrow" Su's Qiu Pond assemblage, so the lord of Zhao did not trust Qin's offer to trade a string of cities for the famous jade disk. Lin Xiangru, a liegeman of Zhao, offered to take the disk to Qin and, if the promise was not going to be fulfilled, to bring the disk back to Zhao. Once in the court of Qin, Lin Xiangru saw clearly that Qin had no intention of giving Zhao the promised cities; on a pretense, Lin Xiangru got hold of the jade disc and threatened to smash it—as Su Dongpo's friends had suggested that he smash the rocks of Qiu Pond rather than yield them to Wang Shen. Afterward Lin Xiangru did successfully return the *bi* to Zhao.

> Someone able to bring back Zhao's jade disk—where is that person now?-
> he has already entered Southern Bough Land where no dreams reach.

There is no Lin Xiangru to bring back "Nine Blossoms Mountain in a Jug"; perhaps Su Dongpo could have done so, but he is dead, gone to the storied ant kingdom in Southern Bough, a Tang dynasty tale in which a man dreamed whole lifetime in the kingdom of ants before waking up only to find that it was an illusion. There is no way to that land now.

Huang Tingjian's process of association will lead him back to Zhao and Qin, the latter having the "greater strength" and the firm sense of purpose that is the criterion of the successful collector. But first Huang's thought turn to another rock, one that remains and can't be carried away, can't be smashed. This is a full-sized mountain, [Stone] Bell Mountain, about which Su Dongpo composed one of his most famous prose accounts. We will come to this account in due time, but it opens with a story about names, with Su Dongpo's predecessors trying to explain how the mountain got its name "Bell." At the beginning of Su's account, an acolyte at a temple there picks up a rock from the mountain and strikes it; but the rock gives off only a comic tinkle—hardly worthy of the name "Stone Bell."

Smashing is on Huang Tingjian's mind—Su Dongpo smashing his infatuating rocks before they are taken by Wang Shen, someone with greater strength; Lin Xiangru threatening to smash the famous disk that belonged to Zhao; and striking the rock of Bell Mountain with an iron bludgeon. And this brings him back to Qin and Zhao, as the Qin army besieged the Zhao capital and Zhao desperately begged for help from the neighboring domain of Wei. The ruler of Wei refused to help, but the Wei Lord of Xinling, the ruler's brother, resolved to save Zhao at any cost. A plan was devised by which the Lord of Xinling would steal the tally of authority and go take command of the Wei army, leading it to relieve the siege of the Zhao capital. But the plotters worried that the general would not yield command of the army so easily, so a strongman, Zhu Hai, with an iron bludgeon in his wide sleeve, accompanied the Lord of Xinling when he presented the tally. The general was indeed unwilling, and Zhu Hai killed him with the bludgeon. Then the Lord of Xinling took command of the army and saved Zhao by forcing the Qin army to withdraw.

> But we do have that frosty Bell that can't be rolled up in a mat,
> bludgeon in sleeve, I'll go listen to its echoes clanging.

We come back at last to the comparison of the more powerful collector, who literally rolled up Nine Blossoms Mountain in a Jug in a mat and carried it away, to Qin, which famously wanted to "roll the world up in a mat." But the real mountain cannot be carried away or smashed; struck, it gives off the sound *linglong*, the final rhyme earlier translated as "twinkling," describing light coming through many interstices. In this context it refers to the sound of fine jade—and the sound of fine jade was often figuratively applied to the quality of great writing—Su Dongpo's "Account of Stone Bell Mountain." And it is the sound of Stone Bell Mountain itself.

These are not erudite allusions; all are famous stories and things generally known, and they all are woven together in stories of rock and death, the contest of strength and will of collectors, and the resistance by smashing what one most loves to keep it from the grasp of greater power, all framed by the dreamlike quality of infatuation. The reader might easily think of another "infatuating creature" in the possession of another collector, Shi Chong 石崇 (249-300)—his surname happens to mean "rock"—who had a favorite concubine named "Green Pearl" 綠珠. A courtier with close ties to the family in political power wanted to take her, but Shi Chong refused—"I love/will hold onto Green Pearl." When they were coming to take her away, she committed suicide by throwing herself off a high terrace. And in the end, this led to Shi Chong's own execution. Death it seems, closely follows upon loss of what one holds most dear.

But "Nine Blossoms Mountain in a Jug" was gone, and then Su Dongpo was gone. In 1101, the year in which Huang wrote his poem, a new emperor took the throne, posthumously known as Huizong. He would prove to be the greatest collector of all, the one with "greater strength"—except for Death. And somehow "Nine Blossoms in a Jug" ended up in his vast collection, no doubt brought to the imperial park "rolled up in a mat." That collection too had a history.

4

ALL MINE

The Poetics of Ownership

We have been considering sites of happiness, tied to some object or set of objects or to some place that is one's own. Such an idea that happiness in sites and objects is linked to the opposite argument, that happiness is a state of mind that permits one to find happiness anywhere and in anything. Often we find the anxiety that the person who finds happiness in things or places will be swallowed up by the things they own or love: the too-much-desired possession will become the "infatuating thing/creature" that can make a person lose oneself.

In his "Account of the Hall of Precious Paintings," Su Dongpo tried to find a middle ground between the new discourse of ownership and the old Buddhist discourse of nonattachment. He suggested a kind of philosophical "flirting" with things—to enjoy them for the moment and let them go. But flirtation is always dangerous, and the person is always in danger of being caught up by the very things he pretends to casually enjoy and finally doomed to experience loss. If Su Dongpo permits himself to want "Nine Blossoms Mountain in a Jug," there will always be another collector to snatch it away and boast about his success, enjoying Su Dongpo's sense of loss.

The anxiety about ownership came in direct proportion to a pervasive awareness of ownership. In the Song we have entered the edge of a modern world in which one is always aware of who owns things. The space in which we now live is divided by an awareness of what is public space and property as opposed to what is private space and property. Both public and private space are often marked with signs of prohibition for those who would enter that space. We do, of course, find occasional references to ownership before the Song dynasty, but they are not pervasive. Ownership had become part of consciousness in the Song, so that even the sternest Daoxue 道學 scholar, who believed that one should not be attached to possessions, may use personal ownership in a metaphor for the perfect absence of alienation. The Confucian scholar Cheng Yi 程頤 (1033–1107) offered the following explanation of the passage in the *Analects* where Confucius says that "loving learning" 好學 is not as good as "being happy in learning" 樂學:

> 學至於樂則成矣。篤信好學未如自得之為樂，好之者如游佗人園圃，樂之者則己物爾。(二程遺書 11)

> When learning reaches the stage of being happy, then it is perfected. A steadfast love of learning is inferior to finding it a self-contained happiness. Those who love it are as if visiting someone else's garden; for those who are happy in it, it is one's own possession (*jiwu*).

This is a remarkable passage; the Confucian philosopher normally disapproves of the absorption of possession but can allow it to return in a simile to clarify the difference between "loving" 好 and "being happy" 樂. Perhaps it is something deeper than a mere simile; perhaps it is a basic change in the consciousness of the lived world, which is the basis of the philosopher's understanding of the world, even though it may be something he wants to transcend. To "love" 好 is also to "want"; it opens the gap of desire. "Happiness" can be found only in "one's own possession."

We might contrast this to Bai Juyi 白居易 (772–846), contesting ownership with a landlord in the Tang in "Visiting Yunju Temple, Given to Landlord Mu" 遊雲居寺，贈穆三十六地主:[1]

> 亂峰深處雲居路，共蹋花行獨惜春。勝地本來無定主，大都山屬愛山人。

> Through the deepest places in tangled peaks, the road to Yunju Temple,
> we both go treading the flowers, but only I feel bad about spring.
> The most scenic spots basically have no fixed owner,
> by and large the mountain belongs to the one who loves the mountain.

The Tang writer dismisses permanent ownership: "basically have no fixed owner" 本來無定主. A claim of ownership is there, but it is irrelevant. In the Song we find similar claims, but legal ownership cannot be ignored.

Suppose you are holding a party on someone else's land. You may claim that it doesn't matter; but in order to make that claim, you have to invoke ownership. Thus when Ouyang Xiu held a party by West Lake (not Hangzhou's West Lake but the West Lake of Yingzhou, where Ouyang Xiu had retired), he had the performer begin a suite of songs with a prose introduction, a *nianyu* 念語. The date was probably 1072, at the very end of Ouyang Xiu's life:[2]

> 昔者王子猷之愛竹，造門不問於主人；陶淵明之臥輿， 遇酒便留於道上。況西湖之勝概，擅東穎之佳名。雖美景良辰，固多於高會；而清風明月，幸屬於閒人。並遊或結於良朋，乘興有時而獨往。鳴蛙暫聽，安問屬官而屬私； 曲水臨流，自可一觴而一詠。至歡然而會意，亦傍若於無人。乃知偶來常勝於特來，前言可信；所有雖非於己有，其得意多。因翻舊闋之辭，寫以新聲之調，敢陳薄伎，聊佐清歡。

> Long ago Wang Huizhi so loved bamboo that when he arrived at someone's gate, he did not greet the master of the house. Tao Yuanming lay recumbent in his palanquin [his feet being sore], but when he chanced upon ale, he would linger on the road. Such events would be even more likely before this splendid scenery of West Lake, peerless among places of renown in Eastern Ying. And though there are lovely scenes and excellent moments, these are indeed enriched by a sophisticated gathering. Moreover, the cool breeze and the bright moon fortunately belong to men at ease.
>
> Here for joint excursions one may meet up with good friends; or following one's whim, one may sometimes go off by oneself. As we listen a while to the croaking of the frogs, why should we care whether they are frogs belonging to the state or the frogs of some private person. Beside the current of winding streams, it is well to drink a cup and recite a verse. And when it happens that a person is delighted by one of these catching his fancy, it is as if there were no one else around. Now we may grasp the credibility of the old adage that coming somewhere by chance always excels coming with some purpose. And one may get much out of it, even though what one has in this is not one's own.
>
> Thus I redid the lyrics of old stanzas and wrote them to the melody of a popular song, daring to offer this minor art to add to our pure pleasures for the while.

The opening reference to insouciant Wang Huizhi 王徽之 (d. 388) is revealing:[3]

> 時吳中一士大夫家有好竹，欲觀之，便出坐輿造竹下，諷嘯良久，主人灑埽請坐，徽之不顧。將出，主人乃閉門。徽之便以此賞之，盡歡而去。
>
> At the time in Wu there was a gentry household that had fine bamboo and he [Wang Huizhi] wanted to go look at them. At once he set out in his palanquin and reached the bamboo, where he chanted a long time. The owner cleaned up a place and begged him to be seated, but Wang Huizhi didn't pay any attention to him. When he was about to leave, the owner shut his gate. Huizhi immediately appreciated him for this; they had a good time, and then he left.

Ouyang Xiu is looking for precedents for stopping off on someone else's land on the whim of the moment. From beginning to end of the prose introduction, he comes back to the fact that he is holding his party on someone else's property; this is *not* space belonging to the state. Ouyang Xiu's eminence probably ensures that the owner will not object, but nevertheless there is a basic awareness of being on someone else's property without their permission. He begins with Wang Huizhi's interest in the bamboo and going to enjoy them without greeting their owner. This is a mark of Wang Huizhi's aristocratic eccentricity, ignoring courtesy in his absorption in the bamboo; it is only incidentally a transgression on someone else's property. If Wang Huizhi is not aware of being on someone else's property, Ouyang Xiu is intensely aware. When Ouyang Xiu talks about pleasure, however, he uses one of the terms of property, "belong to," *shuwu* 屬於: "the cool breeze and the bright moon fortunately belong to men at ease" 而清風明月，幸屬於閒人. He keeps stressing the unpremeditated nature of the party coming here, always returning to ownership and the transcendence of ownership: "As we listen a while to the croaking of the frogs, why should we care whether they are frogs belonging to the state or the frogs of some private person?" 鳴蛙暫聽，安問屬官而屬私.[4] The simple-minded child-emperor of the Jin dynasty, Xiao Huidi, once asked whether the croaking toads were "state" (literally "official") toads or "private" toads. This story was used as an example of his simple-mindedness. The story as it is given in the *Jin History* is an example of an implicitly very foolish question; Ouyang Xiu answers the question that needs no answer, by saying that it doesn't matter. The fact that it is not his own land or state property is on his mind: "And one may get much out of it, even though what one has in this is not one's own" 所有雖非於己有，其得意多.

The role of allusion here is much like a legal argument, citing precedent to justify oneself. Since there is clearly no one present objecting—and who would dare object to someone of Ouyang Xiu's prominence holding a party on one's property?—this is all from within Ouyang Xiu himself, justifying what makes him not entirely comfortable. Cheng Yi was correct about happiness in "one's own garden."

This brings us to one of the most remarkable texts of our period, a text militantly celebrating private property and attempting to defend it against a weight of a classicist ideology that disapproved of property being kept to oneself alone. This is Sima Guang's "Account of My Solitary Happiness Garden" 獨樂園記 of 1073, three years after "The Biography of the Retired Layman Six Ones," during the regime of Wang Anshi, when Sima Guang had withdrawn to private life in Luoyang. It is a garden of contradiction, discursively extensive and physically rather small compared to other famous gardens of Luoyang. He publicly celebrates the garden in detail, not only in the "Account," but also in numerous poems; however, the "Account" affirms exclusion, claiming—rather incongruously—that it provides only enough pleasure for the owner.

In the background is Wang Anshi's program to assert state control of the economy against the private wealth and enterprise of powerful merchant families. Sima Guang's modest garden was hardly in danger of state appropriation, but the factional conflict between Wang Anshi and the so-called conservatives brought the issue of private property and freedom from state interference to the fore. Sima Guang wanted to be left alone; and ownership is the power to exclude others from using or enjoying what one has. When he was in his garden, he famously dressed the part of the antique recluse; but he was the relatively wealthy and famous "recluse" in an age of private property. Solitary Happiness Garden was Sima Guang's small theater of antiquity, and classicist ideology wanted it to be willingly shared.

To name one's garden "Solitary Happiness" stood squarely opposed to the *Mengzi*'s comments on shared happiness, a value that stood behind Ouyang Xiu's "Account of the Pavilion of the Drunken Old Man." It is also an account of privately owned space, as opposed to the public or state-owned space of Ouyang Xiu's Chuzhou accounts. In this new world of Confucian values taken seriously, Sima Guang needs a justification for private ownership. There is nothing he can draw on in the Confucian Classics—the people may have come willingly to build King Wen's Spirit Terrace 靈臺 garden, but King Wen did not first purchase the property and then pay the builders a day-wage. In Solitary Happiness Garden, the property and each building on it cost Sima Guang money.

Sima Guang can account for private ownership of this middling urban estate by a series of negations, attempting to show that the values in the Confucian Classics do not apply in his case. He first directly addresses the problem presented by the values of the Classics by paraphrasing the conclusions of the dialogue between Mengzi 孟子 and King Hui of Liang 梁惠王. Sima Guang then denies that this saying applies to his case because this is "the happiness of kings and lords and great men" 王公大人之樂 and therefore beyond his reach. Then he offers the opposite case in the person of Yan Hui, who was happy despite poverty and hardship. Rather than "the happiness of kings and lords and great men," this is "the happiness of sages and worthies," and again beyond his reach. In effect, Sima Guang has created a "middle class" by opening a space between the rich and powerful and the poor and powerless, but virtuous; the happiness of the former can come only through their public role, and the happiness of the latter can come only from within.[5] This is fine for rulers and impoverished sages, but not for an ordinary person like himself. Middling modesty becomes a refuge.

> 孟子曰:獨樂樂，不如與人樂樂；與少樂樂，不如與衆樂樂。此王公大人之樂，非貧賤者所及也。孔子曰:飯蔬食飲水，曲肱而枕之，樂亦在其中矣。顏子一簞食，一瓢飲。不改其樂。此聖賢之樂，非愚者所及也。
>
> Mengzi said: "Solitary happiness in listening to music is not as good as being happy listening to music with others, and being happy listening to music with few is not as good as being happy listening to music with many." But this is the happiness of kings and lords and great men; it is not something that a poor and ordinary man can achieve. Confucius said: "In eating vegetables and drinking water, crooking your arm and making it your pillow—there is happiness even in this." "Yan Hui ate from a single bamboo plate and drank from a single gourd, but his happiness did not change." But this is the happiness of sages and worthies, and not something that a foolish man like me can achieve.

Sima Guang begins by attempting to forestall the criticism that his name for the garden invites. For the positive model of what a foolish man like himself *can* achieve, he offers this:

> 若夫鷦鷯巢林，不過一枝，鼴鼠飲河，不過滿腹，各盡其分而安之，此乃迂叟之所樂也。

> Now the wren takes no more than a single branch when it nests in the woods; and when the mole drinks from the river, it does no more than fill its belly. Each fulfills its own lot and is content with it. This, in fact, is what I, the Reclusive Old Man, find happiness in.

In a long section, not translated here, Sima Guang goes through the garden, describing each section and naming the name that he gave to it.[6] This verbal itinerary was a miniature theater of display as "solitary happiness," circulated in words for all to imagine.

> 堂北為沼，中央有島，島上植竹。圓若玉玦，圍三丈，攬結其杪，如漁人之廬，命之曰釣魚庵。

> North of the hall I made a pond with an island in the middle, and on the island I planted bamboo. This was round, three yards in circumference, like a jade ring with a gap; I gathered together the tips [of the bamboo] and bound them up, like the hut of a fisherman, calling it "Fishing Cottage."

Any gardener who has worked with bamboo will recognize how much artifice and effort is required to make such a "ring" with living bamboo in order to produce an image of the serene simplicity of a "fishing cottage." Bamboo has a *horror vacui* and will soon fill in an adjacent space. The island would help, but in Qiu Ying's (仇英, ca. 1494–1552) famous painting, the "fishing cottage" is smack in the middle of Sima Guang's herbarium of different plants in neat squares.

We should note that his lodgings were not here in the garden but elsewhere in the city; he purchased the property only for a garden. Sima Guang tells us that his entire Luoyang garden property was twenty *mu* 畝 (over three acres); and while his garden may have seemed cramped in comparison with some of the more spacious Luoyang gardens, it was considerably more than a wren's "single branch." He may be "fulfilling his lot" with twenty *mu*, but his "lot" was quite comfortable—not to mention a comfortable home elsewhere in the city. Everyone has his own standards of what is minimally adequate, but an estate of twenty *mu* in a major city, with a library for five thousand *juan* of books set aside for his "Reading Hall," along with numerous buildings, does not seem to be testing the lower limits of material comfort for a human being. Sima Guang tells us that he purchased the land, but not how much he paid for it. I think it is reasonable to assume that it must have cost at least the forty thousand cash Su Shunqin paid for the land around his Canglang Pavilion outside the old section of Suzhou.

If ownership becomes a question, then it is worth considering prices. It is instructive to compare Su Shunqin's forty thousand cash for his Canglang estate to a story often told about Solitary Happiness Garden. The present version is from *The Recorded Conversations of Yuancheng* 元城語錄, conversations with and anecdotes about Sima Guang by a devoted follower. In this we learn that Sima Guang's gardener earned ten thousand cash from selling admission to the garden when the flowers were in bloom.[7]

> 然獨樂園，在洛中諸園最為簡素，人以公之故，春時必遊。洛中例，看園子所得茶湯錢，閉園日，與主人平分之。一日園子呂直得錢十千，肩來納。公問其故，以衆例對。曰:此自汝錢，可持去。再三欲留，公怒，遂持去，回顧曰:只端明不愛錢者。後十許日，公見園中新創一井亭，問之，乃前日不受十千所創也。

> Nevertheless, Solitary Happiness Garden was the most plain and simple of all the gardens in Luoyang. But on account of Sima Guang, people always visited it in springtime. The norm in Luoyang was that on the day when the garden closed, the gardener would take the "tea money" he had received and divide it evenly with the owner. One day the gardener Lü Zhi got ten thousand cash. He brought it in over his shoulder; and when Sima Guang asked him what was going on, he answered by explaining the general norm. Sima Guang said: "This is your money—take it away." When the gardener tried repeatedly to leave it, Sima Guang got angry, and then he took it away. Looking back, he said: "It's just that the Duanming Academician doesn't care about money." A dozen or so days later, Sima Guang saw a newly constructed well-pavilion in the garden. When he asked about it, it turned out to have been constructed with the ten thousand cash that he wouldn't accept earlier.

The purpose of the anecdote is to demonstrate Sima Guang's disinterest in money and the gardener's ingenious way of balancing accounts, but it is strange to read the story against the "Account of My Solitary Happiness Garden." There is a fine irony of commerce and "solitary happiness." The garden is not at all solitary when the flowers are in full bloom; it is open to anyone who can pay the "tea money," the admission price. Sima Guang not only does not "share their happiness," he won't even accept the cash they pay for their happiness. This is an odd twist on *Mengzi* indeed. Others do indeed come, have access, and enjoy the garden. And yet the owner does not "share their happiness"; they have *paid* for their joy, just as Sima Guang paid for the garden's construction; but it requires the intermediary gardener to take their cash. To return the "master's portion," the gardener builds a new pavilion (one later version of this often-retold anecdote has the gardener building Sima Guang a privy).

We should pause here to consider the relationship between cultural value and commercial value. The account of the gardener's "tea money" hints at it: "But on account of Sima Guang, people always visited it in springtime." Li Gefei's 李格非 "Account of the Famous Gardens of Luoyang" 洛陽名園記 is more explicit:[8]

> 司馬温公在洛陽，自號迂叟，謂其園曰獨樂園。卑小不可與他園班。其曰讀書堂者，數十椽屋；澆花亭者，益小；弄水、種竹軒者，尤小。曰見山臺者，高不過尋丈； . . . 。温公自為之序，諸亭臺詩，頗行於世。所以為人欣慕者，不在於園耳。

> When Sima Guang was in Luoyang, he called himself "the Reclusive Old Man" and referred to his garden as "Solitary Happiness Garden." It was a cramped little place that was not on the same level as the other gardens. What he called "Reading Hall" had a roof of only twenty or so beams; "Flower-watering Pavilion" was even smaller; "Enjoying the Water" and "Planting Bamboo" were extremely small. What he called "Mountain-sight Terrace" was only a yard or so high. . . . Sima Guang wrote a preface for the garden himself, and his poems on the terraces and pavilions were widely circulated in the times. The reason why people regarded it with such loving admiration had nothing to do with the garden itself.

Value is produced through cultural texts—one of which explicitly rejects allowing others to enjoy the garden. That cultural value is translated into commercial value as visitors pay to be allowed to see the garden when the flowers are in bloom. Offered his cut of the profits, Sima Guang, the high-minded literary scholar, must reject commercial gain; but in doing so, the commercial value ultimately returns to him in the form of a new pavilion in his garden. There is little reason to believe anecdotes like the story of the gardener as historically true or true in precise details, but such anecdotes still represent an imagined relation between cultural and commercial value. And there is one point that deserves notice in this story about balancing accounts: the gardener gets ten thousand cash; the custom in

Luoyang is to give *half* to the owner of the garden; but Sima Guang, who disdains profit, finally gets it all—the well pavilion "turned out to have been constructed with the ten thousand cash that he wouldn't accept earlier."

The discursive world of the classical essay is trying to make room for "private property" in the terms it has, but only the miscellany (*biji* 筆記) can represent the full consequences of private property and the commercialization of access. The resonant name "Solitary Happiness" 獨樂, the great fame of Sima Guang, and the aesthetic austerity of the property all certainly added to its attraction and to the flocks of visitors who came to see it. Forces have been introduced into the culture that will split it apart discursively: the miscellany can tell us what is happening behind the scenes; the classical genres are trying to reconcile the new reality with old values—or, more often—concealing the new values. But even the classical genres sometimes show the new world coming through. In the garden Sima Guang tells us: "On the highest level I take the Sages as teachers, on a lower level befriend all the worthies, observe the source of Fellow Feeling and Right, investigate the traces of Music and Rites, from before form had even begun to beyond the boundless tracks, and the principles behind all things appear together before my eyes." Sima Guang here sounds very much like the Confucian master; but soon afterward the new world of private ownership slips in: when he is weary, he works in the garden and enjoys his garden and then exclaims proudly "all mine!" 悉為己有.

> 迂叟平日多處堂中讀書，上師聖人，下友羣賢，窺仁義之原，探禮樂之緒，自未始有形之前，暨四達無窮之外，事物之理，舉集目前。所病者，學之未至，夫又何求於人，何待於外哉。志倦體疲，則投竿取魚，執衽采藥，决渠灌花，操斧剖竹，濯熱盥手，臨高縱目，逍遥徜徉，唯意所適。明月時至，清風自來，行無所牽，止無所柅，耳目肺腸，悉為己有，踽踽焉、洋洋焉，不知天壤之間復有何樂可以代此也。因合而命之曰:獨樂園。

> The Reclusive Old Man spends most of his days in the hall studying. On the highest level I take the Sages as teachers, on a lower level befriend all the worthies, observe the source of Fellow Feeling and Right, investigate the traces of Music and Rites, from before form had even begun to beyond the boundless tracks, and the principles behind all things appear together before my eyes. What I fault myself on are those points where my study has not reached; but I also seek nothing from others and depend on nothing external. If my aims grow weary and my body is tired, I cast my fishing rod and take a fish, pull up my

> sleeves and pick herbs, dig a channel to water flowers, take ax in hand to cut bamboo, wash my hands in hot water, let my eyes rove from a high spot, lingering and roaming freely, whatever suits my mood. Sometimes the bright moon comes or a clear breeze comes of itself; I go with nothing pulling me and stop with nothing blocking me; what I hear and see and feel within is all mine! Going alone, going in vastness, I don't know of any happiness in the whole world that could take the place of this. Thus I combined it all and named it "Solitary Happiness Garden."

There is an important question here. Is Sima Guang's happiness in the garden itself, or in the fact that it is "all mine" 悉為己有? What he has are the experiences of the garden, but the experiences are dependent on having the garden and occur through the garden. Cheng Yi seems to provide the answer: "Those who love it are as if visiting someone else's garden; for those who are happy in it, it is one's own" 好之者如游佗人園圃，樂之者則己物爾. Of course, the fact that it is "all mine" is not just that he paid for the land and the construction, but that he planned it and named all its sites for his experience of happiness. Solitary Happiness Garden 獨樂園 combines happiness, ownership, and naming. It is an assemblage in which to situate the self, just as the Retired Layman Six Ones was defined by his portable possessions. It is not just a place that makes him happy; it makes him happy in no small part because it is his own.

Even having attempted to forestall criticism in the opening, the imaginary faultfinder makes his inevitable appearance. The critique of Sima Guang's choice of name is a common move in "accounts," and it has been amply anticipated.

> 或咎迂叟曰:吾聞君子所樂必與人共之，今吾子獨取足於己，不以及人，其可乎? 迂叟謝曰:叟愚，何得比君子，自樂恐不足，安能及人? 況叟之所樂者，薄陋鄙野，皆世之所棄也，雖推以與人，人且不取，豈得強之乎? 必也有人肯同此樂，則再拜而獻之矣，安敢專之哉。

> Someone criticized the Reclusive Old Man, saying: I have learned that what a superior man finds happiness in he always shares with others, but you now find satisfaction in yourself alone and do not extend it to others—is this all right? The Reclusive Old Man demurred, saying: I am foolish—how can I be compared to a superior man? I fear it will not be enough for my own happiness; how can I offer it to others? On top of that, what I find happiness in is shabby and crude, all the

> sort of things rejected by the world. Even if I pressed all this on others, others would not take it—and how could I force them? But if there inevitably were someone willing to share this happiness, then I would bow and present him with it. How would I dare keep it entirely to myself?

Again, Sima Guang modestly claims that he cannot compare with a superior man, that he scarcely has enough for himself and does not have enough to share with others. Then, having just given an account of the scale, layout, and pleasures of his garden, he now tells us that it is a poor, shabby spot in which no one is interested—that even if he wanted to share it, others wouldn't want it (wonderfully belied by the earnings from admission to the garden in the spring). But, he continues, if anyone were interested, he would share it. What is happening here?

Faced with Confucian values from antiquity at war with new values of joys in private ownership, Sima Guang creates the interlocutor who forces him to imaginatively sacrifice his dearest possession, the sole use of his garden. In contrast to Ouyang Xiu's genial delight in the company of others, Sima Guang wants to hoard these sites of pleasure: there is something essentially bourgeois here, in which personal possession develops into an autonomous value: "keeping it entirely to oneself" remains an issue, even when the possession could be shared without any loss.

"I fear it will not be enough for my own happiness; how can I offer it to others?" We should pause here to notice what a strange thing that Sima Guang has done in trying to argue against sharing his garden. Obviously, others could come and enjoy the garden without detracting in any way from the pleasure it offers the garden's owner. But Sima Guang "capitalizes" the happiness made available by the garden; he quantifies it, so that if others find happiness in the garden, there will somehow be less left for him. The patent selfishness of this position forces him at the end to a grudging offer to share, with a sudden shift to the language of deference whose tone is elusive—as if forced to accept a superior argument. We move from pride in possession to an attempt to "monopolize," *zhuan* 專, possession by disparaging precisely what had been previously praised, to a final surrender.

In the end he offers to "present," *xian* 獻, his beloved garden to others. *Xian* is an interesting word, offering something to a superior, as he is overcome by a "superior" argument. His name for his garden, Solitary Happiness 獨樂, resisted what could not be resisted.

We know that in Sima Guang's day Luoyang was an ancient city, no part of which was without history. When he dug his ponds and built his pavilions, there were certainly artifacts from Luoyang's past.[9] In "Account of My Solitary Happiness Garden," he calls his purchase "buying a field," *mai tian* 買田, and treats his urban estate as if it had no history, as if it began with the construction of his garden. The names are all names he has given. Purchasing land seems to give the new owner the right to start over. It is not just the deed but the publicity that makes it his own.

If we compare Sima Guang's 1073 account of his garden with Ouyang Xiu's accounts written in Chuzhou almost thirty years earlier, the differences are striking, both in the change from shared happiness to solitary happiness and in the interest in the history behind a place. In large measure these differences follow from the difference between a local official working with state resources and a private citizen using his own resources. We see a similar shift from state to private, from shared happiness to solitary happiness, in "The Biography of the Retired Layman Six Ones," written just a few years before Sima Guang's account of Solitary Happiness Garden. For an earlier account of a private garden, we have "Account of Canglang Pavilion," from 1045, the same year as Ouyang Xiu's "Account of the Pavilion of Abundance and Happiness."

The names given to these places achieved immense durability through the publicity of writing. They fell into ruin and were rebuilt over subsequent centuries, so that a famous text would not lose the physical site that it represented; and even now the sites have been lovingly tracked down even when the old place cannot practically be rebuilt. Su Shunqin's Canglang Pavilion has survived, still outside the old city of Gusu, but now well within the urban area of modern Suzhou. The buildings have been rebuilt, and the garden has been restored, with a copy of "Account of Canglang Pavilion" prominently displayed for all to read. Canglang Pavilion is publicly owned, but one has to pay to enter it and remember Su Shunqin's happiness, just as one had to pay Sima Guang's gardener to visit Solitary Happiness Garden.

While Ouyang Xiu was the governor of a secluded prefecture, erecting public works and hauling a large rock over the landscape with oxen, conscript labor, and state funds, Su Shunqin lost his post and went south to Suzhou. Both were victims of factional struggle—though, reading Ouyang Xiu's famous prose works from Chuzhou, we would never know that his post was considered an "exile." Like Ouyang Xiu in Chuzhou, Su Shunqin found himself in the remains of the Five Dynasties Kingdom of Wu. In the "Account of Canglang Pavilion" 滄浪亭記, he tells of purchasing a parcel of land and the price he paid for it—forty thousand cash.

> 予以罪廢無所歸，扁舟南遊，旅於吳中。始僦舍以處，時盛夏蒸燠，土居皆褊狹，不能出氣，思得高爽虛闢之地，以舒所懷，不可得也。一日過郡學，東顧草樹鬱然，崇阜廣水，不類乎城中。並水得微徑於雜花修竹之間，東趨數百步，有棄地，縱廣合五六十尋，三向皆水也。杠之南，其地益闊，旁無民居，左右皆林木相虧蔽，訪諸舊老，云錢氏有國，近戚孫承右之池館也。坳隆勝勢，遺意尚存。予愛而徘徊，遂以錢四萬得之，構亭北碕，號滄浪焉。前竹後水，水之陽又竹，無窮極，澄川翠幹，光影會合於軒户之間，尤與風月爲相宜。

> Because of an offense I lost my post and had nowhere to go; I went south by boat and took up lodgings in Wu. At first, I rented a place to stay, but it was the height of summer, steamy and hot. The places were all very narrow, and I couldn't breathe. I longed to get a place that was brisk and open where I could relax, but I couldn't find one. One day I was passing the district school; I turned to look around east where plants and trees were growing dense and thick, with high hills and broad waters, different from what lies within the city walls. Following along by the water, I found a tiny path among the various flowering trees and tall bamboo. Making my way quickly east several hundred paces, there was abandoned land, in breadth and width some 150 meters, facing water on three sides. South of a bridge of a single plank, the land was even broader, with no one living around, and on either side the trees of a grove concealed it. When I asked older folks about it, they told me that when the Qians ruled the Wu Kingdom, this was the pool and lodge of Sun Chengyou, a close kinsman of the king by marriage. In the scenic form of rises and depressions, some sense of the design still survived. I loved it and lingered there, and subsequently got it for forty thousand cash. I had a pavilion constructed on the winding northern bank and called it Canglang. There were bamboo in front and water behind, and north of the waters there were more bamboo without limit. Light from the clear stream and those pale green stalks gathered on the porch and doors, especially appropriate in breeze and moonlight.

We have spoken of the way in which the owner becomes defined by what he owns. It is a question of identity. The official is defined by his position in the imperial structure; his identity, which to a large degree determines his relations to others, is defined by his rank. The imperial government may move him from place to place, up and down the hierarchy, but it was a stable system in which to understand who and where one was. To lose one's place in that system—as opposed to exile to lowly post far away—was to lose social identity. Su Shunqin says it with poignant simplicity: "Because of an offense I lost my post and had nowhere to go" 予以罪廢無所歸. He is a wanderer, who doesn't belong anywhere anymore. He is a renter in the cramped quarters of old Gusu (the "old city" of Suzhou); Ouyang Xiu in Chuzhou and even Su Dongpo in Fufeng can use the labor and resources of the state to make themselves comfortable with a nice pavilion. The only power that Su Shunqin now has is money—and writing. Ouyang Xiu, who still very much has a place in the imperial system, can write teasingly to Su Shunqin about his new property, noticing the inclusion of price in the "Account":[10]

清風明月本無價，可惜秖賣四萬錢。

> Cool breeze and bright moon are essentially "priceless"—
> too bad that they were sold for only forty thousand cash.

The source is Li Bai's "Song of Xiangyang" 襄陽歌: "The cool breeze and bright moon need not be bought for a single cash" 清風朗月不用一錢買. Song writers, with their interest in costs, often invoked this sentiment. Ouyang Xiu's couplet turned on the double sense of "priceless."

Exploring outside the walls of the old city, he found his place, the former estate of one of the in-law families of the Five Dynasties Kingdom of Wu. He called it "abandoned land," but it still had an owner from whom he had to buy it. Unlike Ouyang Xiu, he did not imagine its splendor in the past; he noted only that it was overgrown with vegetation and the site was good, with water on three sides. He did, however, note: "In the scenic form of rises and depressions, some sense of the design still survives" 坳隆勝勢，遺意尚存. In other words, this was not a natural site, but a site whose fundamental structure retained the memory of purposeful landscape gardening.

In this world of private ownership, there is much concealed. There are negotiations of price, drawing up deeds, hiring laborers to build his pavilion, probably making walls to publicize the fact that this is no longer "abandoned land." Building requires giving a name and an account that publicizes the name of the place and the person giving the name, just as the deed authorizes the purchase of land. But, as Su Shunqin well knows, names can outlast both ownership and buildings. The name Canglang, of course, suggests the site of a recluse. Canglang Pavilion becomes a space outside the imperial system from which he can reflect on the system. And rather than becoming the slave of what one owns, having one's own space becomes the means to reflect on one's life within the imperial system.

> 予時榜小舟，幅巾以往，至則灑然忘其歸，箕而浩歌，踞而仰嘯，野老不至，魚鳥共樂，形骸既適則神不煩，觀聽無邪則道以明，返思向之汩汩榮辱之場，日與錙銖利害相磨戛，隔此眞趣，不亦鄙哉。噫，人固動物耳。情橫於内而性伏，必外寓於物而後遣，寓久則溺，以爲當然。非勝是而易之，則悲而不開。惟仕宦溺人爲至深，古之才哲君子，有一失而至於死者多矣。是未知所以自勝之道。予既廢而獲斯境，安於沖曠，不與衆驅，因之復能乎内外失得之原，沃然有得，笑傲萬古，尚未能忘其所寓目，用是以爲勝焉。

> I would sometimes sail my little boat, going off wearing a headband. When I reached somewhere, I would be free and easy and forget about going back, singing wildly all sprawled out or squatting with my head looking up whistling. Old rustics did not come, and I shared my happiness with the fish and birds. Once my body felt comfortable, my spirit was not disturbed; my powers of observation and listening not being led astray, the Way became clear. Wasn't it vile to be kept away from these genuine impulses by the daily push and pull of some tiny measure of profit or disadvantage? Human beings are, alas, indeed creatures stirred. If the passions run wild within and one's nature submits, then one must invest oneself temporarily in external things, and afterward dispel them. If you invest yourself in external things too long, then you drown in them and think that it is necessarily that way. If you cannot overcome this and change it, then your sadness will never go away. Only service as an official drowns a person most deeply. Many have been the talented and wise superior men of ancient times who met with death from one slip. This is not knowing the way by which to master oneself. Having been dismissed from office and having attained this scene, I am at peace in the calm openness and am not in a race with the crowd. By this I can again wisely learn something about the sources of gain and loss, both in things external and external. I laugh proudly at all times past, and still never forget what my eyes have seen, and by this I consider myself to have achieved mastery.

Su Shunqin uses that same word *yù* 寓, "invest" [one's attention], that Ouyang Xiu and Su Dongpo used. Su Shunqin describes exactly the same process that Su Dongpo described: if one invests one attention too long in something, one will be swallowed up by it. In this case, however, the object is not books, paintings, and precious things but the imperial system itself: "If you invest in external things too long, then you drown in them and think that it is necessarily that way" 寓久則溺，以爲當然. Only in being expelled from the political system and acquiring a space that is "all mine" can he reflect on the compulsion of his former life. He does not have to justify "solitary happiness"—rejected by the state and unvisited by "old rustics," he "shares his happiness" with the fish and birds.

Although private ownership and attachment to precious possessions had begun to provoke discussion after the middle of the eleventh century, "solitary happiness"—the right to exclude others—did not become an issue until Sima Guang explicitly introduced it in his account of his garden in 1073. Once introduced, the discomfort with the pleasure of private ownership later sought a justification.

Zhu Zhangwen's 朱長文 (b. 1039) "Account of Happiness Herbarium" 樂圃記 from 1080 is an account of his Suzhou garden.[11] Like Su Shunqin's Canglang Pavilion, it was built on the ruins of a Five Dynasties garden—but ruins that had, for several generations, been the homes of commoners. His grandmother purchased the property, and his was the third generation it had been in the family. This account too is framed by the question of happiness, the happiness achieved by not participating in political life but achieved in his garden. Like Sima Guang, he divides his time between studying and gardening. But in contrast to Su Shunqin's account, Zhu Zhangwen's happiness has to be justified. In Zhu's case family is the means by which he escaped the charge of "solitary happiness." Brothers, children, and grandchildren do and will "study here, dine here, and that is enough to consider happiness—how could I be able to have solitary happiness?!" 學于斯，食于斯，是亦足以為樂矣，予豈能獨樂哉.

One of the most interesting accounts supplements cash purchase with a more profound claim of possession. This is the "Personal Account of Dream Creek" 夢溪自記 by the remarkable intellectual Shen Gua 沈括 (1031–1095).[12] A standard account of one's garden or estate is framed by a narrative of dream and fulfillment, with a peculiar commercial wrinkle.

Shen Gua begins by telling how in 1060 he repeatedly dreamed of a particular landscape, one he had never seen: "In my dreams I was happy with it and planned to go live there" 夢中樂之，將謀居焉. Through these repeated dreams the place became familiar: "I grew used to it as if I had visited it all my life" 習之如平生之遊. Then in 1077, seventeen years after the earlier dreams, Shen Gua lost his capital post and became governor of Xuancheng 宣城. In Xuancheng, a monk named

Wuwai 無外 described a particularly scenic estate in Jingkou 京口, a property that happened to be for sale. Taken with the monk's description, Shen Gua bought the property, sight unseen, for the sum of thirty thousand cash. But Shen Gua never went to look at his purchase. He didn't even know for sure where it was 翁以錢三十萬得之，然未知圃之所在.

Later in 1084 Shen Gua was in exile and was planning to live out his life in Xunyang 潯陽, but a journey in 1086 took him through Jingkou, and he went to look at the property that he had purchased so long before. Of course, it was the landscape he had dreamed of in 1060, and he decided to take up his dwelling there, giving it the name Dream Creek 夢溪, the name attached to the famous *Dream Creek Miscellany* 夢溪筆談. As he says: "My destiny was here" 吾緣在是矣. Following this account is the standard itemization of names of sites on the estate.

Shen Gua also achieved solitary happiness 獨樂, but with none of the problems of private ownership that had troubled Sima Guang in 1073. We note how he achieves this, not by wanting solitary happiness 獨樂, but by having his estate rejected by visitors: "My dwelling was in the city, but in a wilderness of old trees and living mixed together with deer and wild pigs; whenever a guest came he would always knit his brows and go off, yet I found solitary happiness in it" 居在城邑而荒蕪古木與鹿豕雜處，客有至者，皆顰頟而去，而翁獨樂焉.

Like many other texts, Shen Gua gives us an account of purchasing property that he loved, but he frames acquisition and ownership with the larger workings of fate. Rejected by visitors, he is able to enjoy "solitary happiness" 獨樂 without seeking it. Yet the idea of "destiny" 緣 is peculiar here—it is not a fate to rise or fail, not a fate to do great deeds, not a fate to meet someone. In this case destiny, so often revealed in dreams, is to acquire a particular piece of real estate and enjoy it.

Earlier we discussed "living questions." Many of these texts focus on ownership, particularly the ownership of land, and, as Cheng Yi would say, the happiness of being in one's own garden (or the anxiety of being on someone else's land uninvited). We have seen how the resonant phrase "solitary happiness," drawn from *Mengzi*, is launched into the community through circulating texts and becomes "activated" by a recurrent critique, which is either written directly into a text or forestalled by an implicit defense. In *Mengzi*, however, "solitary happiness" was raised in conjunction with listening to music. In these eleventh-century texts, it is applied to the experience of a garden or a rockery and is entangled with private property and the power to exclude others (obviated by the claim of the disinterest of others in visiting the property).

If we look at these texts chronologically, we see no direct issue of private property in Ouyang Xiu's Chuzhou essays, which focus on public spaces and their relation to the imperial order. Private property is, however, lapping at the shores of public space. Ouyang Xiu's fantasy of the estate of a Five Dynasties general is superimposed on land either that has no owner or whose owner is unknown. Private property is sneaking into that space, snatching away rocks left unattended. Ouyang Xiu would later allude to the famous story of the Jin emperor, whose dimwittedness was embodied in the question whether certain frogs were "frogs belonging to the state" or "private frogs." For Ouyang Xiu, that question ceases to be so foolish when the question arises whether the famous rocks from the abandoned estate are "rocks belonging to the state" or "private rocks." Rock collectors have been taking them away and turning them into "private rocks." Ouyang Xiu recovers the remaining rock and claims it for the empire as a "rock belonging to the state." Most revealing, he also takes a smaller rock—a "private rock"—from a commoner's household and makes it a "rock belonging to the state." This is easily possible because the owner was a commoner rather than gentry, but it is still a chilling reminder for those who believe in private property.

The "Account of Canglang Pavilion," roughly contemporary with Ouyang Xiu's Chuzhou essays, concerns the acquisition of private property, but Su Shunqin does not declare his estate the site of "solitary happiness," even when describing it as such. The famous *Mengzi* passage is indeed there in the background: no one comes to visit him, so he "shares his happiness" with the fish and birds. Since the deprecation of one's property and the putative rejection of that property by others became the most common way to fend off the criticism of "solitary happiness," Su Shunqin's earlier use in 1045 is instructive because it suggests loneliness and local rejection as a parallel to losing his office. It is not a defense against the criticism of selfishness due to the exclusion of others.

But later when "solitary happiness" was a question, exclusion was precisely the point. Su Shunqin was hardly the most gifted writer of his day, but he had one, distinctly Song virtue: he could be brutally honest about matters that others touched on only gracefully and indirectly. Finding some peace in being stripped of office, he reflects on his brief career. He begins with the commonplace claim that attachment to outer things can destroy a person; but the case in point turns out to be life as an official:

> If the passions run wild within and one's nature submits, then one must invest oneself temporarily in external things, and afterward dispel them. If you invest yourself in external things too long, then you drown in them and think that it is necessarily that way. If you cannot overcome this and change it, then your sadness will never go away. Only service as an official drowns a person most deeply.

The term *yu* 寓, translated as "invest oneself," here refers to state service; Su Dongpo was to make a similar distinction between investing oneself temporarily and investing oneself so deeply that one is swallowed up; but for Su Dongpo, the area of investment is not service but books and works of art, possessions.

In "The Biography of the Retired Layman Six Ones" of 1070, Ouyang Xiu's interlocutor offers a critique of ownership that is picked up in Su Dongpo's subsequent defense of the "Biography." Through attachment to possessions, the owner becomes himself owned. In the "Biography," Ouyang Xiu responds, like Su Shunqin, that state service is no less an entrapment. No one was taught the lesson of the entrapment of state service more dramatically than Su Dongpo himself; but the problem of private ownership became the topic of discussion, while the problem of state service fell largely into silence.

We are gradually slipping over into the very old opposition between serving in office and not serving, *chuchu* 出處, but with a distinctly Song dynasty twist. The criticism, even the hatred of serving in office has a greater urgency; and while this is doubtlessly related to the ugly factional struggles of the late eleventh century, the criticism goes beyond the circumstantial. As Tao Yuanming had said many centuries earlier, it makes a person unhappy. Perhaps we should read Ouyang Xiu's constant claims of public happiness in his Chuzhou essays in this context, with his problematic echoes of Tao Yuanming.

Whether being stripped of office or retiring, not serving becomes caught up in questions of possession. It is often in gardens, but Su Dongpo, always in office, wants to own a miniature landscape in a rockery, filled with holes that lead to another world. Again Tao Yuanming's "Peach Blossom Spring," accessible only though a cave, comes to mind.

In "The Magistrate of Peach Blossom Spring," we considered the empire as a structure of names, by which every place within the empire becomes part of the whole. The private garden, the walled space with its own structure of carefully chosen names, becomes the miniature of empire. It is unlike Peach Blossom Spring because it is the miniature of empire rather than an unmapped, invisible space within empire; but it does have one important thing in common with Peach Blossom Spring: its inhabitants (or solitary but happy inhabitant) have fled the empire. For Su Shunqin it was a space of freedom in which he could reflect critically on the empire and state service. Su Dongpo's miniature landscape of "Qiu Pond" was the place to flee once the empire released him, while Sima Guang and Shen Gua had left imperial service. In the oppressive climate of Wang Anshi's regime and that of his followers, it was wise not to speak critically about the polity. The private garden was a space of contradiction, both the small double of empire as well as the escape from and the alternative to empire. Inspired by *Mengzi*, Huang Tingjian will reimagine the private garden as the site where the polity can be rebuilt.

5

THE STONE THAT TELLS ITS NAME

Possessions are slaves. They pass from hand to hand. They do not speak. "Nine Blossoms Mountain in a Jug" was carried away from Su Dongpo by Guo Xiangzheng, and it was carried away again by the collector-emperor Huizong and probably placed in Gen Mount 艮岳, the imperial park.[1] When the Jurchen were besieging the capital, it may well have been one of the famous rocks from the park used as a catapult stone to be shot at the enemy.[2] That is the fate of "infatuating things."

> 夫芻狗之未陳也，盛以篋衍，巾以文繡，尸祝齊戒以將之。及其已陳也，行者踐其首脊，蘇者取而爨之而已。
>
> Before the straw dogs [used in ritual] are presented, they are kept in bamboo baskets and matting, wrapped around with patterned embroidery. The Invocator performs austerities to take them [to the ritual]. But once they have already been presented, people walk on their heads and backs and crush them, then the fuel gatherers pick them up and burn them—and that's it.
>
> *Zhuangzi*, "Heaven in Its Cycles"

> 天地不仁，以萬物為芻狗，聖人不仁，以百姓為芻狗。
>
> The world is not kind; it treats all things as straw dogs. The Sage is not kind; he treats the people as straw dogs.
>
> Laozi

The last rock of Ling Creek, fallen over, was too big to carry away until Ouyang Xiu, the magistrate who could command greater strength, took it. "Nine Blossoms Mountain in a Jug" was snatched away by someone with money and then taken in turn by the emperor, who seemed to have the greatest strength of all. Then, when that emperor was about to be carried away by those with still greater strength, the rock may have been smashed in the futile attempt to save the city. As Huang Tingjian wrote, there was one rock that was just too big to carry away, the "frosty Bell," Stone Bell Mountain.

Su Dongpo's "Account of Stone Bell Mountain" is virtually a set-piece for the Song distrust of received textual opinion in favor of contemporary reconsideration and verification, and such a story of tradition corrected by empirical investigation does indeed explicitly frame the account. As in the Song study of the Classics, textual information from the past may turn out to be wrong, or even absurd. In that spirit Su Dongpo investigates the origin of the name of Stone Bell Mountain, beginning with a critique of earlier interpretations and discovering by observation what seemed to him to be the obvious explanation. Preparing for a visit to Hukou (in modern Jiangxi), he reads about it. He begins his own essay with the received explanations of the name of the mountain:

> 水經云:彭蠡之口，有石鐘山焉。酈元以為下臨深潭，微風鼓浪，水石相搏，聲如洪鐘。是說也，人常疑之。今以鐘磬置水中，雖大風浪，不能鳴也，而况石乎? 至唐李渤始訪其遺蹤，得雙石於潭上，扣而聆之，南聲函胡，北音清越，枹止響騰，餘韻徐歇，自以為得之矣。然是說也，余尤疑之。石之鏗然有聲者，所在皆是也，而此獨以鐘名，何哉?

> The *Classic of Rivers* says that at the mouth of Lake Pengli there is Stone Bell Mountain. Li Daoyuan [the author of the commentary] thought that since it looked down on a deep pooling, when a light breeze stirred the waves, the water and rock would strike each other with a sound like a great bell. People have always had reservations about this explanation. If you put a bell or chimes in the water, it won't make a sound no matter how strong the wind and waves are—much less so for rock. In the Tang, Li Bo first visited the site and got a pair of rocks from a deep pool; he struck them and listened; the southern sounds were blurry, but the northern sounds were sharp and clear. Then he stopped the striker, the echoes rose, and the lingering tones gradually subsided. And he thought that he had found the explanation. Still I doubt this explanation even

> more. Stones that have a clinking sound are found everywhere, but why is it only here that they call it a "bell"?

The account concludes with pride and cultural confidence in the power of empirical investigation and reason to find the truth:

> 事不目見耳聞而臆斷其有無，可乎？酈元之所見聞，殆與余同，而言之不詳。士大夫終不肯以小舟夜泊絶壁之下，故莫能知。而漁工水師，雖知而不能言，此世所以不傳也.
>
> Is it all right to make a speculative determination of how things are unless one has seen it with one's own eyes and heard it with one's own ears? What Li Daoyuan learned was very close to my experience, but he didn't describe it in enough detail. Men of the gentry were never willing to moor in a small boat by night beneath the sheer cliff, and thus they could not know. Even though fishermen and boatmen might know, they cannot account for it in words. These are the reasons why it [the truth of the name] has not been passed on in the world.

Su Dongpo is being rather unfair to Li Daoyuan (c. 472–527), who could not have personally visited Stone Bell Mountain. A loyal subject of the Northern Wei in a divided China, he was in no position to travel deep into the territory of the rival Liang dynasty to investigate their waterways. The larger point is, however, correct: he simply copied what textual information was available to him, and the unexamined reliance on textual authority led to the transmission and accumulation of errors, especially in the context of a conservative community that took umbrage at any disagreement with textual authority. In this particular case, Li Daoyuan was not wrong; he simply did not know enough to explain the phenomenon more clearly.

In contrast to the old gentry, who believe books and will never get in a boat to go investigate, Su Dongpo represents himself as the new Song intellectual who, by his own efforts, will correct errors in the tradition. The commoner boatman may know the truth, but only Su Dongpo can publish that truth. This is what Su Dongpo himself claims, and it is a legitimate reading. However, it overlooks much that is important in the text and complicates it.

The essay opens with the received textual information and Su Dongpo's doubts. This is what Su would have known before visiting the actual place—indeed probably what he read in anticipation of his visit to the mountain on a planned itinerary with his son Su Mai. He continues:

> 元豐七年六月丁丑，余自齊安舟行適臨汝，而長子邁將赴饒之德興尉，送之至湖口，因得觀所謂石鍾者。寺僧使小童持斧，於亂石間擇其一二扣之，硿硿焉。余固笑而不信也。

> On the day *dingchou* of the sixth month of the seventh year of the Yuanfeng reign, I went by boat from Qi'an to Linru; my eldest son Mai was setting off for his post as assistant magistrate of Dexing County in Raozhou. I went along with him to Hukou, and that's how I had a chance to see the so-called Stone Bell. A monk in the temple had an acolyte take an ax and randomly pick up one or two stones and strike them. They clinked a bit. I laughed indeed and didn't credit this [as the explanation].

Su Dongpo notes the date and circumstance, to lend experiential verisimilitude to the account. The qualification "so-called Stone Bell" lets the reader know that he comes with doubts and wants to see for himself. He would have seen what the modern visitor sees, not so much a "mountain" as a rocky hill rising up sharply out of the lake. The two tourists ask about the name and are sent to the local Buddhist temple, where they get a demonstration of folk etymology from a temple acolyte striking some local stones. We may reasonably suspect that the monks in the temple had been doing this demonstration for passing visitors for a very long time. It was one way to collect donations. We might even suspect this was how Li Bo [not the eighth-century poet Li Bai] got his explanation in the ninth century.

> 至暮夜月明，獨與邁乘小舟至絶壁下。大石側立千仞，如猛獸奇鬼，森然欲搏人。而山上栖鶻，聞人聲亦驚起，磔磔雲霄間，又有若老人欬且笑於山谷中者，或曰此鸛鶴也。余方心動欲還，而大聲發於水上，

> That night the moon was bright; Mai and I rode in a small boat to the foot of the sheer cliff. The huge rock stood slanting for a thousand yards up, as if fierce beasts or strange demons were darkly ready to snatch a person. A falcon roosting on the mountain, hearing the sound of human voices, rose up suddenly in alarm, screeching in the clouds. There was also something like an old man

> laughing and coughing in the mountain valley. Some say this was a stork. When I recovered from my agitation, a loud sound came out over the water.

At this point the text does not suggest that Su Dongpo's moonlight excursion with Mai was to find out the origin of the mountain's name. It seems that they were just passing through Hukou and wanted to see the Stone Bell more closely. What they find is, at first, not the satisfying empirical evidence of the origin of the mountain's name but rather a looming mystery, with wild beasts and demons in the moonlit night. It is a threatening scene, quite different from the confidence of the beginning and closing of the account.

The sudden motion of the falcon flying up alarms them, and Su Dongpo masters his alarm by giving it an empirically rational cause: "Hearing the sound of human voices, [it] rose up suddenly in alarm." But then another sound intrudes that is still more mysterious and cannot be explained except by hypothesis: "There was also something like an old man laughing and coughing in the mountain valley. Some say this was a stork."

This passage is the real center of interest in the account. The celebration of empirical verification would still be the lesson, but without this passage the account would be smug and dull. This is what makes it writing with the sound of fine jade, which, after the loss of Nine Blossoms Mountain in a Jug and Su Dongpo himself, survives to be speculatively struck by Huang Tingjian with the iron bludgeon and produce a beautiful, lingering resonance.

But what is the relation between this moment of threatening strangeness and the celebration of empirical investigation? We can note one thing: he did not find the name by investigation but rather because, at that moment of mystery, the stones made music.

> 而大聲發於水上，噌吰如鐘鼓不絕，舟人大恐。徐而察之，則山下皆石穴罅，不知其淺深，微波入焉，涵澹澎湃而為此也。舟廻至兩山間，將入港口，有大石當中流，可坐百人，空中而多竅，與風水相吞吐，有窾坎鏜鞳之聲，與向之噌吰者相應，如樂作焉。因笑謂邁曰:汝識之乎？噌吰者，周景王之無射也。窾坎鏜鞳者，魏獻子之歌鐘也。古之人不余欺也。

> A loud sound came out over the water, booming and ringing like unceasing bells and drums. The boatman was very frightened. When I gradually investigated it,

> there were caves and fissures all around the base of the mountain, of uncertain depth; small waves entered them, and the sloshing and churning produced this. When the boat turned back and reached the space between the two mountains, on the point of entering the mouth of the harbor, there was a large rock midstream, with space enough to seat a hundred people. It was empty inside with many holes, swallowing and spilling out the wind-blown water. It produced a drumming and thrumming sound, which answered the earlier booming and ringing, as if music were being played. And I said to Mai laughing: "Don't you recognize it? The booming and ringing are the Wuye bells of King Jing of Zhou; the drumming and thrumming are the song bells of Lord Xian of Wei. The ancients were not deceiving us."

The sound of the bird "like an old man laughing and coughing" fades into a much louder sound, the sound of the waves in the rocks that gave the mountain its name. The sound of the bird presumes a background of silence. Either the sound of the waves in the rocks had not started yet or the focus of attention in listening led Su Dongpo to notice it. Su Dongpo's pride in his discovery was because he was frightened; the discovery itself was an accident that came with the calming of his alarm and his attention to the new sounds as the mysterious sound faded.

The mystery at the heart of this text that finally celebrates certainty of understanding is a moment of uncertainty. Unlike the surprise of the falcon's sudden flight, the cause and nature of the strange sound echoing in the valleys is uncertain: "some say this was a stork," but *who* says this? Perhaps he told someone of his experience and the person said that the bird that makes a sound "something like an old man coughing and laughing" was a stork. What is that bird doing there in the middle of the night? There is a mystery here, something eerie. The appearance of the rocks on the cliff looking like fierce beasts and demons can be explained, though the effect on Su Dongpo is more direct than the explanation; the falcon suddenly flying up can be explained and is explained in the text, but the surprise precedes the rational explanation—especially following the line "darkly ready to snatch a person" 森然欲搏人. A sense of threat and danger is present.

Su Dongpo does not quite admit to being frightened. He admits to the threatening appearance of the rocks in the darkness; he admits to "alarm" or "agitation," *xin dong* 心動. On hearing the booming of the waters in the fissures in the rock, "the boatman was very frightened" 舟人大恐. But later we learn that "even though fishermen and boatmen know, they cannot account for it in words" 而漁

工水師，雖知而不能言. Fear of the unknown, which occupies a central position in the account, is at last displaced to ordinary gentry, who "do not dare" go riding in a boat in the moonlight.

As there is fear, there is laughter, coming from a superior position, either coming from understanding or mocking the failure to understand. Three occasions of laughter come from Su Dongpo himself. The first laughter occurs when a local has an acolyte strike local rocks. The next time that Su Dongpo laughs is when he interprets the sounds as matching ancient drums and bells: "And I said to Mai laughing: 'Don't you recognize it? The booming and ringing are the Wuye bells of King Jing of Zhou; the drumming and thrumming are the song bells of Lord Xian of Wei. The ancients were not deceiving us.' " And this account that began with a distrust of textual authority comes at last to a reaffirmation of textual authority. The final laugh is pure mockery; once he believes he understands the true source of the mountain's name, he sums up: "Thus I give this account, feeling bad that Li Daoyuan was too cursory, and laughing at Li Bo's vulgarity."

But there is, of course, one more moment of laughter in the account: the sound of the unknown bird in the darkness, with a voice like an old man coughing and laughing. Immediately following this sound, Su Dongpo's agitation calms down; he masters himself, investigates, speaks with pride at his discovery. We cannot say with certainty that he feels as if he himself was the object of laughter, but the sudden change in tone suggests something of that sort.

Perhaps I should make this more explicit. Three times it is Su Dongpo himself laughing, either mocking someone else or expressing delight that he has understood the meaning when others have failed. Only one case of laughter comes from the outside, at a time when Su Dongpo almost admits to having been frightened; and immediately following that laughter, he masters himself. A great writer must include this moment as well as the cases in which he himself laughs.

Although he is, like Li Daoyuan, too cursory, the seventeenth-century critic Lin Yunming also commented on this passage on boating in the darkness:[3]

> 驚起者可以望見，則直言棲鶻。咳笑者之為鸛鶴未必果確，故借或曰二字。寫出何等活動，此處忽撰寂寥動魂奇景，人以為妝點閒話，不知為下文心動張本，且伏末段士大夫不肯泊舟之脈，針縫甚密。

> When what rises up startled can be seen in the distance, he speaks directly of a roosting falcon. But it is not necessarily certain that what is coughing and

> laughing is a stork. This is why he uses the words "some say." The description is so lively, at this point suddenly describing a marvelous scene of vast and dark emptiness that agitates the soul. Some people think it is just ornament and idle comment without realizing that it is the origin of the "agitation" in the following passage; moreover, it adumbrates the line of development to "men of the gentry were never willing to moor in a boat" in the final section—the fabric of the text is woven very tightly.

With his rich seventeenth-century technical vocabulary of critical interpretation, Lin Yunming is very close to Western "New Criticism," trying to reconcile everything in the text into an aesthetic whole. He is not, however, clear about how this passage anticipates the conclusion—though he has good intuition that somehow this moment and the confident conclusion are tied together.

If Lin Yunming seeks to show the unity of the text, the contemporary critic looks at the problems that make Lin Yunming's attempt to demonstrate unity interesting. The very passage that Lin Yunming picks out to show the "tightly woven" unity of the text is also the passage that presents a problem with the unity of the text—as he himself says. If we are here talking about "understanding" in a broad sense, "Account of Stone Bell Mountain" is itself about understanding: it is confident in the beginning and at the end, but in the middle of the text is this moment that cannot be fully understood, something that "agitates" the usually confident Su Dongpo. The text becomes a process and an act; the confidence in empirical knowledge is something achieved, rather than taken for granted.

This is the Song dynasty moment: clearing away the detritus of accumulated tradition, with its errors and mindless repetition, one investigates with mind and the senses the world as it is; and what is discovered in that darkness is not a transcendent truth, as we find in Southern Dynasties writing on landscape, but rather the physical nature of the world here embodied in and mediated by the return of ancient music. By experientially investigating how things are, one rediscovers antiquity. There had been a long history playing on the link between the two pronunciations and meanings of the character 樂: it was *yue* (*ngaewk*), "music," or it was *le* (*lak*), "happiness." Later in this section we will see happiness of antiquity returning in the music of the Song dynasty present.

If "Account of Stone Bell Mountain" were simply a lesson in skepticism about textual tradition and the necessity of empirical investigation for proper understanding, Su Dongpo could have omitted the dark mountain, the sudden flight of the hawk, and the cry of the unknown bird. It would be easy to remove that section and leave a remarkably coherent (but less interesting) text. The passage "interrupts" a linear movement to certain understanding of the origin of the name Stone Bell Mountain. This is a "hole" or a "gap" in the linear text, like the holes in Stone Bell Mountain itself, which in this case are the secret source of its name—and "getting the name right," *zhengming*, is the Confucian promise of an intelligible world.

Su admits to us at the end that fishermen and boatmen already knew what he learned. Of course they did. Had he simply asked them, there would have been no essay. But those fishermen and boatmen would have been "dialect" speakers, and it is not at all clear that Su Dongpo could have asked them about Stone Bell Mountain or understood their answers. As Ouyang Xiu had located Chuzhou within the empire, so Su Dongpo makes knowledge of Stone Bell Mountain's name available to the empire, filling in a troubled spot in the empire's map of names.

In the context of writing "accounts" of places, there is a striking oddity, something that was not usually said and did not need to be said: "Men of the gentry were never willing to moor in a small boat by night beneath the sheer cliff, and thus they could not know." We might reiterate: "exclusion *is* the point." Just as Sima Guang's garden, with all his experiences within it, is "all mine," Su Dongpo's discovery is "all his own."

Su Dongpo did one other thing of note while passing through Hukou. He found a remarkable rock for his rock assemblage and named it "Nine Blossoms Mountain in a Jug." In Huang Tingjian's poem, Stone Bell Mountain is the rock that remains together with Su Dongpo's famous account. Su Dongpo may have named the previously unnamed rock that was carried away, but he no less wrote his name on Stone Bell Mountain—he "signed" it. Even to this day one cannot visit Stone Bell Mountain or even talk about it without bringing up Su Dongpo's name and his account. This mountain cannot be spirited away.

"Nine Blossoms Mountain in a Jug" may have been a good rock with an interesting shape, with the proper peaks and holes. It probably would have fetched a decent price anyway. But the exorbitant value it acquired was because it was "named," and, most of all, because it was named by Su Dongpo. It had his figurative signature, and that signature was worth money. Even if it rested in the cup or "jug" of a Song catapult in the Jurchen siege of Bianjing, if an educated person were standing there (which I very much doubt), he might have said: "There goes Su Dongpo's 'Nine Blossoms in a Jug'!" It would have ended up smashed to pieces in the Jurchen camp—but its name lasted on, still with Su Dongpo's own name written with it. If Zhao Shiyan 趙師嚴 claimed to have recovered the rocks of Su Dongpo's Qiu Pond assemblage from the ruins of the imperial park and carried them south, it might be true—but we should retain the possibility that the name left the original rocks and found other rocks in which to take lodging.[4] The "name" and signature accompanying the name are far more durable than rock—and they, not the rock, carry the prestige and cash value.

We read Sima Guang's "Account of Solitary Happiness Garden" with greater understanding when we become aware of the world of commerce that surrounds the garden. Sima Guang's account has two sides: it makes claims for one set of values, but it is also an act of publicity that adds to the cultural value of the garden, which, in turn, becomes commercial value. The more a world of commercial value pressed all around them, the more publicly Confucian intellectuals signaled their disdain for it. But increasingly it was becoming part of their world and impossible to escape. They constructed spaces of theatrical solitude, but those spaces cost money. We begin to learn how much things cost: forty thousand for a parcel of land just outside old Suzhou, thirty thousand for a parcel of land inside Jingkou, ten thousand for a well pavilion. Where did all this money come from? And what is the point of it all? Can one buy happiness or a site in which one can be happy? Can one use money to restore antiquity, buying a site like the Spirit Terrace of King Wen of Zhou as a place for shared happiness? To reach such a vision of primal shared happiness, perhaps we must follow the money trail.

If someone happened to be the governor of Chuzhou like Ouyang Xiu, he may have gotten enough benefits from his post to live comfortably—though we do not fully understand the relationship between salary and cost of living, much less taking perks and external income into consideration. We know that in the Tang, patrons often supplied income in the form of fungible gifts as well as offering political support. In the Song, however, patronage seems to have been largely political support supplemented with gifts. One important source of income, however, was prose.

You have to write for your friends and prominent officials. Much prose writing was done in response to social obligations or for one's own pleasure. Prose composition was, however, also a potential source of significant income. Su Dongpo's unwillingness to write tomb inscriptions (*muzhiming* 墓誌銘) was a significant decision.[5] The consequence was losing a steady source of income. At least from the Tang on, this is one of the most basic facts of classical prose that one doesn't read about in most literary histories. Only the most down-to-earth of Tang writers, Bai

Juyi, tells us how much he was paid for writing the tomb inscription for his closest friend Yuan Zhen—a great deal of money—and Bai probably tells us the amount only because he donated the money to a Buddhist temple.

Suppose that you were a famous literary man in Bianjing sometime around 1090. Your fame/name is your capital; it has exchange value. You constantly will receive requests for prose. The payment for such writings can be a major source of income. Suppose that you receive a request in a letter from a rich merchant in Sichuan to write an account for a pavilion that he has built.[6] Clearly the Sichuan merchant, one Han Jian 韓漸, wants an account by the famous writer for the prestige it gives. Under what circumstances would you agree to such a request? In all probability the rich merchant sent either money or commensurate gifts with the request, or promised to pay, or it was assumed that he would pay very well. Money or its equivalent is clearly involved; however, literary men were not supposed to talk about the money or large gifts they received for writing texts. That practical truth is repressed. When something outside the text is repressed, it will often return inside the text in a different form. We may expect that our literary man, who receives such a request from a merchant, will talk about the merchant spending his money liberally. And this is exactly what the text does.

The literary man in this case is Huang Tingjian. We do not know exactly when this account was written, but it was sometime between 1086 and 1093. We do know, however, that this was an account of a garden composed after a recent history of famous prose texts on gardens in which the question of happiness was central. Huang Tingjian writes as someone who comes late to a "family" of texts, and he speaks back to those texts even as he writes "for" Han Jian.

The "Account of Pine and Chrysanthemum Pavilion" 松菊亭記 is a much less familiar text than the famous prose accounts we have been discussing. One might argue that its lesser fame is because it has fewer literary merits, but we cannot deny that one important factor in its relative disregard is that it is far too close to the merchant world for a gentleman to read without discomfort. Like so many of the earlier accounts, this account concerns happiness, possession, and a name; and it may come closer to reconciling classical values with the new world of the Song than any of the accounts we have so far read. But the recipient and central figure—the man who is encouraged to spend his wealth—is a merchant.

In Huang Tingjian's age, a lifetime of reading earlier texts was a form of capital, a "store" of accumulated learning, *xueye* 學業. Han Jian is using his own capital, his money, to purchase access to Huang's store of learning. Han Jian probably does not know all the earlier texts that Huang Tingjian uses in his account; but the very reason Han Jian is spending his money is for Huang Tingjian's ability to reference those texts. The merchant is buying cultural prestige; but in this exchange, the literary man has to make a place for a merchant, both through the values of classical antiquity and in the values of recent discourse. This is precisely what Huang Tingjian does with genius.

Perhaps the most powerful discursive structure in a civilization is the nature and range of legitimate choices for life that are normally presented to a socially mobile elite. Tao Yuanming is himself quite explicit in deciding whether to live his life as an official or a farmer; a "farmer"—and we essentially mean a "peasant," as a profession rather than a class—lives with the contingencies of farming and the ever-present danger of starvation. Tao Yuanming made this choice and seems to have worried about and personally experienced the hardships of the farmer's life. In the elite appropriation of Tao Yuanming, however, he is reclassified as a "recluse," which is a legitimate elite choice for one's life—living as a peasant is not legitimate. Members of the "recluse" category may choose to abstain from food, but they usually do not labor in the fields for uncertain outcomes. If one was a member of the elite in the Tang, the choices were also to serve or to live as a recluse. In the Tang, the choice of being a "recluse" simply was a way to refer to anyone who did not hold a position in the government nor was an aspirant for such a position. The older sense of "recluse" as an imagined possibility does not disappear, but it recedes into the background in the Song.

The "Account of Pine and Chrysanthemum Pavilion" offers a choice among *three* possibilities, which profoundly changes the old structure of binary choice.

> 期於名者入朝，期於利者適市。期於道者何之哉。反諸身而已。
>
> Those who aspire to name/fame enter the court; those who aspire to profit go to the marketplace. But those who aspire to the Way—where do they go? They simply turn back to themselves.

Even though these choices fit the new Song world and the increasing commercialization of society, Huang Tingjian, with his immense store of learning, begins with a classical reference, from a famous speech by the Warring States debater Zhang Yi: "Those who struggle for name are in the court; those who struggle for profit are in the marketplace" 爭名者於朝，爭利者於市. With this allusion to the *Stratagems of the*

Warring States, *Zhanguo ce* 戰國策, Huang Tingjian has opened a space for merchants, of which Han Jian was one. The third choice, the Way 道, requires that he change "struggle," *zheng* 爭, to "aspire to," *qi yu* 期於 (you cannot have "struggling for the Way" 爭道者). The phrasing of the passage, however, leaves "aspiration to the Way" as a possibility open to merchants as well as officials. If one tries to reconcile this with earlier gentry statements of value, this is shocking; but it is, at the same time, consistent with what was happening in Song society and intellectual life. If the earlier choice was "service" or "retirement," then either choice could be said to possess the Way. We do not expect the merchant to seek the Way, but we do not expect the official, rising in the government hierarchy, to be excluded from the Way. This strongly reminds us that nascent Daoxue 道學 was not the state-sponsored Daoxue 道學 of a later era but conceived of itself independent of service to the state. In Huang Tingjian's triadic structure of choice, serving the imperial government, "entering the court" 入朝, was not a moral decision but merely a desire for name/fame.

Not only has Huang Tingjian opened a place for the merchant as a way of life, he has made service in the government no longer a moral commitment, no longer part of the Way. Here public life, the quest for name, *ming* 名, balances the merchant's quest for "profit," *li* 利, so that the person who rejects both to seek the Way is someone who does not care about "name and profit" 名利 (rejecting "name and profit" was an established value in the Confucian vision of *Mengzi*). Huang Tingjian offers a subtle but important change: the person who aspires to the Way *no longer* cares about "name and profit"; seeking the Way may be a new phase of life for someone who has understood the limits of "name and profit." Serving the state is here treated as the equal counterpart of being a merchant. The third choice, "aspiring to the Way" 期於道者, also should involve "movement" (as in "entering the court" 入朝 or "going to the marketplace" 適市); the question is: "Where does such a person go?" 何之哉. In this final case, the movement is different from the other two: "they simply turn back to themselves" 反諸身而已. The new configuration of life choices is that you can serve the state to build name/fame, or you can try to accumulate a fortune, or you can study the Way. The first two are movements outward; the third turns back.

Observe Huang Tingjian's rhetoric. Immediately following the first triad of choices, he offers a second triad:

> 鐘鼓管絃以飾喜，鈇鉞干戈以飾怒，山川松菊所以飾燕閒者哉。貴者知軒冕之不可認，而有收其餘日以就閒者矣；富者知金玉之不可守，而有收其餘力以就閒者矣。

> Bells, drums, pipes, and stringed instrument are the adornments of delight; axes, falchions, shields, and pikes are the adornments of rage. And are not mountains, rivers, pines, and chrysanthemums the means to adorn leisure? The noble understand that crowns and coaches cannot be counted on, and they gather their remaining days and seek out leisure; the wealthy realize that gold and jade cannot be kept, and they gather their remaining strength and seek out leisure.

The three terms here are delight, rage, and calm. The "third term" has a different status than the first two; the binary pairs ("name and profit" 名/利; "delight and rage" 喜/怒) are transcended by the third term, which goes beyond both. "Leisure," *xian* 閒, the third term, corresponds to the Way in the first triad and is linked to pines and chrysanthemums, the name of Han Jian's pavilion. "Pine and chrysanthemums" are from Tao Yuanming's "Return" 歸去來辭: "my three paths have been overgrown, / but my pines and chrysanthemums still survive" (三徑就荒，松菊猶存), and refer to a later phase in life in which one "returns." In the first triad, all three terms were on the same level as choices; here, "leisure" or "calm" is clearly the choice to which someone later turns after disillusionment or weariness with one of the first two choices. It is a new way of conceiving of life: in youth one expends efforts for various purposes, whether public office or making money; as one gets older, one turns one's "remaining strength" to finding calm through leisure.

Now we turn to Han Jian, described as an old man, who has the seniority to turn to leisure and calm:

> 蜀人韓漸正翁有范蠡、計然之策，有白圭、猗頓之材，無所用於世，而用於其楮，中更二十年而富百倍。

> Han Jian (Zhengweng) of Shu has the stratagems of Fan Li and Jiran; he has the material of a Bai Gui or a Yi Dun. Not having been used by the age, he made use of his currency bills, and over the course of twenty years his wealth increased a hundredfold.

In addition to the famous merchants of antiquity Bai Gui and Yi Dun, Huang Tingjian chooses as models Fan Li 范蠡 and his supposed teacher Jiran 計然. The inclusion of Fan Li is particularly interesting. In literary references, Fan Li appears as the brilliant advisor of the king of Yue, whose stratagems defeated the enemy state of Wu; offered rich rewards by the king, Fan Li refused and became a recluse-wanderer on the lakes of the Southeast. But the usual literary references almost never mention the part of his biography that tells how, after giving up his post with the king and *before* retiring to a solitary life adrift, Fan Li was a successful merchant. Fan Li was indeed "used by the age" 有所用於世. Han Jian surely knew part of the Fan Li story—his political success and his later withdrawal to the life of a recluse; but he probably did not know that Fan Li had been a merchant. Han Jian should indeed appreciate Huang Tingjian's learning: here is the foremost classical source that links the talents of a statesman with the talents of a merchant. If Han Jian was not used by the state, then that is the error of the state; but once he has amassed his fortune, he should "gather his remaining strength and seek out leisure."

Huang Tingjian then turns to the pavilion, whose name "Pines and Chrysanthemums" suggest genteel reclusion. Huang Tingjian refers this back to the paradigm he has already established: "Master Han, realizing that gold and jade cannot be kept, wants to gather his remaining strength and seek out leisure" 韓子真知金玉之不可守，欲收其餘力而就閒者. At this point the social authority of the literary man shows itself, as Huang responds with a question about how Han Jian is going to use his pavilion. "I would like to ask you now: is it going to be for song and dancing, or is it going to for business dealing?" 予今將問子，斯堂之作，將以歌舞乎？將以研、桑乎？

At this point we should realize that we are in a very sophisticated world. As in our own world, people used sites of pleasure not to be free of the negotiations of power but as a site in which to carry them out more successfully. We can be certain that this was no less true for parties among government officials, those who, "aspiring to name, enter the court" 期於名者入朝. This is a cultural paradigm shift from an antithesis between serving the state and not serving the state, to an antithesis between activities undertaken for their own sake, as opposed to those undertaken for "name and/or profit."

The terms that are used as the antithesis of "name and profit" (encompassing both political office and commercial activities) are various: it can be the Way; it can be leisure; it can even be "song and dancing." This is what we call "negative unity," in which very different phenomena are unified as the negation of something else. Here negative unity conjoins terms that would usually be treated as quite distinct, even opposed. Seeking the Way is not usually associated with pretty young singers and dancers.

What happens next in this account is remarkable and part of a paradigm shift in the culture. First, we have classical values rearticulated, addressing the familiar question from *Mengzi* of "solitary happiness" 獨樂 versus "happiness shared with many" 與眾樂. In the original context in *Mengzi*, the case was enjoying "music" (*yue* 樂), a term with a distinct classical cachet; Huang Tingjian replaces the classical term with the contemporary term, "songs and dancing," not only lacking a classical cachet but suggesting the kind of sensual pleasures that were often disapproved.

> 將以歌舞，則獨歌舞而樂，不若與人樂之；與少歌舞而樂，不若與衆樂之。
>
> If it's going to be songs and dancing, then a solitary happiness in songs and dancing is not as good as happiness shared with others; and happiness in songs and dancing shared with few is not as good as a happiness shared with many.

Encouraging a middle-aged or old Sichuan merchant to enjoy "songs and dancing," which has been rephrased with resonant classical authority, is a surprise that invites a smile, but no less surprising than what follows. Mengzi's singular manner of teaching the princes of the Warring States has been transferred to a wealthy member of a local community. Moral responsibility is no longer the prerogative of the state and family; it is now invested in a community's "leading citizens," including merchants.

> 夫歌舞者豈可以樂此哉。卹饑問寒以拊孤，折券棄責以拊貧，冠婚喪葬以拊宗，補耕助歛以拊客，如是則歌舞於堂，人皆粲然相視曰:韓正翁而能樂之乎。
>
> But as for song and dancing, how may one find happiness in just this? Help the hungry and cold to care for orphans; forgive debts to care for the poor; care for the clan in capping ceremonies, marriages, and funerals; help in plowing and tax demands to care for your tenants. If you do this, then when there are songs and dancing in the hall, everyone will give a broad smile and say: "Isn't old Han Jian good at enjoying himself!"

The rich merchant Han Jian now takes the place of King Wen of Zhou, no longer the representative of the state but the local philanthropist, who takes care of the immediate problems in the world around him and shares his joy and wealth with the people. As in Mengzi's discourse to King Hui of Liang, the "ruler's" happiness is found through the happiness of those around him and their reciprocal delight in his happiness. We have gone beyond the "Account of the Pavilion of the Drunken Old Man," in which the magistrate shows his distinction from the locals by finding happiness in their happiness, but the reason for his happiness is not known to the locals. Instead, here we have the locals happy that old Han Jian is enjoying himself. Since Huang Tingjian would have known the "Account of the Pavilion of the Drunken Old Man," he was surely aware that he was turning it on its head.

We know that a shift from dependence on the central government to local responsibility happened in the Southern Song, but Huang Tingjian shows those values already taking shape in the late Northern Song. Loving the Way, loving leisure, loving song and dancing, and taking care of orphans, the poor, impoverished family members, and landless tenants are all on the same level. We see the figure of the wealthy local gentry figure emerging, the leader of a local community who uses his wealth both for pleasure and for the community good. *Le zhi* 樂之 here means primarily "to be happy in it" or "to enjoy it," but it also means "to make them happy." The use of *neng* 能, "be able" or, as above, "be good at," here recalls *Mengzi*: "It was by sharing their happiness with the people that men of antiquity were *able to be* happy" 古之人與民偕樂，故能樂也.

The argument that follows is even more remarkable, situating the rich Sichuan merchant in relation to his posterity.

> 此樂之情也，將以研桑，何時已哉。金玉之為好貨，怨入而悖出，多藏厚亡，他日以遺子孫，賢則損其志，愚則益其過，韓子知及此，空為之哉。雖然，歌舞就閒之日以休研桑之心，反身以期於道，豈可以無孟獻子之友哉。孟獻子以百乘之家，有友五人，皆無獻子之家者也。必得無獻子之家者與之友，則仁者助施，義者助均，智者助謀，勇者助決，取諸左右而有餘，使宴安而不毒，又使子弟日見所不見，聞所不聞，賢者以成德，愚者以寡怨，於以聽隱居之松風，裛淵明之菊露，可以無愧矣。

> If this mood of happiness is carried through in matters of business, when will that ever end? Gold and jade are the best goods, brought in with rancor and going out in turmoil; the more you keep, the greater your loss. Someday you may give it to your children or grandchildren; if they are worthy, then it saps their ambition; if they are foolish, it increases their errors. If Master Han's understanding reaches this point, then to do this [to keep your wealth for your children] would be in vain. Nevertheless, in the days of leisure for song and

> dancing by which you cease to be preoccupied with business dealings, returning to yourself in aspirations for the Way, how can you fail to have the kind of friends Meng Xianzi had? With a household of five hundred chariots, Meng Xianxi had five friends, none of whom had a household like Xianzi's. He would find only people that did not have a household as great as his own and make friends with them; thus the kindly aided him in giving, the righteous aided him in equity, the clever aided him in planning, and the bold aided him in decisiveness. You draw from those around yourself and have plenty, leading you to enjoy secure peace and never harm yourself. Also, by this you have followers to show you every day what you have never seen and hear what you have never heard; by this the worthy perfect your virtue, and the foolish diminish your resentments. As you listen to the wind in the pines of your secluded dwelling and are soaked by Tao Yuanming's dew on the chrysanthemums, you may be free from shame.

It is in the interest of the rich merchant not to accumulate much wealth, which harms his children, whether good or bad, but rather to take care of the community and gather friends, who in turn contribute their various gifts to his endeavors. Gathering such friends seems remarkably close to a ruler finding worthy ministers. In earlier injunctions, Han Jian was encouraged to care for his family; here his attention is redirected to the local "commonweal." In effect, the local community becomes the "state within a state," drawing always on *Mengzi*, the theorist of the community as the model for the state.

The officials are the mobile servants of the empire. Their "place" is in an imperial structure of positions. Like the aging Ouyang Xiu, the Retired Layman Six Ones, in the end they can locate themselves only within a set of *portable* possessions. Su Dongpo always writes of going back home to Sichuan, but he never goes home. The new world of ownership, especially landownership, ties people to a local place and to a local community. One travels for name/fame, a place in the official hierarchy, as the merchant travels for profit; but to study the Way, one "simply turns back to oneself" 反諸身而已, in a particular place.

There is one more very peculiar thing in this account, which returns to the discussion of spending money with which we began this discussion. In the Tang, a "legacy of virtue," *De ye* 德業, can be passed on to children and grandchildren; even in the Song dynasty, an "accumulation of learning," *xue ye*, 學業 can be passed on. But the merchant's wealth can only harm his children, dulling the ambitions of good children and inviting license in bad children. Thus Huang Tingjian encourages Han Jian to spend what he has, to support the local community, to find pleasure in the present, and to make friends with those who can give him good advice—like Huang Tingjian himself.

THE LEGACY OF THE SPIRIT TERRACE: "FINISHING IT" 成之 AND "DESTROYING IT" 廢之

One of the first texts we discussed in these essays was Mengzi in dialogue with King Hui of Liang, invoking the scene of King Wen of Zhou enjoying the Spirit Terrace with his people. Although the central question was and remained solitary happiness as opposed to shared happiness, the Spirit Terrace was necessary, as both a site and a possession to possibly share.

Huang Tingjian encourages the Sichuan merchant Han Jian to use his Pine and Chrysanthemum Pavilion like the Spirit Terrace, to share his possessions and share his joy with others. He is the local philanthropist as one who "aspires to the Way," who also enjoys leisure, along with song and dancing. As in *Mengzi*, the joys and comforts are not in opposition to moral action but achieved through moral action. Han Jian becomes a local version of King Wen of Zhou, helping his community with his wealth and sharing his pavilion for their delight.

If the local merchant-turned-philanthropist can be a small-scale model ruler, like King Wen, the Song emperor Huizong 徽宗 can become the voracious literati collector like Li Shen. After all, the emperor is, more than anyone, "the one with greater strength." He built his own urban garden in the palace grounds on an unprecedented scale, appropriating the finest rocks and trees from all over the empire. His was the ultimate "solitary happiness," delighting in his private possessions, and he does *not* share them with his people. This is, of course, Huizong's Huayang Palace 華陽宮, also known as Gen Mount 艮岳. The garden was finished in 1122, and Huizong was able to enjoy it only a short while.

As the capital, Bianjing, was falling to the Jin army, the citizens of the city broke into the imperial garden seeking refuge. As the monk Zuxiu describes it:[7]

> 靖康元年閏十一月，大梁陷，都人相與排墻避敵于壽山艮嶽之上，時大雪新霽，丘壑林塘，粲若畫本，凡天下之美，古今之勝在焉。祖秀周覽累日，咨嗟驚愕，信天下之傑觀而天造有所未盡也。明年春，復遊華陽宮，而民廢之矣。

In the eleventh month of the first year of the Jingkang reign, Daliang [Bianjing, Kaifeng] fell. The citizens of the capital joined together to break down the wall and tried to get away from the enemy on Longevity Mountain and Gen Mount. At the time a heavy snowfall had newly cleared up, and the hills, valleys, groves, and pools were sparkling white like a painting. All the beauties of the world and the finest scenes of past and present times were right here. Zuxiu went around looking for a number of days and sighed with shock and amazement, for truly these were the most splendid views of all that is under Heaven and something that Heaven's creation itself had not entirely exhausted.

In spring of the following year he visited Huayang Palace again, and the common people had destroyed it.

Recall:

經始靈臺，經之營之，庶民攻之，不日成之。

He first planned the Spirit Terrace,
Planned it, labored on it,
All the common people worked on it,
In less than a day they finished it.

Against:

明年春，復遊華陽宮，而民廢之矣。

In spring of the following year he visited Huayang Palace again, and the common people had destroyed it.

This is a story of ownership and happiness, along with giving names, in the Northern Song. The authoritative source in the Classics was *Mengzi* writing about the Spirit Terrace. The story of Huizong is the story of the failure of lasting happiness in ownership. The new world belonged to Han Jian, the merchant who shared his gains with his community.

6

THE BAMBOO IN THE BREAST AND IN THE BELLY

Merchants like Han Jian had always been there. They were, perhaps, the most despised estate and not often mentioned in the writings of the literate elite. Fortunes were surely made, especially in the great ports like Guangzhou and Yangzhou; but in contrast to Europe and the Islamic world, we do not read of great merchant families making loans to princes to finance their luxuries and their wars. When we do read about merchants—sometimes in Tang poetry—it is often with indignation about their ability to amass wealth without working the fields and weaving silk. Commerce grew considerably throughout the Song, and we can be reasonably certain that merchants were also literate in varying degrees, but in the eyes of the literate elite, they did not know the texts that "really mattered." This was what Huang Tingjian was selling to Han Jian.

In the context of our discussion here, the growth of commerce in the Song is not an issue in its own right, but it was rather a propensity of thought to understand happiness as contingent on having something substantial—from real estate to a rock to a painting. The failure to acquire that "something" could result in disappointment and unhappiness. The desire for such acquisition naturally involved reference to the means of acquisition, which often involved money. We should also not overlook fungible commodities such as silk. The usual commerce of gifts and favors among the elite continued, but the value of acquisitions, both prestige value for the person and commercial value, increasingly entered discourse. In addition, a true commercial network formed, one that dealt in elite goods—paintings, calligraphy, antiques, and Taihu rocks—changing hands and crisscrossing the empire. A new group of brokers arose, real merchants dealing in elite goods. We again turn to Li Qingzhao, who, in her "Afterword" to her husband's colophons on inscriptions, lets us see the kind of moments that were rarely written by the male elite:[1]

嘗記崇寧間，有人持徐熙《牡丹圖》，求錢二十萬。當時雖貴家子弟，求二十萬錢豈易得耶? 留信宿，計無所出而還之，夫婦相向惋悵者數日。

> I recall that in the Chongning reign a man came with a painting of peonies by Xu Xi and asked twenty thousand cash for it. In those days twenty thousand cash was a hard sum to raise, even for children of the nobility. We kept it with us a few days, and, having thought of no plan by which we could purchase it, we returned it. For several days afterward husband and wife faced one another in deep disappointment.

We should note: "a man came with a painting of peonies by Xu Xi and asked twenty thousand cash for it." Suppose she had written: "a man came with a painting of peonies and asked twenty thousand cash for it" or "a man came with an exceptionally beautiful painting of peonies and asked twenty thousand cash for it." However obvious it may be, Xu Xi's signature had cash value, and this we do not often see in the Tang. Aesthetic value is cash value, which can be guaranteed by a "brand name" (Xu Xi); and this in turn returns to influence aesthetic value.

The Song turn of mind can, perhaps, be best illustrated in the couplet, quoted earlier, from Su Dongpo's "Written on a Painting of a Mist River and Layered Cliffs in the Collection of Wang Dingguo [Wang Gong]" 書王定國所藏煙江疊嶂圖. He begins with a description of the painting, following the course of streams down from the cliffs to the river on open land and off to the horizon. Then he comments:

不知人間何處有此境，徑欲往買二頃田。

> I know not where in this mortal world there is such a scene,
> I want to there straightaway and buy two acres of fields.

It is a compliment, but aesthetic evaluation edges into desire—in Su Dongpo's case, to leave the life of an official and go elsewhere, especially home. When this happens, art and advertising are drawn closer together. To want to go to such a place is one thing; to go and purchase land there is something else. The impulse is coded in the aura of allusion. "Two acres of fields" is an allusion to Su Qin, a wandering persuader of the Warring States, and suggests a place to retire from public life. The allusion to "two acres" was often used, but no one talked about *buying* their two acres. On top of this, praise from the famous Su Dongpo increased the value of the painting, and such "gifts of value" on the part of Su Dongpo were often reciprocated with more material gifts and favors. Such gifts and favors were itemized in detail in the Censorate dossier of his trial for slandering the emperor, creating the impression of corruption. This was an increasingly murky world in which the significance of words, things, and acts was changing as the realities of "value" changed.

Su Dongpo does not seem to have been a wealthy man, but—to the chagrin of his enemies—he was a superstar. Wealth flowed from his brush, as in the famous story that he wrote poems and painted bamboo on twenty fans of a destitute fan-maker to help him with his debts.[2] The fan-maker sold each fan for a thousand cash. This was probably just a Hangzhou urban legend, but it is revealing. We have, to my knowledge, no record that he actually "sold" his writing or calligraphy, but recipients of his "gifts" of text and painting knew quite well what their value was, in terms of both prestige and cash value; and to that degree they were indebted to him.

Elite goods were purchased, traded, "loaned," and displayed—ostensibly because they brought happiness to the owner, but also because, through publicity, they added to the aura of the owner, showing his taste and sensibility. At the same time, we find repeated claims that their passion for acquisition was all right because it differed from the objects desired by ordinary people. As Ouyang Xiu says in his "Preface for the List of My *Records of Collected Antiquities*": "I am by nature naively simple and have a passion for antiquity; there is nothing I want among all those things that are avidly desired by the people of this age, so I am able to achieve a single-minded focus in loving these things." And Li Qingzhao says of the collection she shared with her husband Zhao Defu: "Books lay ranged on tables and desks, scattered on top of one another on pillows and bedding. This was what took our fancy and what occupied our minds, what drew our eyes and what our spirits inclined to; and our happiness was greater than the pleasure others had in dancing girls, dogs, and horses" 於是几案羅列，枕席枕藉，意會心謀，目往神授，樂在聲色狗馬之上.

There were also some occasions of prospective happiness through buying land in the pre-Song tradition. The most famous example is Zhi Dun's 支遁 (314-366) desire to "buy a mountain," *maishan* 買山:[3]

> The monk Zhi Dun through an intermediary once approached the monk Zhu Qian to purchase Yang Mountain (Zhejiang) from him. Qian sent back the answer, "I never heard of Chao Fu or Xu You purchasing a mountain for their hermitage."

Chao Fu and Xu You were exemplary recluses of antiquity. Zhu Qian's retort might be expected, but thereafter "buying a mountain" became the phrase commonly used when looking for a place to retire. Another case of "buying a mountain" (in exile rather than retirement) can be found in Liu Zongyuan's 柳宗元 (773–819) "An Account of the Small Hill West of Gumu Pond" 鈷鉧潭西小丘記, which he purchased for four hundred cash. This became a site for excursions by Liu Zongyuan and his friends. If it had frogs, they were "private frogs" rather than frogs belonging to the state, even though the frogs would neither have known nor cared.

What happened in the Song was on a different scale and circulated discursively through a broad community. Educated gentry were taught to emulate the virtue of Confucius's disciple Yan Hui, whose happiness was indifferent to deprivation. They disapproved of a world dominated by commerce and acquisition, but it was already within them. They tried to resist. Su Dongpo told Li Shen that it was best to get things, enjoy them a while, and let go of them; and in a moment of wise sophistry, he observed that to avoid holding onto things was no less a dependency on things than having them. Then he acquired his Qiu Pond rocks and could not bring himself to let go of them, arguing that he wanted no more than just that—the ancient principle of "knowing what is enough," *zhi zu* 知足. But then he saw "Nine Blossoms Mountain in a Jug" and suddenly felt that his Qiu Pond rocks were too "lonely," and he needed just one more rock to make his assemblage complete. Once one has the conviction that acquisition will make one happy and satisfied, there will always be "just one more rock."

Consciousness of the commodity value of a work of art can spread even to the most unlikely artist, which brings us to Su Dongpo's "An Account of Wen Tong's Painting of the Recumbent Bamboo of Yundang Valley" 文與可畫篔簹谷偃竹記. As in the "Account of Stone Bell Mountain," here too the intellectual historical significance is distinct from the literary significance, which follows from reading the whole account. Perhaps what we think of as "literary significance" should be expanded to fall within the scope of what gets called "intellectual historical significance." That too was part of the thought of the age, even if it is generally excluded because it does not make certain kinds of claims and, as is the case here, can be represented only when safely framed as "joking."

In this account, the intellectual historical "lesson," in the usual sense, is framed as such and placed at the beginning, followed by Su Dongpo's comment: "This was what Wen Tong taught me." This passage is often excerpted, and the rest of the account of Wen Tong's painting is ignored. The passage in question is the source of a set phrase (*chengyu*) in Chinese: "to have the complete bamboo in one's breast [mind]," *xiong you chengzhu* 胸有成竹. I have no doubt that Wen Tong (Wen Yuke 文與可, 1018–1079) did say something to that effect, and it represents a distinct strain in Chinese painting theory, fully developed and no doubt perfected by Su Dongpo's prose. When we read it in the context of the rest of the account, however, it becomes, at the very least, complicated. If challenged, Wen Tong would probably have answered that this was how paintings of bamboo "should" be done. But that it not necessarily the living context in which a painting might be done.

Following the famous lesson, the account becomes primarily reminiscences of joking with Wen Tong. Joking was a way Su Dongpo was able to address difficult questions that were not considered in the lesson and probably could not be considered. Most of the rest of the account makes no grand claims as the lesson does, but it takes certain things for granted that are no less a part of thought than the lesson itself.

Michael Fuller has an excellent article entitled "Pursuing the Complete Bamboo in the Breast: Reflections on a Classical Chinese Image for Immediacy."[4] The title of this essay borrows part of his title but supplements the beginning of the account with the end, which involves bamboo in the stomach. Fuller's discussion focuses on the "lesson" in the context of its history in the Chinese tradition, in comparison with "immediacy" in the European tradition.

Fuller omits the first lines of the "lesson," which deserve some consideration:

> 竹之始生，一寸之萌耳，而節葉具焉。自蜩腹蛇蚹以至於劍拔十尋者，生而有之也。今畫者乃節節而為之，葉葉而累之，豈復有竹乎！
>
> When a bamboo is first born, it is just an inch-long sprout, yet the segments and leaves are complete in it. Going from a cicada or snake molting to reach up ten yards, like a sword held upright, is something that it has from birth. Nowadays painters do it segment by segment and burden it with leaf after leaf—how can there still be a bamboo?!

The essential problem is that the bamboo is not just an image in the eyes or mind but a growing organism, with a "propensity" (to borrow François Cheng's translation of the term *shi* 勢). "Propensity," *shi*, was already a standard term in calligraphy theory to describe the kinetic form of brush strokes, the way that momentum can inhere in an essentially static image. Calligraphic brushstrokes occur in ink-painting of bamboo and match up with the "propensity" of the organism to grow. Su Dongpo does not use the term *shi* here, but it informs his description of bamboo's inherent capacity for growth. Su Dongpo invokes neither the "ideal" bamboo nor the mimesis of any particular bamboo, but rather a shape that embodies growth.

The sprout is a Chinese "inch," *cun* 寸. No Chinese reader of the time would miss the fact that the seat of consciousness (the "breast" or "mind" that houses the image of bamboo) was commonly referred to as a "square inch," *fangcun* 方寸. Indeed "square inch" is an elegant way of saying "mind." So the sprout, already complete in its parts and with a propensity to grow, literally fits exactly into the mind. What the artist paints, as described in the next section, is the "fully grown" bamboo. But the artist must somehow invest organic growth in the visual representation. The most taxonomically perfect representation, done "segment by segment" and "leaf by leaf," betrays what the bamboo essentially "is."

Here we pick up the part of the lesson discussed by Fuller:

> 故畫竹必先得成竹於胸中，執筆熟視，乃見其所欲畫者，急起從之，振筆直遂，以追其所見，如兔起鶻落，少縱則逝矣。與可之教予如此。予不能然也，而心識其所以然。夫既心識其所以然而不能然者，內外不一，心手不相應，不學之過也。故凡有見於中而操之不熟者，平居自視了然，而臨事忽焉喪之，豈獨竹乎？

> For this reason, in painting bamboo you must get a fully grown bamboo in your breast. Holding your brush, observe it fully, and only when you see what you want to paint do you stir your brush and go after it directly to catch what you have seen. Like a rabbit jumping into motion as a hawk descends—the slightest laxness and it's gone. This was what Wen Tong taught me. I am not able to carry through that way, but in my mind, I recognize why it is that way. Now if in the mind you recognize why it is a certain way but cannot carry though that way, then inside and outside are not one, mind and hand are not mutually responsive, which is the failure of not studying. Whenever you see something inside you, but you can grasp it securely, ordinarily you consider it perfectly

clear, but when you are about to do something, you suddenly lose it—this is not just with bamboo.

The problem here is that the hawk acts "by nature," but the human being acts only after study, at least according to Su Dongpo's explanation of his failure to carry out Wen Tong's instruction—he has not studied enough. If the hawk acts by nature, the human is supposed to act by "second nature," that imagined point at which, after study, the human being acts as if unselfconsciously. The hawk does not need the image in its mind—it sees the rabbit. Any hawk that must "study" how to strike and catch a rabbit will be a dead hawk. Su Dongpo fails because there is a split second between proposal and action, and he imagines that there will be a time when mind and hand are one.

Su Dongpo's self-criticism of his failure takes us back to Confucius: "Confucius said: 'Those who are born knowing it are the best; those who know it by studying are next best' " 孔子曰，生而知之者，上也；學而知之者，次也 (*Analects* XVI.9). "To be born knowing it" is the mark of sages and hawks; it is to "be" nature. Apart from sages, human beings must study to "know it." They hope to overcome their alienation from nature and be "like" the sage, knowing how a human being should act by "second nature." This brings us to *Analects* II.4: "When I was fifteen, I set my mind on study; at thirty I was established; at forty I was free of doubts; at fifty I understood what Heaven ordained; at sixty my ears did not resist; at seventy I followed my heart's desires without transgressing the set norm" 吾十有五而志于學，三十而立，四十而不惑，五十而知天命，六十而耳順，七十而從心所欲，不踰矩. That is, by a life of study, the lessons learned in the long process may eventually become second nature. It is such perfection of "second nature" that Su Dongpo claims to have not yet achieved.

That process of long study and concentration on the image formed is anything but "immediacy," which lies only in the moment when the image is fully formed and flows out through the hand. And then there is the *Zhuangzi*'s Wheelwright Bian, who explains to Duke Huan why he can't explain his craft or teach it to his son: in the interesting formulation there: "I achieve it in my hand, and it responds to the mind" 得之於手而應於心. Here it seems that it is the hand that learns. If this is the case, Wen Tong's lesson is futile.

The "lesson" has a complex and resonant history, which is why it became the most often quoted part of the account; the narrative that follows the lesson is a new phenomenon of the Song dynasty, without precedent; and while anyone then and later would understand the truth of it, it lacked the historical resonance of the "lesson." Yet the lesson is an easy, comfortable argument—predictable profundity. It is serious—or at least pretends to be. But much of the rest of the essay consists of jokes exchanged between Su Dongpo and Wen Tong.

Before that, however, Su Dongpo's brother intervenes to praise Wen Tong's lesson and Wen Tong as "having the Way."

> 子由為《墨竹賦》以遺與可曰：庖丁，解牛者也，而養生者取之。輪扁，斫輪者也，而讀書者與之。今夫夫子之托於斯竹也，而予以為有道者，則非耶？子由未嘗畫也，故得其意而已。若予者，豈獨得其意，並得其法。

> [My brother] Ziyou [Su Che] wrote a "Poetic Exposition on Ink-Painting of Bamboo" and sent it to Wen Tong. It said: "Butcher Ding was someone who cut apart oxen, yet those who would nurture life learned something from him. Wheelwright Bian was someone who cut wheels, yet the one who was reading [Duke Huan] agreed with him. You, sir, have invested [such an idea] in bamboo, yet would anyone disagree if I think that you possess the Way?" Ziyou never practiced painting; he simply got the idea. As for myself, I didn't just get the idea, I also got the method [for painting].

Su Che makes reference to two famous stories in the *Zhuangzi*, in which two commoners each show a mastery of his skill that is "immediate" or prereflective. Butcher Ding cut up the carcasses of oxen without ever dulling his cleaver because he followed the "empty spaces" in the carcass. Wheelwright Bian, referenced earlier, cut wheels with a skill that could not be put into words or taught, even to his own son. The latter case, of course, invalidates Wen Tong's "lesson" on ink-painting of bamboo. In failing to be able to execute the principles Wen Tong set forth, Su Dongpo verifies Wheelwright Bian's lesson about lessons. The conclusion drawn by Su Che is predictably banal: Wen Tong "possesses the Way," for which painting bamboo is merely the empirical vessel.

This is the moment when Su Dongpo's wicked wit takes over the account—he cannot take banality, even from his brother. If Su Che offers the standard line that "possessing the Way" is the ultimate value, and ink-painting is merely a case that leads to the ultimate value. Su Dongpo turns that hierarchy upside down, in effect suggesting that Wen Tong's lesson not merely teaches the Way, it also gives Su Dongpo the method of painting.

This little twist of humor is the point where the texts turns and leaves the easy lesson. Something pesky and disruptive intrudes into the neatly enclosed world of art theory, confined to mind, object, and hand. The essay that begins with a lesson about the "bamboo in the breast" ends up with Wen Tong having a picnic of roasted bamboo shoots, which he spits out on the table in laughter upon receiving a joking poem from Su Dongpo. When this happens, Su Dongpo is playing. When Su Dongpo plays, it is often because he has no other way to discuss something important. If we don't look at the essay as a whole, we will miss the intellectual point and the fun.

Su Dongpo has been using the high rhetoric of art theory and the great issues of the day, and the intellectual historians take the bait. But all of a sudden, he drops that discourse entirely and switches over to a very different way to talk about painting "in the world." Here there is no authoritative truth or lesson but rather changing meaning of painting for a person (Wen Tong), who is also himself changing. This is our second "moment," and it becomes comic—and then painfully sad.

It is no easy matter to recover the humor of poems written almost a thousand years ago in an entirely different language, but an essay like this one depends on its humor. Turning the topic to Wen Tong himself, Su Dongpo begins: "When Wen Tong painted bamboo, at first he didn't watch out for himself." All Su Dongpo's readers knew that phrase "didn't watch out for himself." It comes from one of Han Yu's most famous essays, his "Tomb Inscription for Liu Zongyuan" 柳子厚墓誌銘, referring to Liu Zongyuan (773–819) in his youth, when he joined the faction of Wang Shuwen, which essentially staged a coup d'état, taking over the powers of government when the new emperor Shunzong was incapacitated by a stroke. When Shunzong's heir, later known as Xianzong, took over the throne, Wang Shuwen was executed, and members of his faction were exiled to exceedingly unpleasant posts in the wilds of South China. For his rash incaution ("not watching out for himself"), Liu Zongyuan spent the rest of his life in exile. This was a weighty allusion for Su Dongpo, whose own career had been wrecked by factional struggle and his own incaution.

But that weight of the phrase sits uncomfortably in the sentence: "When Wen Tong painted bamboo, at first he didn't watch out for himself." And we wonder how painting bamboo could put one in such peril. The next sentences are the punch lines.

與可畫竹，初不自貴重，四方之人持縑素而請者，足相躡於其門。與可厭之，投諸地而罵曰：吾將以為襪。士大夫傳之以為口實。

> At first when Wen Tong painted bamboo, he didn't watch out for himself. People, carrying plain silk, came from every direction to ask for a painting, and would line up toe to heel at his gate. Wen Tong was sick of this and threw the silk on the ground, cursing: "I'm going to make socks out of this." Gentlemen passed this around as a good anecdote.

Wen Tong's rash imprudence was letting his gift for painting bamboo be known. Into the world of lofty art theory, forming the image in the mind and the hand instantly executing the painting, comes the outside world of gentry commerce of favors and gifts, in a queue of gentlemen all carrying silk.

Wen Tong was, evidently, not a rich man. No doubt that when he painted bamboo, he painted on paper. Silk was expensive, and, like gold or silver, it was a fungible commodity that could be used like cash in exchange. Bringing silk, on which Wen Tong was supposed to paint bamboo, was a mark of how easily aesthetic value translated into commercial value—and we can assume that these silk-bearing gentlemen knew that whatever Wen Tong doodled bamboo on would become far more valuable. The artist becomes a factory with a backlog of orders awaiting his inspiration.

It is also not unreasonable to suppose that the silk-bearing gentlemen would not cut the silk at the best size for display in their personal reception rooms. That would suggest parsimony. They probably brought extra silk, both as a "present" and on the possibility that Wen Tong's inspiration might stir him to paint still more bamboo on them. The joking that follows is premised on surplus silk.

Wen Tong tries to escape the bamboo-painting factory and has a fit, throwing the silk on the ground and saying he wants to make socks out of it—transforming a medium of artistic expression and commodity exchange into something of practical use value. But no escape from "name" is possible: this becomes a good story passed around, adding to his aura of eccentricity and thus the value of his "products."

At last Wen Tong thinks of a way to escape.

> 及與可自洋州還，而余為徐州。與可以書遺余曰：近語士大夫，吾墨竹一派，近在彭城，可往求之。襪材當萃於子矣。

> When Wen Tong returned from Yangzhou and I was governing Xuzhou, he sent me a letter which said: "Recently I have been saying to the gentry, 'My lineage of

> ink-painting of bamboo has recently relocated in Pengcheng [Xuzhou]. Why don't you go look for it *there*?' So, the material for socks is going to flock to *you*!"

In effect Wen Tong is pretending to retire and pass the mantle of "master of ink bamboo" on to Su Dongpo. That was a strategy that the gentry would understand.

Commercialism, on the margin between the bamboo in the mind and the bamboo on silk, is beginning to enter the picture. And in the joking poems that follow, the medium of silk becomes the point of contact for an analogy between bamboo and capital. Bamboo begins as a tiny, inch-long sprout in the ground or in the mind, but it has the "propensity" to keep growing and increasing.

In the poem accompanying the letter, Wen Tong imagines painting a "super-bamboo"; Su Dongpo thinks of the material medium of representation, the silk, requisite for a "super-bamboo"; the increase in size of the representation is also an increase in money-value in the material medium, the silk.

> 書尾復寫一詩，其略曰：擬將一段鵝溪絹，掃取寒梢萬尺長。予謂與可，竹長萬尺，當用絹二百五十匹，知公倦於筆硯，願得此絹而已。

> At the end of the letter Wen Tong copied out a poem that said, in excerpt:
>
> I plan to take a piece of Goose Creek silk
> and sweep forth wintry stalks ten thousand feet long.
>
> I told Wen Tong: "If you are going to have bamboo ten thousand feet tall, you are going to need 250 bolts of silk. I realize that you are going to wear yourself out with brush and ink-stone [i.e., in painting] simply from your desire to get so much silk."

As Wen Tong imagines that inch-long sprout becoming a painted bamboo ten thousand feet tall, Su Dongpo immediately calculates the number of bolts of silk that such a painting would require. Conventional poetic hyperbole is translated into silk inventory, so that the artist's dream resolves into the growth of the artist's capital.

The two friends, older and younger, have descended to witty banter, but Su Dongpo was the unchallenged wit of his age and the master of banter. Wen Tong is confounded.

> 與可無以答，則曰：吾言妄矣，世豈有萬尺竹也哉。余因而實之，答其詩曰：世間亦有千尋竹，月落庭空影許長。與可笑曰：蘇子辯則辯矣。然二百五十匹，吾將買田而歸老焉。因以所畫篔簹谷偃竹遺予，曰：此竹數尺耳，而有萬尺之勢。
>
> Since Wen Tong couldn't make a good retort, he said: "I was wrong. How could there ever be bamboo ten thousand feet tall?" I followed up on this and offered a concrete example, answering his poem:
>
> In this world there are indeed
> bamboo a thousand yards tall—
> when the moon sets in the empty courtyard,
> its shadows are just that long.
>
> Wen Tong laughed and said: "Su Dongpo can really make a witty case! Still, with 250 bolts of silk I could buy fields and retire." Then he sent me "The Recumbent Bamboo of Yundang Valley" that he had painted, commenting: "These bamboos are just several feet long, but they have the propensity to become ten thousand feet tall.

No one is supposed to be thinking about money—this is not proper for a gentleman—but one does not have to read far and long in Northern Song texts to realize that many gentlemen are indeed thinking about money.

Su Dongpo has infected the discourse not with wealth but with fantasies of wealth. This sets Wen Tong to thinking. Su wants to demonstrate his cleverness—he always does—and gives Wen Tong an example of how there can indeed be bamboo as tall as Wen Tong imagines. His figure of bamboo growing even taller as dark shadows in the sinking moonlight uncannily evokes the black and white of ink-painting, where the "inch" of bamboo in the mind can grow to any imagined height on white silk. This is the "propensity" of bamboo to grow tall. Wen Tong's disavowal of his fantasy of increase collapses before Su Dongpo's affirmation, and at this point Wen Tong starts thinking that he might make enough money from his painting to buy a retirement home.

Wen Tong, who rashly let the world know about his ink bamboo, has now brought up a fantasy of 250 bolts of silk and the possibility of buying a retirement home. The elite disdained commerce and professed lofty ideals, but the realities of commerce and economic life easily crept in around the edges—especially when they considered retiring. In his next poem, Su Dongpo will "grow" Wen Tong's imaginary capital accumulated from painting silk to even more fabulous wealth.

"Ink bamboo" was considered one of the most aesthetically noble forms of literati art. But in this famous text, bamboo is the counterpart of capital, beginning small—the "inch" that fits the "square inch" of the painter's mind—but with the propensity to grow to ten thousand feet, and requiring vast quantities of silk—indeed it is the very Warren Buffet of bamboo. The small bamboos of Yundang Valley have that propensity within them.

> 篔簹谷在洋州，與可嘗令予作《洋州三十詠》，篔簹谷其一也。予詩云：漢川修竹賤如蓬，斤斧何曾赦籜龍。料得清貧饞太守，渭濱千畝在胸中。與可是日與其妻游谷中，燒筍晚食，發函得詩，失笑噴飯滿案。
>
> Yundang Valley is in Yangzhou [where Wen Tong served], and he commissioned me to write thirty verses on Yangzhou, one of which was to be on Yundang Valley. My poem went:
>
> > The tall bamboo of the River Han are cheap as dandelions,
> > did the hatchet ever spare these sheathed dragons?[5]
> > I reckon they feed the hungry governor in his austere poverty,
> > but a thousand acres by the Wei's shores are in his breast.
>
> On that day Wen Tong was visiting the valley with his wife, and they were roasting bamboo shoots for their evening meal. When he opened the letter packet and found this poem, he was so overcome by laughter that he spit out his food all over the table.

The noble bamboo was a signifying plant whose image invited contemplation. It was referred to poetically as *ci jun* 此君, "this gentleman," and was famous for integrity (*jie* 節, also the segmented joints of the bamboo) and for its perseverance, staying green though the winter. It was the icon of the Confucian gentleman. As a shoot it was also a delicious vegetable.

It is difficult to explain a thousand-year-old joke, but Su Dongpo's poem is very funny. The question of commercial value is part of the joke. *Jian* 賤, translated as "cheap" in its commercial context ("acquire cheap, sell dear"), is also a class term, "base," the very opposite of the bamboo as *ci jun*, "this gentleman." Does this growth of the base/cheap sprout into superbamboo have anything to do with social mobility as well as capital, and transformation of *jian* to *gui* ("noble," "expensive")? The opening "bamboo in the breast" of the artist here becomes a veritable bamboo plantation in the breast, providing the artist with income of a great lord.

At first, we may not know why they are being cut indiscriminately with a hatchet—bamboo has many uses—but when we see "sheathed dragons" with purplish skins, we know that these are supremely edible bamboo shoots. Dragons can contract into something very small but can extend onto something huge and grand, just as the bamboo begins with an inch-long shoot but can grow, in the imagination, to ten thousand feet. The "governor," Wen Tong, lives in noble poverty and eats cheap bamboo shoots. But he is dreaming of wealth: he does have "bamboo in his breast," as well as in his belly—indeed he has the famous thousand acres of bamboo by the Wei River. Wen Tong will, of course, recognize the allusion to the "Treatise on Commerce" 食貨志 in the *Grand Historian's Records*, the *Shiji*, by Sima Qian from around the turn of the first century BCE.[6] There it speaks of "a thousand acres of bamboo by the Wei River," commenting that anyone who owns the bounty of a place like that in the empire is the equal of a duke with the income of ten thousand households. Roughly speaking, you live in poverty, eating the cheapest and most humble of foods, but in your heart are the bamboo, which are both a dream of wealth and that inch-long sprout that grows into the painting for which others bring you silk.

Su Dongpo's poem by chance reaches Wen Tong at the very moment he is having a picnic in Yundang Valley, eating bamboo shoots. In Chinese one would say that is *qiao* 巧, a remarkable coincidence. Our essay begins with a bamboo shoot in the breast and comes at last to bamboo shoots in the stomach. The former, the bamboo shoot in the breast, grows to maturity and at exactly the right moment emerges through the hand of the artist; those bamboo on silk are valuable and bring a queue of seekers bearing silk. The roasted bamboo shoots in the stomach are disgorged onto the picnic table with uncontrollable laughter. A hand, like Su Dongpo's, may falter an instant in painting the image of the bamboo in the breast, but the bamboo in the stomach come forth with true unselfconscious "immediacy." The former belongs to the artist; the latter belongs to the governor who lives simply, without luxury, who thinks of making socks with his surplus silk and eats roasted bamboo shoots.

The straightforward idea in the "lesson" followed by the complicating supplement recalls the famous passage on language and meaning or "idea" in the "Outer Things," *Waiwu* 外物," chapter of *Zhuangzi*:

> 荃者所以在魚，得魚而忘荃;蹄者所以在兔，得兔而忘蹄;言者所以在意，得意而忘言。吾安得忘言之人而與之言哉?
>
> The purpose of the lure is for the fish; when you get the fish, you forget the lure. The purpose of the snare is for the rabbit; when you get the rabbit, you forget the snare. The purpose of words is for the idea; when you get the idea, you forget the words. How can I find someone who forgets words and have a word with him?

Like the "account" by Su Dongpo, the first part of the *Zhuangzi* passage is often quoted, and the last part—in *Zhuangzi* the final sentence—adding something to the already "complete" idea, is usually omitted. Although *Zhuangzi*'s commentators try desperately to make the last sentence serious, it sounds very much like a joke at the expense of the clear idea just articulated. The often-quoted passage is generally known to Chinese readers, at least in the set phrase "get the idea and forget the words" 得意忘言. There is, of course, an irony in so often repeating the analogy in words, since the words supposedly self-destruct—or at least fade from memory—on being understood. This is even more ironic with the apparently garrulous speaker looking for someone else to talk to—probably about "forgetting words." Moreover, the person with whom he wants to speak already has "forgotten words" and so is in no need of the lesson.

Even though this famous passage is not from the core *Zhuangzi* chapters, whoever set this down had fully mastered the philosophically significant wit of Zhuang Zhou. He loves words and sometimes loves to undermine or complicate what he just said with more words. There is *always* something else to be said. So too Su Dongpo's account of Wen Tong's lesson is not contradicted by what follows, but rather the lesson is irrevocably complicated by placing the painter in the human world. We are invited to imagine a long queue of silk-bearing gentlemen, each in turn reminding the artist to first form the complete bamboo in the breast and then to execute the painting spontaneously at exactly the right moment. Or worse still, one gentleman saying to the gentleman behind him: "Now he's forming the idea of a complete bamboo in his mind; watch how quickly he paints it on the silk!"

When we finally come to Wen Tong spitting out his bamboo shoots in uncontrollable laughter at Su Dongpo's joking poem, the words are still not over, and there is more to be said. And again, the supplement changes everything.

> 元豐二年正月二十日，與可沒於陳州。是歲七月七日，予在湖州曝書畫，見此竹，廢卷而哭失聲。昔曹孟德《祭橋公文》，有車過、腹痛之語，而予亦載與可疇昔戲笑之言者，以見與可於予親厚無間如此也。

> On the 20th day of the first month in the second year of the Yuanfeng Reign (1079), Wen Tong passed away in Chenzhou. On the seventh day of the seventh month that year, I was in Huzhou and was airing my books and paintings. When I saw these bamboo [in the painting], I put aside the scroll, choked up with tears. Long ago Cao Cao's sacrificial address to Qiao Xuan used the phrases "my carriage passed" and "I felt a pain in the belly." And those playful words I wrote earlier for Wen Tong show my feeling of perfect closeness to him.

We come at last to the occasion for writing, the autumn airing of Su Dongpo's scrolls. He had not been initially thinking of Wen Tong, but seeing the painting reminded him of his very dear friend who had passed away earlier that year. The painting is a trace of a moment in their long relationship, a story he wants to tell. It is a trace that leads to the memory of laughter; but the death of the person who shared that laughter changes it, without extinguishing the laughter. And in giving us the history behind the painting, we see it as more than an aesthetic object, more than a trophy of the famous painter of ink bamboo.

As Chinese writers so often did, Su Dongpo looks for a past example though which to understand his situation. Perhaps only Su Dongpo would so daringly compare himself to Cao Cao, the great warlord at the end of the Han. Qiao Xuan was the man who first told Cao Cao that he had genius (as Wen Tong passed the "mantle" of mastery in ink-painting bamboo on to Su Dongpo). After Qiao Xuan passed away, Cao Cao was passing by his tomb engaged in pleasantries with others, but a few paces later he felt the pain of memory in his belly. And we can't forget about the bamboo shoots in Wen Tong's belly.

We might reflect on the nature of knowledge embodied in literary texts. It is clearly not the kind of knowledge offered in Wen Tong's "lesson" about knowing the moment to strike or use the brush. Perhaps the best way to approach it is the knowledge that we must presume in the reader in order for him or her to make sense of or see the humor of the text. This is a special kind of historical knowledge in which we suddenly realize they know what we know. They can make endless claims about immediacy, but they know the real complications of the world, how things are embedded in social relationships—which include those values that can be realized in the human world only imperfectly.

It is worthwhile reflecting on the question of knowledge here. Wen Tong's authoritative lesson on painting bamboo is a variation on conventional values. In the background is the assumption of a long phase of practice, after which "mastery" is achieved. That mastery justifies the "lesson," given to Su Dongpo. There is no hint that such mastery will change or evolve further. It is represented as a stable, unchanging truth.

This stage of mastery involves the internalization of value to the degree that action is prereflective. Such a notion of final, prereflective knowledge does have a long tradition in China. This can indeed be taught as "traditional Chinese values," a novel reiteration of something familiar, and it is satisfying as such.

At a certain stage in a civilization, that no longer seems adequate. It is important to realize that Wen Tong's lesson, the idea that can be "trapped" in words and consumed, cannot be reconciled with the representation of Wen Tong in the second half of the essay—though that too can be reached through words. There Wen Tong never has unqualified mastery; he is in the world, either not entirely aware of what he is doing or almost helpless in face of the social forces that treat him as a "master." In the first version of Wen Tong, Su Dongpo can understand but not live up to the teaching of the master; in the second version, Su Dongpo easily understands Wen Tong's unwilling role as the master of bamboo ink-painting. Flustered, worried about retirement, there is nothing in the second version of Wen Tong that offers a lesson in standard values. Nevertheless, the second version is someone we can all recognize, just as Su Dongpo took for granted that his readers could also recognize such a person.

To reach a representation of a human being in the world, Su Dongpo has to go through standard values to show something beyond them. These standard values are not false, but they are inadequate, or perhaps simply incomplete. There is more to be said.

CLOSURE

Let us return to Ouyang Xiu's joke with which we began. Ouyang Xiu tells a joke; we laugh and share the humor. Suddenly Ouyang Xiu adds a final comment of moral criticism and disapproval: this behavior is not appropriate for ministers of state. Although we, the audience caught laughing, are not the objects of his criticism, it is an uncomfortable shift of discursive spheres from one in which we are encouraged to laugh to another in which stern moral judgment is called for and not laughter.

We reflect that if he hadn't told the joke and simply described the situation, it would have been very different. "Minister Feng Dao played a joke on Minister He Ning, and everyone in the hall of the Secretariat roared with laughter. Such behavior harmed their authority to supervise their subordinates." In this case the reader might feel comfortable by the disapproving judgment; but few, I suspect, would read or remember it.

The twinge of readerly discomfort is not from the content of the anecdote, but from the way it is written. It makes us share the laughter and then leaves us there, with the author assuming a different role as moral judge. A joke is supposed to be a protected discursive space in which the rules of social discourse are temporarily suspended. In our own world we understand the dangers of jokes, how easily they can transgress some moral boundary of the community. But if such a judgment is made, we expect that it come from the audience and not the person telling the joke.

Here and in many of the texts discussed, the speaker is under surveillance, even by himself. Always present is the imaginary "visitor" who may step in to criticize and demand an explanation. Usually the primary speaker crumbles, concedes, or tries to change the topic. Su Dongpo's "poetry trial," in which the Censorate scrutinized all his texts for anything politically or ethically objectionable, was just one extreme instance of something that seems to have been widespread in authors themselves. Su Dongpo was far more brash and incautious than others. Perhaps it was not the rise of Daoxue in itself that led to a diminished importance of literature, but rather simple fear. Even in Su Dongpo's perfectly innocent "Account of Stone Bell Mountain," the sound of mocking laughter flies above him, unseen in the dark.

No small part of Ouyang Xiu's impulse to offer criticism was due to historicizing the joke. If such a joke were told in the Warring States, it could easily be dehistoricized, with the actors being "men from the state of Song" (the often-mocked Warring States domain rather than the dynasty), with no loss to the humor. From early in the tradition, historical acts and events called for moral judgment, but the call was not always an urgent one. It seems that Ouyang Xiu cannot let pass a scene of subordinates laughing at their superiors in the Secretariat, even in a joke he himself is telling.

Ouyang Xiu does not include this joke in his "classical" writings. The term "classical" is not used in Chinese, but it is a useful term to suggest the formal decorum and gravity of genres included in an author's official "literary collection," his *wenji* 文集. This is much like the textual counterpart of the Secretariat, where the appearance of dignity must be maintained. The joke we have been discussing is included in his *Return to the Fields*, *Guitian lu* 歸田錄, which consists of less serious "entries" rather than genres.

During the eleventh century new kinds of prose were appearing outside the received system of genres. This is often referred to as "informal prose," because it was generally less crafted than the genres in the "collection." Such works often circulated independently. A few such forms made it into the standard collection as new genres, but the doors were closing on the classical genre system. The new, informal genres had less strict rules, but we can see from Ouyang Xiu's joke that the surveillance of writing spread out to include the informal genres as well. Su Dongpo, who wrote both in classical genres and in informal kinds of prose and verse, stood in that shrinking gap in the closing doors—probably with his foot in the doors.

There was seepage across this barrier, and fine works were still to be written within the classical genres, but by the Southern Song something had changed. Thereafter the best of "old-style prose" was represented by the famous "eight masters": two from the Tang and six from the Northern Song. But when we look more closely, nearly seven hundred years of prose was represented by only one short generation in the Tang and by two generations in the Northern Song, the generations of Ouyang Xiu and Su Dongpo.

FURTHER READINGS

Scholarship on Song dynasty history is a field of study far more developed than Song literary studies. In Song dynasty literary studies, scholarship has generally focused on poetry rather than on essayistic prose. The works of Ronald Egan, addressing both poetry and prose, are a major exception. Egan has published a series of books on major authors and on the growth of aesthetics. These are *The Literary Works of Ou-yang Hsiu (1007–72)* (Cambridge: Cambridge University Press, 1984); *Word, Image, and Deed in the Life of Su Shi* (Cambridge, Mass.: Council in East Asian Studies Publications, 1994); *The Problem of Beauty: Aesthetic Thought and Pursuits in Northern Song Dynasty China* (Cambridge, Mass.: Harvard Asia Center Publications, 2006); and *The Burden of Female Talent: The Poet Li Qingzhao and Her History in China* (Cambridge, Mass.: Harvard University Asia Center, 2013).

Michael Fuller's *The Road to East Slope: The Development of Su Shi's Poetic Voice* (Stanford, Calif.: Stanford University Press, 1990) is an excellent study of Su Shi's poetry but also contains some valuable discussions of Su's prose. An interesting discussion of Ouyang Xiu's prose, including some of the texts discussed here, is to be found in Xianda Lian, "The Old Drunkard Who Finds Joy in His Own Joy—Elitist Ideas in Ouyang Xiu's Informal Writings," *Chinese Literature: Essays, Articles, Reviews (CLEAR)* 23 (December 2001): 1–29.

Art history is a field allied to literary studies and one in which the social situation of production—the creation of different kinds of social value—has been studied. We have some exemplary works here, such as Peter Sturman's *Mi Fu: Style and the Art of Calligraphy in Northern Song Culture* (New Haven, Conn.: Yale University Press, 1997); Robert Harrist's *Painting and Private Life in Eleventh Century China: Mountain Villa by Li Gonglin* (Princeton, N.J.: Princeton University Press, 1998);

Alfreda Murck's *Poetry and Painting in Song China: The Subtle Art of Dissent* (Cambridge, Mass.: Harvard University Asia Center, 2002); and Maggie Bickford's *Ink Plum: The Making of a Chinese Scholar-painting Genre* (Cambridge: Cambridge University Press, 1996).

Song dynasty history is a large field and dwarfs Song literary studies. Perhaps the best introduction is Denis Twitchett and Paul Jakov Smith, eds., *The Cambridge History of China*, vol. 5, part 1: *The Sung Dynasty and Iits Precursors, 907–1279* (Cambridge: Cambridge University Press, 2009). Paul Jakov Smith's chapter, "Shen-tsung's Reign and the New Policies of Wang An-shih, 1067-1085," is helpful in sorting out the complexities the economic situation and the introduction of the divisive "New Policies."

For the eleventh-century forces leading to the rise of Daoxue (Neo-Confucianism), I have been heavily influenced by my colleague Peter Bol—both his books *"This Culture of Ours": Intellectual Transitions in T'ang and Sung China* (Stanford, Calif.: Stanford University Press, 1994) and *Neo-Confucianism in History* (Cambridge, Mass.: Harvard University Asia Center, 2008), as well as over thirty years of conversations. The books, however, are accessible. Any misunderstandings of conversations are entirely my own.

For Song printing and its troubled relationship with a manuscript culture, one should read Susan Cherniack, "Book Culture and Textual Transmission in Sung China," *Harvard Journal of Asiatic Studies* 54, no. 1 (June 1994): 5–125.

For many aspects of Song history, I depend on the works of Patricia Ebrey. For women's history, one can do no better that her *The Inner Quarters: Marriage and the Lives of Chinese Women in the Sung Period* (Berkeley: University of California Press, 1993). For the reign of Huizong, we have Ebrey's *Emperor Huizong* (Cambridge, Mass.: Harvard University Press, 2014), and a volume edited by Ebrey and Maggie Bickford, *Emperor Huizong and Late Northern Song China: The Politics of Culture and the Culture of Politics* (Cambridge, Mass.: Harvard University Asia Center, 2006).

A defining moment in Northern Song literature was the Censorate trial of Su Shi for slandering the emperor by means of poems that were presumed to be critical of the "New Policies," which were supported by the emperor. Although Su Shi's sudden arrest and the prosecutorial examples of literary interpretation (and misinterpretation) were political rather than moral, the event brings the anxiety of a culture of surveillance to the surface. The texts I discuss in this book abound in procatalepsis; that is, anticipating objections and criticism. Charles Hartmann has written two excellent articles on the Censorate dossier of Su Shi's "poetry trial":

"Poetry and Politics in 1079: The Crow Terrace Case of Su Shih," *Chinese Literature: Essays, Articles, Reviews* (*CLEAR*) 12 (December 1990): 15–44; and "The Inquisition Against Su Shih: His Sentence as an Example of Song Legal Practice," *Journal of the American Oriental Society* 113, no. 2 (April–June 1993): 228–43.

Since ownership is one of the topics running through these essays, we are led to economy and ultimately to production. As someone raised on Mark Elvin's *The Pattern of the Chinese Past* (Stanford, Calif.: Stanford University Press, 1977), I was inclined to think of the Song in terms of an agricultural "revolution." While there is no doubt that the Song dynasty was far more economically developed than the Tang, I have gradually learned that agricultural change came more gradually than I had believed (though widespread double-cropping was an important boost). For a more up-to-date look at Song economy, the curious reader should turn to Richard von Glahn's *The Economic History of China* (Cambridge: Cambridge University Press, 2016).

The best account of the conflict of values for an individual in this period, when the practical demands of life encountered aesthetic pleasures, can be found in Stephen H. West, "Zhu Changwen and His 'Garden of Joy,'" in *The Transmission and Interpretation of the Chinese Literary Canon: Papers from the Fourth International Conference on Sinology* (Taipei: Academia Sinica, 2013).

SOURCES AND TRANSLATIONS

Here I include the sources, texts, and translations for texts extensively discussed in these essays. Several of these texts were shortened for readability and marked with ellipses in the essay. In one case, "The Account of Stone Bell Mountain," I included the concluding paragraph with the opening paragraph for discussing the frame. In all cases, the reader can here find the whole translation without it being broken up by discussion.

1. WHAT'S IN A NAME?

六一居士傳

六一居士初謫滁山，自號醉翁。既老而衰且病，將退休於潁水之上，則又更號六一居士。客有問曰:六一，何謂也。居士曰:吾家藏書一萬卷，集録三代以來金石遺文一千卷，有琴一張，有碁一局，而常置酒一壺。客曰:是爲五一爾，奈何？居士曰:以吾一翁，老於此五物之間，是豈不爲六一乎？客笑曰:子欲逃名者乎，而屢易其號，此莊生所誚畏影而走乎日中者也；余將見子疾走大喘渴死，而名不得逃也。居士曰:吾固知名之不可逃，然亦知夫不必逃也。吾爲此名，聊以志吾之樂爾。客曰:其樂如何？居士曰:吾之樂可勝道哉？方其得意於五物也，太山在前而不見，疾雷破柱而不驚；雖響九奏於洞庭之野，閱大戰於涿鹿之原，未足喻其樂且適也。然常患不得極吾樂於其間者，世事之爲吾累者衆也。其大者有二焉，軒裳珪組勞吾形於外，憂患思慮勞吾心於內，使吾形不病而已悴，心未老而先衰，尚何暇於五物哉。雖然，吾自乞其身於朝者三年矣，一日天子惻然哀之，賜其骸骨，使得與此五物偕返於田廬，庶幾償其夙願焉。此吾之所以志也。客復笑曰:子知軒裳珪組之累其形，而不知五物之累其心乎？居士曰:不然。累於彼者已勞矣，又多憂；累於此者既佚矣，幸無患。吾其何擇哉？於是與客俱起，握手大笑曰:置之區區不足較也。

已而歎曰:夫士少而仕，老而休，蓋有不待七十者矣。吾素慕之，宜去一也。吾嘗用於時矣，而訖無稱焉，宜去二也。壯猶如此，今既老且病矣，乃以難彊之筋骸，貪過分之榮祿，是將違其素志而自食其言，宜去三也。吾負三宜去，雖無五物，其去宜矣，復何道哉。熙寧三年九月七日，六一居士自傳。

"The Biography of the Retired Layman Six Ones"

When the Retired Layman "Six Ones" was banished to the mountains of Chuzhou, he called himself "The Drunken Old Man." When he became old, frail, and sick, he was going to retire to the waters of the River Ying. Then he once again changed how he called himself: the "Retired Layman Six Ones."

It happened that someone asked him: "What do you mean by 'Six Ones'?" The Retired Layman said: "My home library is one of myriad scrolls and I have gathered one thousand scrolls of records of texts surviving on metal and stone since the Three Dynasties; I have one zither and one chess set; and one jug of ale is always set out before me." The person then said: "This is just five 'ones'; what about that?" The Retired Layman then said: "By adding this one old man, me, aging among these five things, how can this not make *six* ones?"

The person then laughed, saying: "Do you really want to escape from having a name/fame? To so often change how you call yourself is what Zhuangzi made fun of as 'someone who fears his shadow yet runs in the sunlight.' As I see it, you are running swiftly, panting, dying of thirst, yet you will never manage to escape your name."

The Retired Layman replied: "I know quite well that having a name cannot be escaped; nevertheless, I also understand that one doesn't have to escape it. I made this name ("Six Ones") just to commemorate my happiness."

The other person asked: "What is that happiness like?" The Retired Layman replied: "Can my happiness ever be fully told? When I find satisfaction among these five things, Mount Tai can be right in front of me, but I don't see it; peals of thunder can smash a column, but I won't be alarmed. Even the echoes of the Nine Shao in the wilderness of Dongting or viewing the great battle on the plain of Zhuolu are inadequate to figure such happiness and contentment. Still I have always counted it a misfortune not to be able to enjoy the fullest measure of happiness among them, for many were the worldly concerns that have encumbered me. On the outside, carriage, gown, badge, and ribbons tasked my physical form; on the inside, worries, troubles, concerns, and cares tasked my mind. These made my physical form decrepit though not sick and my heart waste away though not old—what free time was there for my five things? Even so, for three long years I begged for my person from the court; then one day the Son of Heaven sympathetically felt my distress and granted me back my bones, making it possible for me to go back to my cottage in the fields together with these five things. And I hope that I can enjoy the fulfillment of this abiding desire here. This is why I commemorated it."

The other person once again laughed, saying: "You understand that carriage, gown, badge, and ribbons encumber your physical form, but don't you also understand that the five things encumber your heart?" The Retired Layman said: "It's not that way. To be encumbered by the former is indeed being put to task, and in addition brings many cares; to be encumbered by the latter is an indulgence and fortunately brings no misfortune. What is there to choose between the two?" Thereupon I stood up together with my visitor, clasped his hand, and said with a loud laugh: "Let's drop the matter. These petty things are not worth comparing."

After that I gave a sigh and said: "A gentleman takes service in his youth and retires when he is old. There are indeed those who do not wait until they are seventy. I've always yearned to do so—that's the first reason that it is appropriate to quit. I have indeed been employed in my day yet have done nothing of note—that's the second reason it is appropriate to quit. I was still this way when I was in my prime, and now I am old and sick; in fact, to be greedy for fame and salary with these old bones and sinews that are so hard to force would be to go against my lifelong aims and to eat my own words—that is the third reason it is appropriate to quit. Given these three reasons that it is appropriate to quit, it would be indeed appropriate to quit even without these five things. What more is there to say!"

The third year of the Xining reign, seventh day of the ninth month, the self-account of the Retired Layman Six Ones.

Li Yi'an, *Ouyang Xiu quanji*, 634

蘇東坡, 書六一居士傳後

蘇子曰:居士可謂有道者也。或曰:居士非有道者也。有道者無所挾而安。居士之於五物，捐世俗之所爭，而拾其所棄者也，烏得為有道乎。蘇子曰:不然。挾五物而後安者，惑也；釋五物而後安者，又惑也。且物未始能累人也，軒裳圭組，且不能為累，而況此五物乎。物之所以能累人者，以吾有之也。吾與物俱不得已而受形於天地之間，其孰能有之。而或者以為己有，得之則喜，喪之則悲。今居士自謂六一，是其身均與五物為一也。不知其有物耶，物有之也。居士與物均為不能有，其孰能置得喪於其間。故曰:居士可謂有道者也。雖然，自一觀五，居士猶可見也。與五為六，居士不可見也。居士殆將隱矣。

Su Dongpo, "Written After 'The Biography of the Retired Layman Six Ones' "

Master Su says: The Retired Layman may be thought of as one who possesses the Way. Some have said: "The Retired Layman is not someone who possesses the Way. One who possesses the Way is at peace without holding onto anything. In his relation to his five things, the Retired Layman gave up what ordinary people in the age struggle for yet picked up what they rejected—how can this be considered possessing the Way?"

Master Su says: This is wrong. One who is at peace only after holding onto these five things would be deluded, and one who is at peace only after letting go of these five things would be also deluded. For material things have never had the capacity to encumber a person; even coach and uniform and seal and ribbons of office don't have the capacity to be encumbrances, much less these five things. The reason why things have the capacity to encumber a person is because "I" possess them. Both I and external things could not help receiving form in this world, so who has the capacity to possess them? Yet there are some who consider them their own; they are happy when they gain such things and sad when they lose them.

Now the Retired Layman refers to himself as "Six Ones," which is to say that his person is just one together with the five things. I don't know whether he possesses the things, or the things possess him. And if the Retired Layman and his things equally do not have the capacity to possess, then who can put questions of gain and loss to them? This is the reason I say: The Retired Layman may be thought of as one who possesses the Way. Nevertheless, in observing the five from the perspective of one, the Retired Layman still can be seen; joining the five to become six, the Retired Layman cannot be seen. The Retired Layman has virtually become hidden.

Zhang Zhilie, Ma Defu, and Zhou Yukai, *Su Shi quanji jiaozhu*, 7349

2. THE MAGISTRATE OF PEACH BLOSSOM SPRING

歐陽修，豐樂亭記

修既治滁之明年，夏，始飲滁水而甘。問諸滁人，得於州南百步之近。其上豐山，聳然而特立；下則幽谷窈然而深藏；中有清泉滃然而仰出。俯仰左右，顧而樂之。於是疏泉鑿石，闢地以爲亭，而與滁人往遊其間。

滁於五代干戈之際，用武之地也。昔太祖皇帝，嘗以周師破李景兵十五萬於清流山下，生擒其將皇甫暉、姚鳳於滁東門之外，遂以平滁。修嘗考其山川，按其圖記，升高以望清流之關，欲求暉鳳就擒之所，而故老皆無在者。蓋天下之平久矣。自唐失其政，海内分裂，豪傑並起而爭，所在爲敵國者，何可勝數。及宋受天命，聖人出而四海一。嚮之憑恃險阻，剗削消磨，百年之間，漠然徒見山高而水清。欲問其事，而遺老盡矣。今滁介於江淮之間，舟車商賈，四方賓客之所不至。民生不見外事，而安於畎畝衣食，以樂生送死，而孰知上之功德，休養生息，涵煦百年之深也。

修之來此，樂其地僻而事簡，又愛其俗之安閑。既得斯泉于山谷之間，乃日與滁人仰而望山，俯而聽泉。掇幽芳而蔭喬木，風霜冰雪，刻露清秀，四時之景無不可愛。又幸其民樂其歲物之豐成，而喜與予遊也。因爲本其山川，道其風俗之美，使民知所以安此豐年之樂者，幸生無事之時也。

夫宣上恩德，以與民共樂，刺史之事也。遂書以名其亭焉。慶曆丙戌六月日，右正言知制誥知滁州軍州事歐陽修記。

Ouyang Xiu, "The Account of the Pavilion of Abundance and Happiness"

It was in summer of the year after I took up the governorship of Chuzhou, that I first drank Chu's water and found it sweet. I asked the locals about it and found it nearby, a hundred paces south of the prefectural seat. Above was Abundance Mountain, rising up and standing apart. Below was Secluded Valley, keeping it deeply hidden. Between these two was a clear spring, coming out upward from the ground and welling over. Looking about, above and below and all around, I was delighted. Thereupon I had a channel dredged and had the rock cut, opening the spot in order to make a pavilion. And I would go there on excursions with the natives of Chuzhou.

During the warfare of the Five Dynasties, Chuzhou had been a place of battle. Long ago our emperor Taizu had once led the Zhou army and smashed one hundred and fifty thousand troops of Li Jing at the foot of Clearcurrent Mountain and captured the generals Huangfu Hui and Yao Feng outside the eastern gate. Thereafter Chuzhou was pacified. I have studied the mountains and rivers, checking them against maps and accounts, and I climbed a high place to view Clearcurrent Pass, hoping to find the spot where Huangfu Hui and Yao Feng were captured—but no old people survive from that time. Truly the world has been at peace for a long time. From the time that the Tang government collapsed, and the world split apart with bold, outstanding men rising everywhere in contention, how can one count all the places that became enemy realms? When the Song dynasty received the Mandate of Heaven, a Sage Ruler emerged, and the sea-girt world became one. The defensible fastness on which they once relied has been obliterated and wiped away; and in the span of a hundred years one sees only a blur of high mountains and clear rivers. And if one wants to ask about what happened here, the old survivors of that age are all gone.

Now Chuzhou is bounded by the Yangzi and the Huai, a place where boats and wagons and merchants and visitors from all over do not come. The people see nothing of what happens outside, but they are content with the food and clothing provided by their fields, whereby they are happy during their lives and see off their dead. Who among them understands the depth of the Emperor's achievement and virtue, nurturing them and giving them ease, achievements and virtue that have shed grace on them for a hundred years?

When I came here, I was happy with the remoteness of the place and the simplicity of its affairs; I also loved the contentment and ease of local customs. Having found this spring between the mountain and the valley, I daily join the people of Chuzhou in gazing up at the mountain and listening to the spring run down below. Whether picking secluded blossoms and being shaded by tall trees, or in frosty wind or ice and snow, it reveals its pure excellence—the scenery of all the four seasons is lovable. I also feel fortunate in how the people are happy in the abundance of their harvests and enjoy going on excursions with me. Thus I have told the basics of their mountains and rivers and stated the beauty of their customs, so that the people will know why it is that they can be content in the happiness of this abundant year and feel fortunate that they are living in these times without problems.

To proclaim the Grace and Virtue of the Sovereign in order to share happiness with the people is the business of the governor. Consequently, I wrote this to name the pavilion. An account made on a certain day of the sixth month of the sixth year of the Qingli reign by Ouyang Xiu.

Li Yi'an, *Ouyang Xiu quanji*, 575

曾鞏, 醒心亭記

滁州之西南，泉水之涯，歐陽公作州之二年，搆亭曰豐樂，自為記，以見其名之意。既又直豐樂之東幾百步，得山之高，搆亭曰醒心，使鞏記之。

凡公與州賓客者遊焉，則必即豐樂以飲，或醉且勞矣，則必即醒心而望。以見夫羣山之相環，雲烟之相滋，曠野之無窮，草樹衆而泉石嘉，使目新乎其所覩，耳新乎其所聞，則其心洒然而醒，更欲久而忘歸也。故即其所以然而為名，取韓子退之北湖之詩云。噫。其可謂善取樂於山泉之間，而名之以見其實又善者矣。

雖然，公之樂，吾能言之:吾君優游而無為於上，吾民給足而無憾於下，天下學者皆為才且良，夷狄鳥獸草木之生者皆得其宜，公樂也。一山之隅，一泉之旁，豈公樂哉？乃公所以寄意於此也。若公之賢，韓子歿數百年而始有之。今同遊之賓客，尚未知公之難遇也。後百千年，有慕公之為人，而覽公之跡，思欲見之，有不可及之歎，然後知公之難遇也。則凡同遊於此者，其可不喜且幸歟？而鞏也，又得以文詞託名於公文之次，其又不喜且幸歟？慶曆七年八月十五日記。

Zeng Gong, "An Account of the Pavilion That Sobers the Mind"

Southwest of Chuzhou on the bank of a stream, Master Ouyang, in the second year of his governorship of the prefecture, constructed a pavilion called "Abundance and Happiness" and himself wrote the account to show the significance of the name. Thereafter, several hundred paces directly east of "Abundance and Happiness" reaching the heights of the mountain, he constructed another pavilion called "Sobers the Mind"; and he had me, Gong, write the account for it.

Whenever His Excellency and his guests from the prefecture come on an excursion, they always go to "Abundance and Happiness" to drink; and when they happen to get drunk and uncomfortable, they always go to "Sobers the Mind" for the view.

By seeing all the mountains circling around, made lush by the clouds and mist, the endlessness of the broad wilderness, the multitude of plants and trees, and the excellence of rocks and streams, it makes their eyes renewed by what they observe and their ears renewed by what they hear. Then their minds grow expansive and sober up, and they stay on longer, heedless of going back. Thus he gave it a name for how it is there, borrowing what Han Yu had said in his poem on North Lake. Indeed, he may be considered good at finding happiness among the mountains and streams, but he is someone even better at giving names that show the reality.

Still I am able to tell of His Excellency's happiness: Our Ruler is at perfect ease and governs by nonaction above; our common folk are well-provided and have no resentments below; all over the world men of learning are universally talented and virtuous; all living things, frontier peoples, birds and beasts, plants and trees, attain what is appropriate for them–all this is His Excellency's happiness. How could His Excellency be made happy merely by a nook in a mountain or a streamside? In fact, this is why His Excellency only invests his thoughts in such. One of worthiness such as that of His Excellency has been found only after several centuries following the death of Han Yu. The guests who go on excursions with him scarcely realize how rare it is to encounter His Excellency. In the centuries and millennia to follow, some will adore the kind of person His Excellency was; and in looking on his traces, they will yearn to see him and sigh that they are too late. Only after this will they understand how rare it is to encounter His Excellency. Can all those who come on excursions here with him not feel delighted and fortunate? And can I, Zeng Gong, being able to add my own name by writing in sequence after His Excellency's writing, not feel even more delighted and fortunate? An account on the fifteenth day of the eighth month in the seventh year of the Qingli reign.

Chen Xingzhen and Chao Jizhou, *Zeng Gong ji*, 276

歐陽修，醉翁亭記

環滁皆山也。其西南諸峯，林壑尤美。望之蔚然而深秀者，琅邪也。山行六七里，漸聞水聲潺潺，而瀉出于兩峯之間者，釀泉也。峯回路轉，有亭翼然，臨于泉上者，醉翁亭也。作亭者誰？山之僧智僊也。名之者誰，太守自謂也。

太守與客來飲於此，飲少輒醉，而年又最高，故自號曰醉翁也。醉翁之意不在酒，在乎山水之間也。山水之樂，得之心而寓之酒也。

若夫日出而林霏開，雲歸而巖穴暝，晦明變化者，山間之朝暮也。野芳發而幽香，佳木秀而繁陰，風霜高潔，水落而石出者，山間之四時也。朝而往，暮而歸，四時之景不同，而樂亦無窮也。

至於負者歌于途，行者休於樹，前者呼，後者應，傴僂提攜，往來而不絕者，滁人遊也。臨溪而漁，溪深而魚肥；釀泉爲酒，泉香而酒洌，山肴野蔌，雜然而前陳者，太守宴也。宴酣之樂，非絲非竹，射者中，弈者勝，觥籌交錯，起坐而喧嘩者，衆賓歡也。蒼顏白髮，頹然乎其中者，太守醉也。

已而夕陽在山，人影散亂，太守歸而賓客從也。樹林陰翳，鳴聲上下，遊人去而禽鳥樂也。然而禽鳥知山林之樂，而不知人之樂；人知從太守遊而樂，而不知太守之樂其樂也。醉能同其樂，醒能述以文者，太守也。太守謂誰？廬陵歐陽修也。

Ouyang Xiu, "Account of the Pavilion of the Drunken Old Man"

Surrounding Chuzhou everywhere are mountains. The forests and ravines of the many peaks to the southwest are especially beautiful. The place rising with thick verdure in one's gaze is Langya. When you go six or seven leagues into the mountain, the burbling sound of water gradually comes to ear, and what spills forth between the two peaks is Brewer's Stream. The peak turns, the road bends around, and there is a pavilion with wings outspread; looking out over the stream, is the Pavilion of the Drunken Old Man. Who was it made the pavilion?–a monk of the mountain known as Zhixian. Who was it named the pavilion?–the governor claims this for himself.

The governor comes and drinks here with his guests; and no sooner does he drink a little than he gets drunk. And being also the most advanced in years, he calls himself the "Drunken Old Man." The Drunken Old Man's thoughts are not in the ale but in this space of mountains and waters. The happiness of the mountains and waters is attained in the heart and invested in the ale.

When the sun comes out, the haze in the forest lifts, and when the clouds come back, the crevices in the cliff darken. These transformations of darkness and light are the dawns and dusks in the mountains. Wildflowers come out and secluded spots grow fragrant; fine trees burgeon and their thick leafage casts shade. The wind and frost are high and pure, then the water level sinks and rocks emerge. These are the four seasons in the mountains. At dawn we set off and at twilight we return; and though the scenery of the four seasons is not the same, the happiness in it is endless.

Those carrying things sing on the path; those just walking rest among the trees. The ones in front shout; the ones behind answer; hunched down and leading by the hand, they go back and forth continuously—these are the excursioners of Chuzhou. Standing by the stream and fishing: the stream is deep and the fish are fat; brewing spring water to make ale; the spring waters are sweet and the ale is cold and sharp; herbal relishes from the mountains and greens from the wilds, all mixed together and set before us: this is the governor's feast. The music when the feast gets tipsy is neither of strings nor of woodwinds. The tosspot player gets one in the pot; the chess player wins a game; goblets and forfeit tallies lie mixed up together; the buzz of chatter as they get up and sit down—these are the guests having a good time. Darkening complexion and white hair, collapsed in their midst—this is the governor, drunk.

At last the evening sunlight is in the mountains, and the shadows of the people scatter in confusion; the governor sets out for home, and the guests follow. The trees in the forest shade them over, with the sounds of birdsong above and below. The excursioners leave, and the birds are happy. However, the birds know the happiness of the mountain forest, but they don't know the happiness of people; people know to follow the governor on his excursion and be happy, but they don't know the governor's happiness in their happiness. The one who can be drunk and share their happiness and who, sobering up, can give an account of it in writing is the governor. And who is the governor? Ouyang Xiu of Luling.

Li Yi'an, *Ouyang Xiu quanji*, 575

蘇東坡，喜雨亭記

亭以雨名，志喜也。古者有喜，則以名物，示不忘也。周公得禾，以名其書；漢武得鼎，以名其年；叔孫勝狄，以名其子。喜之大小不齊，其示不忘一也。

余至扶風之明年，始治官舍，為亭於堂之北，而鑿池其南，引流種樹，以為休息之所。是歲之春，雨麥於岐山之陽，其占為有年。既而彌月不雨，民方以為憂。越三月乙卯，乃雨，甲子又雨，民以為未足，丁卯大雨，三日乃止。官吏相與慶於庭，商賈相與歌於市，農夫相與抃於野，憂者以樂，病者以愈，而吾亭適成。

於是舉酒於亭上，以屬客而告之曰:五日不雨，可乎？曰:五日不雨，則無麥。十日不雨，可乎？曰:十日不雨，則無禾。無麥無禾，歲且薦饑，獄訟繁興，而盜賊滋熾。則吾與二三子，雖欲優游以樂於此亭，其可得耶。今天不遺斯民，始旱而賜之以雨，使吾與二三子，得相與優游而樂於此亭者，皆雨之賜也。其又可忘耶?

既以名亭，又從而歌之。曰:使天而雨珠，寒者不得以為襦。使天而雨玉，飢者不得以為粟。一雨三日，繄誰之力? 民曰太守，太守不有。歸之天子，天子曰不。然歸之造物，造物不自以為功。歸之太空，太空冥冥，不可得而名，吾以名吾亭。

Su Dongpo, "Account of the Pavilion of Delighting in the Rain"

The pavilion is named for the rain, commemorating my delight. When the ancients had cause for delight, they named things for it to show that it was not to be forgotten. When the Duke of Zhou got [auspicious] grain, he named one of his writings for it; when Emperor Wu of Han got a cauldron, he named the year for it; when Shusun vanquished the Di people, his son was named for it. Though these occasions for delight differed in magnitude, they were the same in showing that these were not to be forgotten.

In the year after I reached Fufeng, I first had my official lodgings taken care of and made a pavilion north of the hall. South of it I dredged out a pond, brought in a stream of water, and planted trees to make it a place where I could rest. In the spring of that year, it had rained grain on the southern slopes of Mount Qi, and the prognostication was for a good harvest. But then it didn't rain for a full month, and the common people thought that was worrisome. By the eighth day of the third month it rained; on the seventeenth it rained again, but the common people thought that it wasn't enough. On the twentieth there was a big rain that lasted three days. Officials and clerks got together to offer congratulations in the courtyard; merchants got together to sing in the marketplace; peasants got together to clap their hands out in the wilds. Those who were worried became happy; those who were ill were cured; and it was then that my pavilion happened to be completed.

Thereupon I raised my ale-mug in the pavilion to urge my guests to drink and said to them: "Is it all right if it doesn't rain for five days?" They said, "If it doesn't rain for five days, there will be no wheat." "Is it all right if it doesn't rain for ten days?" They said, "If it doesn't rain for ten days, there will be no rice." With no wheat and no rice, the harvest will fail, lawsuits will abound, and bandits will run amok. And if that happens, how will you and I get to take our ease, being happy in this pavilion, even if we want to? But now Heaven has not abandoned these common folk, first with a drought but then granting them the gift of rain; and the fact that you and I have been able to get together to take our ease and find happiness in this pavilion is entirely a gift granted by the rain. Can it be all right to forget that?

This said, I named the pavilion for it, and followed with a song about it:
Supposing Heaven rained pearls,
those who were cold could not make a jacket of them.
Supposing Heaven rained jade,
those who were starving could not use it as grain.
A rain that lasted three days long–
to whose power was that due?
The common folk say "the governor";
the governor says, "Not me!"
Then attribute it to the emperor;
the emperor says, "O no!"
So attribute it to the Maker of Things;
the Maker of Things won't take credit.
Then attribute it to the Great Void,
the Great Void is a dark mystery,
you cannot grasp it to give a name,
and so I named my pavilion.

Zhang Zhilie, Ma Defu, and Zhou Yukai, *Su Shi quanji jiaozhu*, 1095.

3. MISSING STONES

歐陽修，菱谿石記

菱谿之石有六。其四為人取去；其一差小而尤奇，亦藏民家；其最大者，偃然僵臥於谿側，以其難徙，故得獨存。每歲寒霜落，水涸而石出，谿旁人見其可怪，往往祀以為神。

菱谿，按圖與經皆不載。唐會昌中，刺史李濆為荇谿記，云水出永陽嶺，西經皇道山下。以地求之，今無所謂荇谿者。詢於滁州人，曰:此谿是也。楊行密有據淮南，淮人為諱其嫌名，以荇為菱。理或然也。

谿傍若有遺址，云故將劉金之宅，石即劉氏之物也。金，偽吳時貴將，與行密俱起合淝，號三十六英雄，金其一也。金本武夫悍卒，而乃能知愛賞奇異，為兒女子之好，豈非遭逢亂世，功成志得，驕於富貴之佚欲而然邪？想其陂池臺榭，奇木異草與此石稱，亦一時之盛哉。今劉氏之後散為編民，尚有居谿旁者。

予感夫人物之興廢，惜其可愛而棄也。乃以三牛曳置幽谷；又索其小者，得於白塔民朱氏，遂立于亭之南北。亭負城而近，以為滁人歲時嬉遊之好。

夫物之奇者，棄没於幽遠則可惜，置之耳目則愛者不免取之而去。嗟夫。劉金者雖不足道，然亦可謂雄勇之士，其平生志意，豈不偉哉。及其後世，荒堙零落至於子孫泯沒而無聞，况欲長有此石乎？用此可為富貴者之戒。而好奇之士聞此石者，可以一賞而足，何必取而去也哉。

Ouyang Xiu, "Account of the Rocks of Ling Creek"

There are six rocks at Ling Creek. Four have been taken away by people; and there is one, quite small and remarkable, that is kept at a commoner's home. The largest lies fallen over by the edge of the creek; and being hard to move, it managed to be the only one to remain. Every year when the cold frosts fall, the water level sinks, and the rock emerges. Seeing how amazing it is, people by the creek often worship it as a god.

On consultation, none of the maps or canonical texts record a "Ling Creek." In the Huichang reign of the Tang (841–846), the governor Li Fen wrote an "Account of Xing Creek," saying that the waters came from Yongyang Ridge and then went west at the foot of Huangdao Mountain. When one looks for it, there is now nothing called Xing Creek. I inquired of someone from Chuzhou, who said that it is this creek [that is, Ling Creek]. When Yang Xingmi occupied Huainan, the people of Huainan avoided the taboo on his name and changed Xing to Ling. That may be how it was.

By the creek there seem to be some traces of ruins. They say that this was the home of the former general Liu Jin and that the rocks were in fact the possessions of the Liu family. Liu Jin was an exalted general of the illegitimate Wu regime, who rose in arms together at Hefei with Yang Xingmi. They were called the "Thirty-six Heroes," and Liu Jin was one of them. Jin was basically a military man and a tough soldier, and his capacity to appreciate marvelous things was a child's passion. How could this have occurred had he not encountered an age of turmoil, and, achieving deeds and fulfilling his aims, let his arrogance carry him into the unbounded desires of the rich and noble? I imagine his pools and terraces with kiosks, rare trees, and wondrous plants, renowned along with the rocks—it was the splendor of a single moment. Now the posterity of the Liu family has scattered into the registry of commoners, and some still live beside the creek.

I then was moved at how people and things have their moments of glory and then decline, and I thought it a pity that something so attractive be left abandoned. I had three oxen haul it [the largest rock] away and put it in Secluded Valley. I also sought out the smaller one and found it at the home of the commoner Zhu family at White Pagoda. Then I set them [the rocks] up to the north and south of the pavilion. The pavilion has the city wall to its back nearby, and they can be good things for the seasonal excursions of the people of Chuzhou.

If you leave the most remarkable things abandoned in some secluded and remote place, then it is a pity; but if you put one where it can be heard of and seen, then someone who covets it will inevitably take it away. Although Liu Jin is not worth consideration, still he may be considered a brave and heroic man; and his life's goals were certainly grand! But when it came to his posterity, they fell in the world to the point that his descendants disappeared from note and are not heard of. How much less could he want to hold onto these rocks forever. Let this be a warning for the rich and noble. Yet now gentlemen who love remarkable things and hear of these rocks may be satisfied just to come and appreciate them—why must they take them away?

Li Yi'an, *Ouyang Xiu quanji*, 578

歐陽修，集古錄目序

物常聚於所好，而常得於有力之強。有力而不好，好之而無力，雖近且易，有不能致之。

象犀虎豹蠻夷山海殺人之獸，然其齒角皮革，可聚而有也。玉出崑崙，流沙萬里之外，經十餘譯乃至乎中國。珠出南海，常生深淵，採者腰絙而入水，形色非人，往往不出，則下飽蛟魚。金礦于山，鑿深而穴遠，篝火餱粮而後進，其崖崩窟塞，則遂葬於其中者，率常數十百人。其遠且難而又多死禍，常如此。然而金玉珠璣，世常兼聚而有也。凡物好之而有力，則無不至也。

湯盤，孔鼎，岐陽之鼓，岱山、鄒嶧、會稽之刻石，與夫漢、魏已來聖君賢士桓碑、彝器、銘詩、序記，下至古文、籀篆、分隸諸家之字書，皆三代以來至寶，怪奇偉麗，工妙可喜之物。其去人不遠，其取之無禍。然而風霜兵火，湮淪磨滅，散棄於山崖墟莽之間未嘗收拾者，由世之好者少也。幸而有好之者，又其力或不足，故僅得其一二，而不能使其聚也。夫力莫如好，好莫如一。予性顓而嗜古，凡世人之所貪者皆無欲於其間，故得一其所好於斯。好之已篤，則力雖未足，猶能致之。

故上自周穆王以來，下更秦、漢、隋、唐、五代，外至四海九州，名山大澤，窮崖絕谷，荒林破塚，神仙鬼物，詭怪所傳，莫不皆有，以為《集古錄》。以謂轉寫失真，故因其石本，軸而藏之。有卷帙次第，而無時世之先後，蓋其取多而未已，故隨其所得而錄之。又以謂聚多而終必散，乃撮其大要，別為錄目，因並載夫可與史傳正其闕謬者，以傳後學，庶益於多聞。

或譏予曰：物多則其勢難聚，聚久而無不散，何必區區於是哉？予對曰：足吾所好，玩而老焉可也。象犀金玉之聚，其能果不散乎？予固未能以此而易彼也。廬陵歐陽修序。

Ouyang Xiu, "Preface for the List of My *Records of Collected Antiquities*"

Things are always gathered by those who love them, and they are always obtained by the one with the greater strength. If there is someone with the strength who doesn't love them or someone who loves them but lacks the strength, then he cannot acquire them, even if they are close at hand and easy.

The elephant, rhinoceros, tiger, and leopard are man-killing creatures of the mountains and seas of foreign lands, yet their tusks and horns, and skins and pelts can be gathered and possessed. Jade comes from the Kunlun Mountains, ten thousand leagues beyond the Drifting Sands, and it reaches the heartland only after passing through over a dozen languages as it changes hands. Pearls come from the Southern Ocean, always growing in the deep abyss. Those who gather them tie a rope to their waists and dive into the water; they don't look like other people; and when often they don't come to the surface, then they have fed the sharks down below. Metals are mined in the mountains; they dig deep and tunnel far, going in only when they have torches and dried provisions; but when the mountain collapses and the tunnels are blocked, those who are consequently buried inside are usually dozens or hundreds. It is always this way with distances and hardships and, moreover, this causes frequent deaths. Nevertheless, people of the time always can gather together metal, jade, and pearls and possess them. If one loves something and has the strength, anything can be acquired.

The washbasin of Tang [the Shang king], the Kong family tripod [belonging to Zheng Kaofu], the "stone drums" of Qiyang, the inscriptions in stone [by the First

Emperor] on Mount Dai [Taishan], Zou Ridge, and Kuaiji, along with great tomb stelae, the vessels of ancestral temples, inscription poems, and accounts by sage rulers and worthy gentlemen since the Han and Wei, on down in time to writings in ancient script, seal script, *bafen* and clerical scripts, all are the most perfect treasures from the Three Dynasties [of high antiquity] on, marvels of exceptional beauty, things of rare workmanship that give delight. They are not far away from us, and no disaster is involved in obtaining them. Nevertheless, the fact that they have become buried and eroded by the frost and wind and fires of war, abandoned and scattered on mountainsides and in desolate wilderness, is because few in the age love them. And if by lucky chance there is someone who loves them but who at the same time lacks enough strength, then he can only get a few and cannot gather them.

Given the strength, nothing is better than loving something; and in loving something, nothing is better than single-mindedness. I am by nature naively simple and have a passion for antiquity; there is nothing I want among all those things that are avidly desired by the people of this age, so I am able to achieve a single-minded focus in loving these things. Being steadfast in my love for them, I am still able to acquire them, even though my strength is inadequate.

Thus what has been handed down from the days of King Mu of Zhou down through the Qin, Han, Sui, Tang, and Five Dynasties, and outward through the nine continents and the sea-girt world, from famous mountains and large swamps, from remote mountain slopes and precipitous valleys, from overgrown forests and broken tombs, from gods, immortals, and otherworldly beings—there is nothing I do not have and have made my *Record of Collected Antiquities*. And thinking that the accuracy might be lost in copying, I made rubbings, storing them in scrolls. There is sequence in the scroll cases, but without regard to chronological sequence. This is because I have gotten a great many and kept at it, making a record of each when I got it. I also recognize that what when so many have been accumulated, in the end they will inevitably be scattered, so I selected the main pieces and made a separate list of them. Thus *what is included may be used in conjunction with* the histories to correct omissions and errors, to be handed down to later scholars, hopefully with benefit for widely knowledgeable.

Someone criticized me: "When there are many things, the situation makes it hard to gather them; and after they have been gathered for a long time, they are always scattered again. Why then should you be so preoccupied with this?" I answered, "This satisfies what I love, and it's all right to enjoy them and grow old in this. When [ivory of] elephants and rhinoceroses or gold and jade are gathered, in the end how can they not be scattered? I absolutely cannot exchange these for that sort of thing."

Preface by Ouyang Xiu of Luling.

Li Yi'an, *Ouyang Xiu quanji*, 599

4. ALL MINE

司馬光，獨樂園記

孟子曰:獨樂樂，不如與人樂樂；與少樂樂，不如與衆樂樂。此王公大人之樂，非貧賤者所及也。孔子曰:飯蔬食飲水，曲肱而枕之，樂亦在其中矣。顏子一簞食，一瓢飲。不改其樂。此聖賢之樂，非愚者所及也。

若夫鷦鷯巢林，不過一枝，鼴鼠飲河，不過滿腹，各盡其分而安之，此乃迂叟之所樂也。

熙寧四年迂叟始家洛，六年買田二十畝於尊賢坊北關，以為園。其中為堂，聚書出五千卷，命之曰讀書堂。堂南有屋一區，引水北流，貫宇下。中央為沼，方深各三尺。疏水為五派，注沼中，若虎爪。自沼北伏流出北階，懸注庭中，若象鼻。自是分而為二渠，繞庭四隅，會於西北而出，命之曰弄水軒。堂北為沼，中央有島，島上植竹。圓若玉玦，圍三丈，攬結其杪，如漁人之廬，命之曰釣魚庵。沼北橫屋六楹，厚其墉茨，以御烈日。開戶東出，南北列軒牖，以延涼颸。前後多植美竹，為清暑之所，會之曰種竹齋。

沼東治地為百有二十畦，雜蒔草藥，辨其名物而揭之。畦北植竹，方若棋局。徑一丈，屈其杪，交相掩以為屋。植竹於其前，夾道如步廊，皆以蔓藥覆之。四周植木藥為藩援，命之曰：採藥圃。圃南為六欄，芍藥、牡丹、雜花各居其二。每種止植兩本，識其名狀而已，不求多也。欄北為亭，命之曰：澆花亭。洛城距山不遠，而林薄茂密，常若不得見。乃於園中築臺，構屋其上，以望萬安、軒轅，至於太室。命之曰：見山臺。

迂叟平日多處堂中讀書，上師聖人，下友羣賢，窺仁義之原，探禮樂之緒，自未始有形之前，暨四達無窮之外，事物之理，舉集目前。所病者，學之未至，夫又何求於人，何待於外哉。志倦體疲，則投竿取魚，執衽采藥，決渠灌花，操斧剖竹，濯熱盥手，臨高縱目，逍遥徜徉，唯意所適。明月時至，清風自來，行無所牽，止無所柅，耳目肺腸，悉為己有，踽踽焉、洋洋焉，不知天壤之間復有何樂可以代此也。因合而命之曰:獨樂園。

或咎迂叟曰:吾聞君子所樂必與人共之，今吾子獨取足於己，不以及人，其可乎？迂叟謝曰:叟愚，何得比君子，自樂恐不足，安能及人？況叟之所樂者，薄陋鄙野，皆世之所棄也，雖推以與人，人且不取，豈得強之乎？必也有人肯同此樂，則再拜而獻之矣，安敢專之哉。

Sima Guang, "Account of My Solitary Happiness Garden"

Mengzi said: "Solitary happiness in listening to music is not as good as being happy listening to music with others, and being happy listening to music with few is not as good as being happy listening to music with many." But this is the happiness of kings and lords and great men; it is not something that a poor and ordinary man can achieve. Confucius said: "In eating vegetables and drinking water, crooking your arm and making it your pillow—there is happiness even in this." "Yan Hui ate from a single bamboo plate and drank from a single gourd, but his happiness did not change." But this is the happiness of sages and worthies, and not something that a foolish man like me can achieve.

Now the wren takes no more than a single branch when it nests in the woods; and when the mole drinks from the river, it does no more than fill its belly. Each fulfills its own lot and is content with it. This, in fact, is what I, the Reclusive Old Man, find happiness in.

In the fourth year of the Xining reign (1072), this Reclusive Old Man moved his home to Luoyang; in the sixth year I bought twenty *mu* of farmland by the northern gate of the Zunxian Ward and made a garden there. I took five thousand scrolls from my book collection for the "Reading Hall." South of the hall there is a small area with a building, and I channeled water to flow north, passing under its roof. In the middle I made a pond three feet square and three feet deep. I dug five channels for the water and fed these into the pond like a tiger claw. From the pool it flowed north out of sight and came out by the north stairs, spilling down into the courtyard like an elephant's trunk. From there I divided it into two courses, circling the four corners of the courtyard, coming together and emerging to the northwest, and I called it "Enjoying Water Balustrade." North of the hall I made a pond with an island in the middle, and on the island I planted bamboo. This was round, three yards in circumference, like a jade ring with a gap; I gathered together the tips [of the bamboo] and bound them up, like the hut of a fisherman, calling it "Fishing Cottage." North of the pond is a six-bay building with thick walls and roof-thatch to fend off the heat of the sun. A door opens out to the east, where a balustrade with windows is oriented north to south, to let in cool gusts of breeze. In front and behind I planted fine bamboo as a place to clear away muggy heat; and I called the area "Planted Bamboo Studio."

East of the pond I cleared the land into one hundred and twenty little plots where I grew various kinds of herbs and plants, with signs giving their names. North of these plots I planted bamboo in a square like a chessboard; along a yard-long path I bent their tips to crisscross like a roof. I planted bamboo in front of this, with a narrow way like a corridor, all covered over with herbs and vines. All around I planted shrubs to serve as a hedge and called it "Herb-Picking Patch." South of the patch I made six trellises, with paeonias, tree peonies, and various flowers each occupying two of these. I planted only two of each kind, just to recognize its name and what it looked like, but not trying to have more. North of the trellises I made a pavilion and named it "Flower-watering Pavilion." Luoyang is not far from mountains, and usually you can't catch sight of them for the density of the trees and vegetation. So in the garden I built a terrace with a roofed building on top to gaze at Wan'an, Xuanyuan, all the way to Taishi Peak. I called this the "Terrace of Seeing the Mountains."

The Reclusive Old Man spends most of his days in the hall studying. On the highest level I take the Sages as teachers, on a lower level befriend all the worthies, observe the source of Fellow Feeling and Right, investigate the traces of Music and Rites, from before form had even begun to beyond the boundless tracks, and the principles behind all things appear together before my eyes. What I fault myself on are those points where my study has not reached; but I also seek nothing from others and depend on nothing external. If my aims grow weary and my body is tired, I cast my fishing rod and take a fish, pull up my sleeves and pick herbs, dig a channel to water flowers, take ax in hand to cut bamboo, wash my hands in hot water, let my eyes rove from a high spot, lingering and roaming freely, whatever suits my mood. Sometimes the bright moon comes or a clear breeze comes of itself; I go with nothing pulling me and stop with nothing blocking me; what I hear and see and feel within is all mine! Going alone, going in vastness, I don't know of any happiness in the whole world that could take the place of this. Thus I combined it all and named it "Solitary Happiness Garden."

Someone criticized the Reclusive Old Man, saying: I have learned that what a superior man finds happiness in he always shares with others, but you now find satisfaction in yourself alone and do not extend it to others—is this all right? The Reclusive Old Man demurred, saying: I am foolish—how can I be compared to a superior man? I fear it will not be enough for my own happiness; how can I offer it to others? On top of that, what I find happiness in is shabby and crude, all the sort of things rejected by the world. Even if I pressed all this on others, others would not take it–and how could I force them? But if there inevitably were someone willing to share this happiness, then I would bow and present him with it. How would I dare keep it entirely to myself?

Quan Song wen, 56:236

蘇舜欽，滄浪亭記

予以罪廢無所歸，扁舟南遊，旅於吳中。始僦舍以處，時盛夏蒸燠，土居皆褊狹，不能出氣，思得高爽虛闢之地，以舒所懷，不可得也。一日過郡學，東顧草樹鬱然，崇阜廣水，不類乎城中。並水得微徑於雜花修竹之間，東趨數百步，有棄地，縱廣合五六十尋，三向皆水也。杠之南，其地益闊，旁無民居，左右皆林木相虧蔽，訪諸舊老，云錢氏有國，近戚孫承右之池館也。坳隆勝勢，遺意尚存。予愛而徘徊，遂以錢四萬得之，構亭北碕，號滄浪焉。前竹後水，水之陽又竹，無窮極，澄川翠榦，光影會合於軒户之間，尤與風月爲相宜。

予時榜小舟，幅巾以往，至則灑然忘其歸，箕而浩歌，踞而仰嘯，野老不至，魚鳥共樂，形骸既適則神不煩，觀聽無邪則道以明，返思向之汩汩榮辱之場，日與錙銖利害相磨戛，隔此眞趣，不亦鄙哉。噫，人固動物耳。情橫於内而性伏，必外寓於物而後遣，寓久則溺，以爲當然。非勝是而易之，則悲而不開。惟仕宦溺人爲至深，古之才哲君子，有一失而至於死者多矣。是未知所以自勝之道。予既廢而獲斯境，安於沖曠，不與衆驅，因之復能乎内外失得之原，沃然有得，笑傲萬古，尚未能忘其所寓目，用是以爲勝焉。

Su Shunqin, "Account of Canglang Pavilion"

Because of an offense I lost my post and had nowhere to go; I went south by boat and took up lodgings in Wu. At first, I rented a place to stay, but it was the height of summer, steamy and hot. The places were all very narrow, and I couldn't breathe. I longed to get a place that was brisk and open where I could relax, but I couldn't find one. One day I was passing the district school; I turned to look around east where plants and trees were growing dense and thick, with high hills and broad waters, different from what lies within the city walls. Following along by the water, I found a tiny path among the various flowering trees and tall bamboo. Making my way quickly east several hundred paces, there was abandoned land, in breadth and width some 150 meters, facing water on three sides. South of a bridge of a single plank, the land was even broader, with no one living around, and on either side the trees of a grove concealed it. When I asked older folks about it, they told me that when the Qians ruled the Wu Kingdom, this was the pool and lodge of Sun Chengyou, a close kinsman of the king by marriage. In the scenic form of rises and depressions, some sense of the design still survived. I loved it and lingered there, and subsequently got it for forty thousand cash. I had a pavilion constructed on the winding northern bank and called it Canglang. There were bamboo in front and water behind, and north of the waters there were more bamboo without limit. Light from the clear stream and those pale green stalks gathered on the porch and doors, especially appropriate in breeze and moonlight.

I would sometimes sail my little boat, going off wearing a headband. When I reached somewhere, I would be free and easy and forget about going back, singing wildly all sprawled out or squatting with my head looking up whistling. Old rustics did not come, and I shared my happiness with the fish and birds. Once my body felt comfortable, my spirit was not disturbed; my powers of observation and listening not being led astray, the Way became clear. Wasn't it vile to be kept away from these genuine impulses by the daily push and pull of some tiny measure of profit or disadvantage? Human beings are, alas, indeed creatures stirred. If the passions run wild within and one's nature submits, then one must invest oneself temporarily in external things, and afterward dispel them. If you invest yourself in external things too long, then you drown in them and think that it is necessarily that way. If you cannot overcome this and change it, then your sadness will never go away. Only service as an official drowns a person most deeply. Many have been the talented and wise superior men of ancient times who met with death from one slip. This is not knowing the way by which to master oneself. Having been dismissed from office and having attained this scene, I am at peace in the calm openness and am not in a race with the crowd. By this I can again wisely learn something about the sources of gain and loss, both in things external and external. I laugh proudly at all times past, and still never forget what my eyes have seen, and by this I consider myself to have achieved mastery.

Quan Song wen, 41:83

5. THE STONE THAT TELLS ITS NAME

蘇東坡，石鐘山記

水經云:彭蠡之口，有石鐘山焉。酈元以為下臨深潭，微風鼓浪，水石相搏，聲如洪鐘。是說也，人常疑之。今以鐘磬置水中，雖大風浪，不能鳴也，而况石乎？至唐李渤始訪其遺蹤，得雙石於潭上，扣而聆之，南聲函胡，北音清越，枹止響騰，餘韻徐歇，自以為得之矣。然是說也，余尤疑之。石之鏗然有聲者，所在皆是也，而此獨以鐘名，何哉?

元豐七年六月丁丑，余自齊安舟行適臨汝，而長子邁將赴饒之德興尉，送之至湖口，因得觀所謂石鍾者。寺僧使小童持斧，於亂石間擇其一二扣之，硿硿焉。余固笑而不信也。

至暮夜月明，獨與邁乘小舟至絶壁下。大石側立千仞，如猛獸奇鬼，森然欲搏人。而山上栖鶻，聞人聲亦驚起，磔磔雲霄間，又有若老人欬且笑於山谷中者，或曰此鸛鶴也。余方心動欲還，而大聲發於水上，噌吰如鐘皷不絶，舟人大恐。徐而察之，則山下皆石穴罅，不知其淺深，微波入焉，涵澹澎湃而為此也。舟廻至兩山間，將入港口，有大石當中流，可坐百人，空中而多竅，與風水相吞吐，有窾坎鏜鞳之聲，與向之噌吰者相應，如樂作焉。因笑謂邁曰:汝識之乎？噌吰者，周景王之無射也。窾坎鏜鞳者，魏獻子之歌鐘也。古之人不余欺也。

事不目見耳聞而臆斷其有無，可乎？酈元之所見聞，殆與余同，而言之不詳。士大夫終不肯以小舟夜泊絶壁之下，故莫能知。而漁工水師，雖知而不能言，此世所以不傳也。而陋者乃以斧斤考擊而求之，自以爲得其實。余是以記之，蓋歎酈元之簡，而笑李渤之陋也。

Su Dongpo, "Account of Stone Bell Mountain"

The *Classic of Rivers* says that at the mouth of Lake Pengli there is Stone Bell Mountain. Li Daoyuan [the author of the commentary] thought that since it looked down on a deep pooling, when a light breeze stirred the waves, the water and rock would strike each other with a sound like a great bell. People have always had reservations about this explanation. If you put a bell or chimes in the water, it won't make a sound no matter how strong the wind and waves are—much less so for rock. In the Tang, Li Bo first visited the site and got a pair of rocks from a deep pool; he struck them and listened; the southern sounds were blurry, but the northern sounds were sharp and clear. Then he stopped the striker, the echoes rose, and the lingering tones gradually subsided. And he thought that he had found the explanation. Still I doubt this explanation even more. Stones that have a clinking sound are found everywhere, but why is it only here that they call it a "bell"?

On the day *dingchou* of the sixth month of the seventh year of the Yuanfeng reign, I went by boat from Qi'an to Linru; my eldest son Mai was setting off for his post as assistant magistrate of Dexing County in Raozhou. I went along with him to Hukou, and that's how I had a chance to see the so-called Stone Bell. A monk in the temple had an acolyte take an ax and randomly pick up one or two stones and strike them. They clinked a bit. I laughed indeed and didn't credit this [as the explanation].

That night the moon was bright; Mai and I rode in a small boat to the foot of the sheer cliff. The huge rock stood slanting for a thousand yards up, as if fierce beasts or strange demons were darkly ready to snatch a person. A falcon roosting on the mountain, hearing the sound of human voices, rose up suddenly in alarm, screeching in the clouds. There was also something like an old man laughing and coughing in the mountain valley. Some say this was a stork. When I recovered from my agitation, a loud sound came out over the water, booming and ringing like unceasing bells and drums. The boatman was very frightened. When I gradually investigated it, there were caves and fissures all around the base of the mountain, of uncertain depth; small waves entered them, and the sloshing and churning produced this. When the boat turned back and reached the space between the two mountains, on the point of entering the mouth of the harbor, there was a large rock midstream, with space enough to seat a hundred people. It was empty inside with many holes, swallowing and spilling out the wind-blown water. It produced a drumming and thrumming sound, which answered the earlier booming and ringing, as if music were being played. And I said to Mai laughing: "Don't you recognize it? The booming and ringing are the Wuye bells of King Jing of Zhou; the drumming and thrumming are the song bells of Lord Xian of Wei. The ancients were not deceiving us."

Is it all right to make a speculative determination of how things are unless one has seen it with one's own eyes and heard it with one's own ears? What Li Daoyuan learned was very close to my experience, but he didn't describe it in enough detail. Men of the gentry were never willing to moor in a small boat by night beneath the sheer cliff, and thus they could not know. Even though fishermen and boatmen might know, they cannot account for it in words. These are the reasons why it [the truth of the name] has not been passed on in the world. And yet the ignorant will strike a rock with an ax to find out and think that they have discovered the truth. This is why I made this account, sighing over Li Daoyuan's excessive concision and laughing at Li Bo's ignorance.

Zhang Zhilie, Ma Defu, and Zhou Yukai, *Su Shi quanji jiaozhu*, 1170

黃庭堅，松菊亭記

期於名者入朝，期於利者適市。期於道者何之哉。反諸身而已。

鐘鼓管絃以飾喜，鈇鉞干戈以飾怒，山川松菊所以飾燕閒者哉。貴者知軒冕之不可認，而有收其餘日以就閒者矣；富者知金玉之不可守，而有收其餘力以就閒者矣。

蜀人韓漸正翁有范蠡、計然之策，有白圭、猗頓之材，無所用於世，而用於其楮，中更三十年而富百倍。乃築堂於山川之間，自名松菊，以書走京師，乞記於山古道人。山谷逌然笑曰:韓子真知金玉之不可守，欲收其餘力而就閒者。予今將問子，思堂之作，將以歌舞乎，將以研桑乎。將以歌舞，則獨歌舞而樂，不若與人樂之；與少歌舞而樂，不若與衆樂之。

夫歌舞者豈可以樂此哉。卹饑問寒以拊孤，折券棄責以拊貧，冠婚喪葬以拊宗，補耕助斂以拊客，如是則歌舞於堂，人皆粲然相視曰:韓正翁而能樂之乎。

此樂之情也，將以研桑，何時已哉。金玉之為好貨，怨入而悖出，多藏厚亡，他日以遺子孫，賢則損其志，愚則益其過，韓子知及此，空為之哉。雖然，歌舞就閒之日以休研桑之心，反身以期於道，豈可以無孟獻子之友哉。孟獻子以百乘之家，有友五人，皆無獻子之家者也。必得無獻子之家者與之友，則仁者助施，義者助均，智者助謀，勇者助決，取諸左右而有餘，使宴安而不毒，又使子弟日見所不見，聞所不聞，賢者以成徳，愚者以寡怨，於以聽隱居之松風，裛淵明之菊露，可以無愧矣。

Huang Tingjian, "Account of Pine and Chrysanthemum Pavilion"

Those who aspire to name/fame enter the court; those who aspire to profit go to the marketplace. But those who aspire to the Way—where do they go? They simply turn back to themselves.

Bells, drums, pipes, and stringed instrument are the adornments of delight; axes, falchions, shields, and pikes are the adornments of rage. And are not mountains, rivers, pines, and chrysanthemums the means to adorn leisure? The noble understand that crowns and coaches cannot be counted on, and they gather their remaining days and seek out leisure; the wealthy realize that gold and jade cannot be kept, and they gather their remaining strength and seek out leisure.

Han Jian (Zhengweng) of Shu has the stratagems of Fan Li and Jiran; he has the material of a Bai Gui or a Yi Dun. Not having been used by the age, he made use of his currency bills and over the course of thirty years his wealth increased a hundredfold. Now he had built a hall among the mountains and river, giving it the name "Pine and Chrysanthemum"; thus he sent a letter to the capital, asking for a prose account of it from The Man of the Way Shan'gu [Huang Tingjian]. Shan'gu gave a mellow smile and said: Master Han truly understands that gold and jade cannot be kept, and he wants to gather his remaining strength and seek out leisure. But now I am going to ask him whether he made this hall for songs and dancing or for business dealings. If it's going to be songs and dancing, then a solitary happiness in songs and dancing is not as good as happiness shared with others; and happiness in songs and dancing shared with few is not as good as a happiness shared with many.

But as for song and dancing, how may one find happiness in just this? Help the hungry and cold to care for orphans; forgive debts to care for the poor; care for the clan in capping ceremonies, marriages, and funerals; help in plowing and tax demands to care for your tenants. If you do this, then when there are songs and dancing in the hall, everyone will give a broad smile and say: "Isn't Han Jian good at enjoying himself!"

If this mood of happiness is carried through in matters of business, when will that ever end? Gold and jade are the best goods, brought in with rancor and going out in turmoil, the more you keep the greater your loss. Someday you may give it to your children or grandchildren; if they are worthy, then it saps their ambition; if they are foolish, it increases their errors. If Master Han's understanding reaches this point, then to do this [to keep your wealth for your children] would be in vain. Nevertheless, in the days of leisure for song and dancing by which you cease to be preoccupied with business dealings, returning to yourself in aspirations for the Way, how can you fail to have the kind of friends Meng Xianzi had? With a household of five hundred chariots, Meng Xianxi had five friends, none of whom had a household like Xianzi's. He would find only people that did not have a household as great as his own and make friends with them; thus the kindly aided him in giving, the righteous aided him in equity, the clever aided him in planning, and the bold aided him in decisiveness. You draw from those around yourself and have plenty, leading you to enjoy secure peace and never harm yourself. Also, by this you have followers to show you every day what you have never seen and hear what you have never heard; by this the worthy perfect your virtue, and the foolish diminish your resentments. As you listen to the wind in the pines of your secluded dwelling and are soaked by Tao Yuanming's dew on the chrysanthemums, you may be free from shame.

Liu Lin, Li Yongxian, and Wang Ronggui, *Huang Tingjian quanji*, 438

蘇東坡，文與可畫篔簹谷偃竹記

竹之始生，一寸之萌耳，而節葉具焉。自蜩腹蛇蚹以至於劍拔十尋者，生而有之也。今畫者乃節節而為之，葉葉而累之，豈復有竹乎！故畫竹必先得成竹於胸中，執筆熟視，乃見其所欲畫者，急起從之，振筆直遂，以追其所見，如兔起鶻落，少縱則逝矣。與可之教予如此。予不能然也，而心識其所以然。夫既心識其所以然而不能然者，內外不一，心手不相應，不學之過也。故凡有見於中而操之不熟者，平居自視了然，而臨事忽焉喪之，豈獨竹乎？

子由為《墨竹賦》以遺與可曰：庖丁，解牛者也，而養生者取之。輪扁，斫輪者也，而讀書者與之。今夫夫子之托於斯竹也，而予以為有道者，則非耶？子由未嘗畫也，故得其意而已。若予者，豈獨得其意，並得其法。

與可畫竹，初不自貴重，四方之人持縑素而請者，足相躡於其門。與可厭之，投諸地而罵曰：吾將以為襪。士大夫傳之以為口實。及與可自洋州還，而余為徐州。與可以書遺余曰：近語士大夫，吾墨竹一派，近在彭城，可往求之。襪材當萃於子矣。

書尾復寫一詩，其略曰：擬將一段鵝溪絹，掃取寒梢萬尺長。予謂與可，竹長萬尺，當用絹二百五十匹，知公倦於筆硯，願得此絹而已。與可無以答，則曰：吾言妄矣，世豈有萬尺竹也哉。余因而實之，答其詩曰：世間亦有千尋竹，月落庭空影許長。與可笑曰：蘇子辯則辯矣。然二百五十匹，吾將買田而歸老焉。因以所畫篔簹谷偃竹遺予，曰：此竹數尺耳，而有萬尺之勢。

篔簹谷在洋州，與可嘗令予作《洋州三十詠》，篔簹谷其一也。予詩云：漢川修竹賤如蓬，斤斧何曾赦籜龍。料得清貧饞太守，渭濱千畝在胸中。與可是日與其妻游谷中，燒筍晚食，發函得詩，失笑噴飯滿案。

元豐二年正月二十日，與可沒於陳州。是歲七月七日，予在湖州曝書畫，見此竹，廢卷而哭失聲。昔曹孟德《祭橋公文》，有車過，腹痛之語，而予亦載與可疇昔戲笑之言者，以見與可於予親厚無間如此也。

6. THE BAMBOO IN THE BREAST AND IN THE BELLY

Su Dongpo, "An Account of Wen Tong's Painting of the Recumbent Bamboo of Yundang Valley"

When a bamboo is first born, it is just an inch-long sprout, yet the segments and leaves are complete in it. Going from a cicada or snake molting to reach up ten yards, like a sword held upright, is something that it has from birth. Nowadays painters do it segment by segment and burden it with leaf after leaf—how can there still be a bamboo?!

For this reason, in painting bamboo you must get a fully- grown bamboo in your breast. Holding your brush, observe it fully, and only when you see what you want to paint do you stir your brush and go after it directly to catch what you have seen. Like a rabbit jumping into motion as a hawk descends—the slightest laxness and it's gone. This was what Wen Tong taught me. I am not able to carry through that way, but in my mind, I recognize why it is that way. Now if in the mind you recognize why it is a certain way but cannot carry though that way, then inside and outside are not one, mind and hand are not mutually responsive, which is the failure of not studying. Whenever you see something inside you, but you can grasp it securely, ordinarily you consider it perfectly clear, but when you are about to do something, you suddenly lose it—this is not just with bamboo.

[My brother] Ziyou [Su Che] wrote a "Poetic Exposition on Ink-painting of Bamboo" and sent it to Wen Tong. It said: "Butcher Ding was someone who cut apart oxen, yet those who would nurture life learned something from him. Wheelwright Bian was someone who cut wheels, yet the one who was reading [Duke Huan] agreed with him. You, sir, have invested [such an idea] in bamboo, yet would anyone disagree if I think that you possess the Way?" Ziyou never practiced painting; he simply got the idea. As for myself, I didn't just get the idea, I also got the method [for painting].

At first when Wen Tong painted bamboo, he didn't watch out for himself. People, carrying plain silk, came from every direction to ask for a painting, and would line up toe to heel at his gate. Wen Tong was sick of this and threw the silk on the ground, cursing: "I'm going to make socks out of this." Gentlemen passed this around as a good anecdote.

When Wen Tong returned from Yangzhou and I was governing Xuzhou, he sent me a letter which said: "Recently I have been saying to the gentry, 'My lineage of ink painting of bamboo has recently relocated in Pengcheng [Xuzhou]. Why don't you go look for it *there*?' So, the material for socks is going to flock to *you*!"

At the end of the letter Wen Tong copied out a poem that said, in excerpt:

I plan to take a piece of Goose Creek silk
and sweep forth wintry stalks ten-thousand feet long.

I told Wen Tong: "If you are going to have bamboo ten thousand feet tall, you are going to need two hundred and fifty bolts of silk. I realize that you are going to wear yourself out with brush and ink-stone [i.e, in painting] simply from your desire to get so much silk."

Since Wen Tong couldn't make a good retort, he said: "I was wrong. How could there ever be bamboo ten-thousand feet tall?" I followed up on this and offered a concrete example, answering his poem:

In this world there are indeed
bamboo a thousand yards tall—
when the moon sets in the empty courtyard,
the shadows are just that long.

Wen Tong laughed and said: "Su Dongpo can really make a witty case! Still, with two hundred and fifty bolts of silk I could buy fields and retire." Then he sent me "The Recumbent Bamboo of Yundang Valley" that he had painted, commenting: "These bamboos are just several feet long, but they have the propensity to become ten-thousand feet tall.

Yundang Valley is in Yangzhou [where Wen Tong served], and he commissioned me to write thirty verses on Yangzhou, one of which was to be on Yundang Valley. My poem went:

The tall bamboo of the River Han are cheap as dandelions,
did the hatchet ever spare these sheathed dragons?
I reckon they feed the hungry governor in his austere poverty,
but a thousand acres by the Wei's shores are in his breast.

On that day Wen Tong was visiting the valley with his wife, and they were roasting bamboo shoots for their evening meal. When he opened the letter packet and found this poem, he was so overcome by laughter that he spit out his food all over the table.

On the 20th day of the first month in the second year of the Yuanfeng Reign (1079), Wen Tong passed away in Chenzhou. On the seventh day of the seventh month that year, I was in Huzhou and was airing my books and paintings. When I saw these bamboo [in the painting], I put aside the scroll, choked up with tears. Long ago Cao Cao's sacrificial address to Qiao Xuan used the phrases "my carriage passed" and "I felt a pain in the belly." And those playful words I wrote earlier for Wen Tong show my feeling of perfect closeness to him.

Zhang Zhilie, Ma Defu, and Zhou Yukai, *Su Shi quanji jiaozhu*, 1153

NOTES

INTRODUCTION

1. 馮相道、和相凝，同在中書。一日，和問馮曰：公靴新買，其值幾何？馮舉左足示和，曰：九百。和性褊急，遽回顧小吏，云：吾靴何得用一千八百？因詬責。久之，馮徐舉其右足曰：此亦九百。於是哄堂大笑。時謂宰相如此，何以鎮服百僚？ Li Yi'an 李逸安, *Ouyang Xiu quanji* 歐陽修全集 (Beijing: Zhonghua shuju, 2001), 1911.
2. For a succinct account of the "Niece Zhang (Chang)" affair, see Ronald Egan, *The Literary Works of Ou-yang Hsiu (1007–72)* (Cambridge: Cambridge University Press, 1984), 6.
3. For a good account of the economic background of Wang Anshi's "New Policies," see Paul Jakov Smith, "Shen-tsung's Reign and the New Policies of Wang An-shih," in *The Cambridge History of China*, vol. 5, part 1: *The Sung Dynasty and Its Precursors, 907–1279*, ed. Denis Twitchett and Paul Jakov Smith (Cambridge: Cambridge University Press, 2009), 347–464.
4. For problems arising in Song government imprints, see Susan Cherniack, "Book Culture and Textual Transmission in Sung China," *Harvard Journal of Asiatic Studies* 54, no. 1 (June 1994): 5–125.
5. For a discussion of Shao Yong's discourse on happiness, see Xiaoshan Yang, *Metamorphosis of the Private Sphere: Gardens and Objects in Tang-Song Poetry* (Cambridge, Mass.: Harvard University Asia Center, 2003), 197–228.
6. Following the Eastern Han interpretation, which would still have been predominant in the Northern Song.
7. I will avoid the old argument of whether 獨樂樂 is *du le yue* or *du yue le*. It is clear that in the Northern Song, 獨樂 was understood as *du le*.
8. For the definitive studies in English, see Charles Hartmann, "Poetry and Politics in 1079: The Crow Terrace Case of Su Shih," *Chinese Literature: Essays, Articles, Reviews* (*CLEAR*) 12 (December 1990): 15–44; and "The Inquisition Against Su Shih: His Sentence as an Example of Song Legal Practice," *Journal of the American Oriental Society* 113, no. 2 (April–June 1993): 228–43.

1. WHAT'S IN A NAME?

1. For another discussion of this work, see Ronald Egan, *The Literary Works of Ou-yang Hsiu (1007–72)* (Cambridge: Cambridge University Press, 1984), 163–64.

2. See also Ronald Egan, *The Problem of Beauty: Aesthetic Thought and Pursuits in Northern Song Dynasty China* (Cambridge, Mass.: Harvard Asia Center Publications, 2006), 185–86.
3. Zhang Zhilie 張志烈, Ma Defu 馬德富, and Zhou Yukai 周裕鍇, *Su Shi quanji jiaozhu* 蘇軾全集校注, 12 vols. (Shijiazhuang: Hebei renmin chubanshe, 2010), 7567.

2. THE MAGISTRATE OF PEACH BLOSSOM SPRING

1. Li Yi'an 李逸安, *Ouyang Xiu quanji* 歐陽修全集 (Beijing: Zhonghua shuju, 2001), 563; *Quan Song wen* 全宋文 (Shanghai and Hefei: Shanghai cishu chubanshe and Anhui jiaoyu chubanshe, 2006), 32:103–4. 某有罪來是邦，朱公於某有舊，且哀其以罪而來，為至縣舍，擇其廳事之東以作斯堂，度為疏潔高明，而日居之以休其心。堂成，又與賓客偕至而落之。
2. Zhang Zhilie 張志烈, Ma Defu 馬德富, and Zhou Yukai 周裕鍇, *Su Shi quanji jiaozhu* 蘇軾全集校注 (Shijiazhuang: Hebei renmin chubanshe, 2010), 1104. For other discussions, see Ronald Egan, *The Problem of Beauty: Aesthetic Thought and Pursuits in Northern Song Dynasty China* (Cambridge, Mass.: Harvard Asia Center Publications, 2006), 179–82; and Michael Fuller, *The Road to East Slope: The Development of Su Shih's Poetic Voice* (Stanford, Calif.: Stanford University Press, 1990), 210–12.
3. Li Yi'an, *Ouyang Xiu quanji*, 568.
4. Li Yi'an, *Ouyang Xiu quanji*, 575; *Quan Song wen*, 35:114–15. For another discussion, see Egan, *The Problem of Beauty*, 40–43.
5. Zhao Kuangyin 趙匡胤, Song Taizu, the founder of the Song dynasty, was earlier a general of the Later Zhou dynasty.
6. Note Lin Yunming 林雲銘 in *Guwen xiyi* 古文析義 (Photo reprint, Taipei: Guangwen shuju, 1976): "All at once in regard to Chuzhou he calls to mind how it had originally been a place of military conflict" 忽就滁州想出原是用武之地.
7. Chen Xingzhen 陳杏珍 and Chao Jizhou 晁繼周, *Zeng Gong ji* 曾鞏集 (Beijing: Zhonghua shuju, 1984), 276.
8. Qian Zhonglian 錢仲聯, *Han Changli shi xinian jishi* 韓昌黎詩繫年集釋 (Shanghai: Shanghai guji chubanhe, 1984), 892. The passage referred to can be translated: "You should leave a place for the mind to sober up, / Intending to come here when drunk."
9. Li Yi'an, *Ouyang Xiu quanji*, 575.
10. *Quan Song wen*, 35:115–16.
11. In drinking games, the drinkers who lose get "forfeits," requiring that they consume a designated amount of spirits.
12. *Quan Song shi* 全宋詩 (Beijing: Beijing daxue chubanshe, 1991), 4637. For Shao Yong on happiness, see Xiaoshan Yang, *Metamorphosis of the Private Sphere: Gardens and Objects in Tang-Song Poetry* (Cambridge, Mass.: Harvard University Asia Center, 2003), 202–5.
13. Zhang, Ma, and Zhou, *Su Shi quanji jiaozhu*, 1095.

3. MISSING STONES

1. Li Yi'an 李逸安, *Ouyang Xiu quanji* 歐陽修全集 (Beijing: Zhonghua shuju, 2001), 578; *Quan Song wen* 全宋文 (Shanghai and Hefei: Shanghai cishu chubanshe and Anhui jiaoyu chubanshe,

2006), 35:117–18. See also Xiaoshan Yang, *Metamorphosis of the Private Sphere: Gardens and Objects in Tang-Song Poetry* (Cambridge, Mass.: Harvard University Asia Center, 2003), 139–41; and Ronald Egan, *The Literary Works of Ou-yang Hsiu (1007–72)* (Cambridge: Cambridge University Press, 1984), 41–42.

2. *Quan Song wen*, 33:320.
3. Li Yi'an, *Ouyang Xiu quanji*, 599. See also an extensive discussion of the preface and project in Ronald Egan, *The Problem of Beauty: Aesthetic Thought and Pursuits in Northern Song Dynasty China* (Cambridge, Mass.: Harvard Asia Center Publications, 2006), 7–20.
4. *Quan Song wen*, 174:117.
5. Zhang Zhilie 張志烈, Ma Defu 馬德富, and Zhou Yukai 周裕鍇, *Su Shi quanji jiaozhu* 蘇軾全集校注 (Shijiazhuang: Hebei renmin chubanshe, 2010), 1122. See also discussion in Egan, *The Problem of Beauty*, 165–69, 179.
6. Yang, *Metamorphosis of the Private Sphere*, 179–96; and Egan, *The Problem of Beauty*, 218–34. Both scholars focus primarily on the Qiu Pond assemblage and less on "Nine Blossoms Mountain in a Jug." I wrote about these three poems more than thirty years ago in *Traditional Chinese Poetry and Poetics* (Madison: University of Wisconsin Press, 1985). Tian Xiaofei also touched on these poems in her *Tao Yuanming and Manuscript Culture: The Record of a Dusty Table* (Seattle: University of Washington Press, 2005), 38–40, since Hukou was part of Tao Yuanming's home territory. After about thirty years and three scholars adding their comments that have given depth and thickness to the record, I would like to return to these poems, which embody all the problems of possession.
7. Xiao Difei 蕭滌非, chief ed., *Du Fu quan ji jiaozhu* 杜甫全集校注 (Beijing: Renmin wenxue chubanshe, 2014), 3:1448.
8. Zhang, Ma, and Zhou, *Su Shi quanji jiaozhu*, 4355.
9. Wang Wengao 王文誥, *Su Shi shiji* 蘇軾詩集 (Beijing: Zhonghua shuju, 1982), 6:2047.
10. Like Qiu Pond, Nine Blossoms was the name of a mountain, this one in modern Anhui.
11. Zhang, Ma, and Zhou, *Su Shi quanji jiaozhu*, 5320.
12. Jibei was the region that produced fine horses.
13. Liu Shangrong 劉尚榮, ed., *Huang Tingjian shiji zhu* 黃庭堅詩集注 (Beijing zhonghua shuju, 2003), 596.
14. Here we keep the received text of 山, "mountain." The *Zhuangzi* text may suggest that the mountain was taken away as well as the boat.
15. Zhang, Ma, and Zhou, *Su Shi quanji jiaozhu*, 3379. See also Egan, *The Problem of Beauty*, 189.

4. ALL MINE

1. Zhu Jincheng 朱金城, ed., *Bai Juyi ji jianjiao* 白居易集箋校 (Shanghai: Shanghai guji chubanshe, 1988), 2:747.
2. Qiu Shaohua 邱少華, *Ouyang Xiu ci xinshi jiping* 歐陽修詞新釋輯評 (Beijing: Zhongguo shudian, 2001), 1.
3. *Jin shu* 晉書 [The Jin history] (Beijing: Zhonghua shuju, 1974), 2103.
4. *Jin shu*, 108.

5. Although the implications are profoundly different, this technique of double negation to create an intermediary space was that used by Bai Juyi in "The Middling Hermit"; see Xiaoshan Yang, *Metamorphosis of the Private Sphere: Gardens and Objects in Tang-Song Poetry* (Cambridge, Mass.: Harvard University Asia Center, 2003), 36–50.
6. See the complete translation in the appendix.
7. Ma Yongqing 馬永卿, *The Recorded Conversations of Yuancheng* 元城語錄, in *Congshu jicheng xinbian* [Assemblage of collectanea, new series] (Taibei: Xinwenfeng chuban gongsi), 21:201, *juan* 2, p. 23.
8. *Quan Song biji* 全宋筆記, series 3 (Zhengzhou: Daxiang chubanshe, 2008), 1:171.
9. This would be the Tang past. Eastern Han Luoyang, continuing through the Western Wei, was situated to the east of the Tang city, whose location has remained the same to the present.
10. *Quan Song shi* 全宋詩 (Beijing: Beijing daxue chubanshe, 1991), 3608.
11. *Quan Song wen* 全宋文 (Shanghai and Hefei: Shanghai cishu chubanshe and Anhui jiaoyu chubanshe, 2006), 93:160–62.
12. This account was preserved in Yu Xilu 俞希魯, *Zhenjiang zhi* 鎮江志, ed. Ruan Yuan 阮元, *Xuxiu Siku quanshu* (*SKQS*), 698:666–67. It is not in the current version of the *Changxing ji* 長興集 or in *Quan Song wen*. There is a summary version in the late Southern Song *Jingkou qijiu zhuan* 京口耆舊傳 [Biographies of the gaffers of Jingkou], *SKQS*, under Shen Gua.

5. THE STONE THAT TELLS ITS NAME

1. Zhu Yu 朱彧, *Pingzhou ketan* 萍洲可談, *Quan Song biji* 全宋筆記, series 2 (Zhengzhou: Daxiang chubanshe, 2006), 6:160.
2. Patricia Ebrey, *Emperor Huizong* (Cambridge, Mass.: Harvard University Press, 2014), 451.
3. Lin Yunming 林雲銘, *Guwen xiyi* 古文析義 (Taipei: Guangwen shuju, 1976), 312–14.
4. See Xiaoshan Yang, *Metamorphosis of the Private Sphere: Gardens and Objects in Tang-Song Poetry* (Cambridge, Mass.: Harvard University Asia Center, 2003), 196. Yang is more certain than I that these were indeed the original rocks of Qiu Pond.
5. Su Dongpo did indeed write some tomb inscriptions, but he was explicit about his dislike of doing so. See "Ji Zhang Wending gong" 祭張文定公 [Funerary address to Zhang Wending, second of three], in Zhang Zhilie 張志烈, Ma Defu 馬德富, and Zhou Yukai 周裕鍇, *Su Shi quanji jiaozhu* 蘇軾全集校注 (Shijiazhuang: Hebei renmin chubanshe, 2010), prose 9:7035.
6. Huang also has a poem to Han Jian and mentions him in a letter, apparently to Han Jian's brother, an acquaintance whose letter he once answered. Liu Lin 劉琳, Li Yongxian 李勇先, and Wang Ronggui 王蓉貴, *Huang Tingjian quanji* 黃庭堅全集 (Chengdu: Sichuan daxue chubanshe, 2001), 3:1297, 1378.
7. This is the account as it appears in the monk Zuxiu's 祖秀 *Huayang gong ji* 華陽宮記 [Account of Huayang Palace], recorded in the Southern Song writer Zhang Hao's 張淏 *Genyue ji* 艮岳記 [Account of Gen Mount], *Quan Song wen* 全宋文 (Shanghai and Hefei: Shanghai cishu chubanshe and Anhui jiaoyu chubanshe, 2006), 308:231–35.

6. THE BAMBOO IN THE BREAST AND IN THE BELLY

1. *Quan Song wen* 全宋文 (Shanghai and Hefei: Shanghai cishu chubanshe and Anhui jiaoyu chubanshe, 2006), 174:117.
2. He Wei 何薳, *Chunzhu jiwen* 春渚紀聞, *Quan Song biji* 全宋筆記, series 3 (Zhengzhou: Daxiang chubanshe, 2008), 3:244.
3. Liu Yiqing, *Shih-shuo Hsin-yü—A New Account of Tales of the World*, trans. Richard Mather, 2nd ed. (Ann Arbor: Center for Chinese Studies, University of Michigan, 2002), 445. Wade-Giles changed to pinyin.
4. Michael Fuller, "Pursuing the Complete Bamboo in the Breast: Reflections on a Classical Chinese Image for Immediacy," *Harvard Journal of Asiatic Studies* 53, no. 1 (June 1993): 5–23.
5. Bamboo shoots have purplish sheathes. "Dragons" here is a figure for bamboo.
6. *Shi ji* 史記 (Beijing: Zhonghua shuju, 1982), 3272.

BIBLIOGRAPHY

Chen Xingzhen 陳杏珍 and Chao Jizhou 晁繼周. *Zeng Gong ji* 曾鞏集 [The works of Zeng Gong]. Beijing: Zhonghua shuju, 1984.

Cherniack, Susan. "Book Culture and Textual Transmission in Sung China." *Harvard Journal of Asiatic Studies* 54, no. 1 (June 1994): 5–125.

Ebrey, Patricia. *Emperor Huizong*. Cambridge, Mass.: Harvard University Press, 2014.

Egan, Ronald. *The Literary Works of Ou-yang Hsiu (1007–72)*. Cambridge: Cambridge University Press, 1984.

—. *The Problem of Beauty: Aesthetic Thought and Pursuits in Northern Song Dynasty China*. Cambridge, Mass.: Harvard Asia Center Publications, 2006.

—. *Word, Image, and Deed in the Life of Su Shi*. Cambridge, Mass.: Council in East Asian Studies Publications, 1994.

Fuller, Michael. "Pursuing the Complete Bamboo in the Breast: Reflections on a Classical Chinese Image for Immediacy." *Harvard Journal of Asiatic Studies* 53, no. 1 (June 1993): 5–23.

—. *The Road to East Slope: The Development of Su Shi's Poetic Voice*. Stanford, Calif.: Stanford University Press, 1990.

Hartmann, Charles. "The Inquisition Against Su Shih: His Sentence as an Example of Song Legal Practice." *Journal of the American Oriental Society* 113, no. 2 (April–June 1993): 228–43.

—. "Poetry and Politics in 1079: The Crow Terrace Case of Su Shih." *Chinese Literature: Essays, Articles, Reviews (CLEAR)* 12 (December 1990): 15–44.

He Wei 何薳.*Chunzhu jiwen* 春渚紀聞 [Spring Isle's notes on what I learned]. *Quan Song biji* 全宋筆記 [The complete Song miscellaneous notes], series 3. Zhengzhou: Daxiang chubanshe, 2008.

Li Yi'an 李逸安. *Ouyang Xiu quanji* 歐陽修全集 [The complete works of Ouyang Xiu]. Beijing: Zhonghua shuju, 2001.

Lin Yunming 林雲銘. *Guwen xiyi* 古文析義 [Analysis of the significance in old-style prose]. Photo reprint. Taipei: Guangwen shuju, 1976.

Liu Lin 劉琳, Li Yongxian 李勇先, and Wang Ronggui 王蓉貴. *Huang Tingjian quanji* 黃庭堅全集 [The complete works of Huang Tingjian]. Chengdu: Sichuan daxue chubanshe, 2001.

Liu Shangrong 劉尚榮, ed. *Huang Tingjian shiji zhu* 黃庭堅詩集注 [The collected poems of Huang Tingjian with annotation]. Beijing: Zhonghua shuju, 2003.

Liu Yiqing. *Shih-shuo Hsin-yü—A New Account of Tales of the World*. Trans. Richard Mather. 2nd ed. Ann Arbor: Center for Chinese Studies, University of Michigan, 2002.

Ma Yongqing 馬永卿. *The Recorded Conversations of Yuancheng* 元城語錄. *Congshu jicheng xinbian* [Assemblage of collectanea, new series]. Taibei: Xinwenfeng chuban gongsi, introduction 1984.

Qian Zhonglian 錢仲聯. *Han Changli shi xinian jishi* 韓昌黎詩繫年集釋 [Collected explications of the poetry of Han Changli, chronologically arranged]. Shanghai: Shanghai guji chubanhe, 1984.

Qiu Shaohua 邱少華. *Ouyang Xiu ci xinshi jiping* 歐陽修詞新釋輯評 [Ouyang Xiu's song lyrics with a new explication and collected critical comments]. Beijing: Zhongguo shudian, 2001.

Quan Song biji 全宋筆記 [The complete Song miscellaneous notes]. 10 series. Zhengzhou: Daxiang chubanshe, 2003–2018. Each volume in each series numbered independently.

Quan Song shi 全宋詩 [The complete poems of the Song]. 72 vols. Beijing: Beijing daxue chubanshe, 1991. Volumes numbered consecutively.

Quan Song wen 全宋文 [The complete Song prose]. 360 vols. Shanghai and Hefei: Shanghai cishu chubanshe and Anhui jiaoyu chubanshe, 2006. Volumes numbered independently. Reference by volume and page number.

Shi ji 史記 [The historian's records]. Beijing: Zhonghua shuju, 1982.

Tian, Xiaofei. *Tao Yuanming and Manuscript Culture: The Record of a Dusty Table*. Seattle: University of Washington Press, 2005.

Twitchett, Dennis, and Paul Jakov Smith, eds. *The Cambridge History of China*. Vol. 5, part 1: *The Sung Dynasty and Its Precursors, 907–1279*. Cambridge: Cambridge University Press, 2009.

Wang Wengao 王文誥. *Su Shi shiji* 蘇軾詩集 [The poems of Su Shi]. Beijing: Zhonghua shuju, 1982.

Xiao Difei 蕭滌非, chief ed. *Du Fu quan ji jiaozhu* 杜甫全集校注 [The complete works of Du Fu with annotation and collation]. Beijing: Renmin wenxue chubanshe, 2014.

Yang, Xiaoshan. *Metamorphosis of the Private Sphere: Gardens and Objects in Tang-Song Poetry*. Cambridge, Mass.: Harvard University Asia Center, 2003.

Yu Xilu 俞希魯. *Zhenjiang zhi* 鎮江志 [Gazetteer of Zhenjiang]. Ed. Ruan Yuan 阮元. *Xuxiu Siku quanshu* [Continuation of the complete books of the four treasuries]. 1996–2002.

Zhang Zhilie 張志烈, Ma Defu 馬德富, and Zhou Yukai 周裕鍇. *Su Shi quanji jiaozhu* 蘇軾全集校注 [The complete works of Su Shi, with annotation and collation]. 12 vols. Shijiazhuang: Hebei renmin chubanshe, 2010.

Zhu Jincheng 朱金城, ed. *Bai Juyi ji jianjiao* 白居易集箋校 [The works of Bai Juyi with notes and collation]. Shanghai: Shanghai guji chubanshe, 1988.

Zhu Yu 朱彧. *Pingzhou ketan* 萍洲可談 [Topics for chit-chat by Master Duckweed Flats]. *Quan Song biji*, series 2. Zhengzhou: Daxiang chubanshe, 2006.

INDEX